DRY **ICE**

DRY **ICE**

The true story of a false rape complaint

PETER JOYCE

Published 2016
by Peter Joyce

Print ISBN 978-0-473-37701-4
Kindle ISBN 978-0-473-37891-2
Epub ISBN 978-0-473-37890-5

Originally printed by The Copy Press, Nelson, New Zealand. www.copypress.co.nz

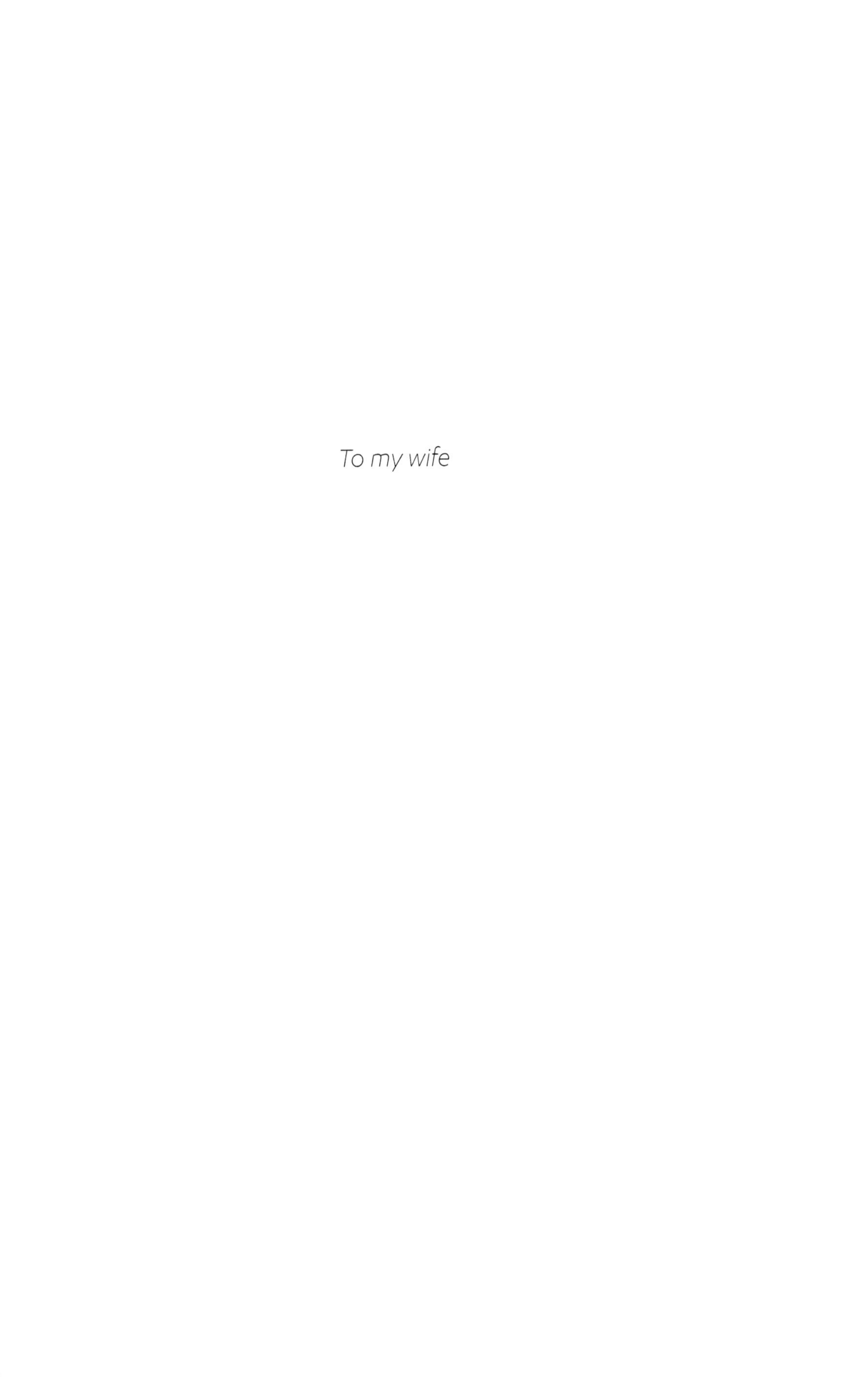

To my wife

Beware the fury of a patient man

John Dryden

Anonymity be damned. My name is Peter Joyce. I am a law-abiding and unassuming middle-class man: embezzlement, arson, rape and assault are just four of the many crimes I have never committed.

I have changed some names of the innocent, the loyal, the honest and the rational, because it is the ethical thing to do…and all names of the guilty, the vindictive, the dishonest and the deluded, because it is the legally necessary thing to do. Some place names have also been changed. For example, the city where we live is now Draketown, the featured North Island city of over 55,000 has become Houwhanga, and the nearby small town where nothing occurred is now Westchester.

Prologue

John and Charlotte Rigby married in England some time before they arrived together in New Zealand to start a new life in the early 1970s. The marriage produced two daughters, first Verity (in the late 1970s) and then Jennifer three years later. John was a high school teacher with a special interest in outdoor education, and Charlotte was a primary school teacher. The couple followed work across the North Island. For reasons unknown to me, by the mid-1980s John and Charlotte had drifted apart. John eventually got a divorce. This was hard on the children, as these things always are. John started a new relationship with Gloria and the two married in late 1988. They settled in Houwhanga. Charlotte did not remarry.

When her marriage ended, Charlotte moved down to Draketown to make a fresh start, taking her daughters with her.

Gloria is the best friend of my wife Angela from university days in the 1970s. It was only after Angela and I married that I met John and Gloria.

August 18 1952

I am born in St Helen's Hospital, Christchurch, the last of three children. Seven pounds ten ounces. Mother and baby are fine.

One Friday night in about 1971

I sit in Mum's kitchen with my friends Rod and George. We have drunk a few too many Lion Browns and get to talking about our future, mainly concerning jobs and girls. We float all sorts of possibilities, many of them far-fetched. The only thing we all agree on is that nothing will happen after thirty: either we will be dead or – even worse – we will still be alive and have to face the prospect of forgetting what day it is and being wheeled around our retirement village.

January 26 1979

I move to sunny, arty and sleepy Draketown.

April 1981

I am hitchhiking in California. A middle-aged guy gives me a ride and we solve most of the world's problems. I ask him if he often picks up hitchhikers. From time to time, he says, but it depends on the person on the roadside. If he's well enough turned out, maybe yes...especially if he looks like a genuine traveller and not some junkie who's run out of gas. No females, of course. "Why?" I ask. He chuckles and throws me a glance that suggests I must have been living in a cave in the highlands of Cameroon.

July 8 1988

Angela and I marry.

August 18 2014

I turn sixty-two. Sixty-two! Not only have I more than doubled the original prediction, but life still offers much more than just a pulse. Angela and I have passed the silver anniversary mark, we owe nobody one red cent and I do part-time work that I would happily do for nothing. I'm still nimble enough to intercept my opponent's forehand passing shots – most of the time. Life is so satisfying that I often walk through the local park counting my blessings with every stride. Things are great the way they are. I am a be-er rather than a doer, so none of that bucket list nonsense.

Part One

February 1 2015

The day we get hit by a train.

I arrive home from "church" – the Sunday morning tennis game against my regular opponent, Les. Angela tells me that a policewoman has been here looking for me. Angela was still in bed when the doorbell rang, but when she peered through the curtains and saw a police uniform she thought she'd better put her dressing-gown on and see what was up. The policewoman wouldn't tell her anything. Angela suggested meeting me at the tennis courts just round the corner, but the policewoman wasn't keen. I immediately rule out the most terrifying possibility – that something dire has happened to our son, who lives in Wellington – because then the policewoman would surely have told Angela. She did leave her card, with the name "Eva B, Child Protection Team", and so I call her.

She says that a sexual complaint has been made against me. Sexual? She reveals no more over the phone, but suggests I come in to the station to talk to her. What on earth can this be? As I drive in, I ponder the possibilities. Whatever it was, it wasn't deliberate. But how could it have been accidental? Maybe our bedroom curtains aren't as opaque as I always assumed, and a neighbour has complained. Indecent exposure – oh my god, how embarrassing! How will I ever live this down?

I arrive at Draketown central police station, my heart thumping and palms clammy. Detective Eva B, tall and uniformed, introduces herself with professional detachment. I say something awkward like "Nice to meet you. Pity it's not in different circumstances," but no light comes into her eyes. I suppose a policewoman's lot is not a happy one. She leads me to an interview room deep inside the blue sanctum. It is cramped and dingy. She tells me that a complaint "of a sexual nature" has been made against me by a woman called Verity Rigby. Here it is – the biggest, the most transforming statement of my life. And it is a lie. Disbelief wallops me in the face. "You mean John's daughter? You're pulling my leg." A dopey thing to say. But no such event occurred, and if what's happening now is a strippergram, what's the point if none of my friends are here and it's not even my birthday?

"I'm quite serious," she says. Of course she is. So this is worse than an accidental and unlikely indecent exposure. Then it must be some kind of sexual assault accusation. Why? Why would she do this to someone she can only have heard of?

"But I've never even met her...I know who she is, but I've never met her." At least, not that I can remember. If I did, it was only fleeting and obviously less than memorable.

Eva asks me if I have ever lived in Houwhanga. I confirm that I have, briefly – back in 1974. She asks what I know of Verity. All I can say is that her father has told me she has had a rather mixed up and unhappy life, and that she and her mother uncritically buy into all kinds of bizarre beliefs: tarot, astrology...in fact, anything alternative or paranormal. Eva sits me down and reads me my rights, including the right to remain silent and to have a lawyer. She asks if I want to make a statement now, and I agree to. After all, what do I – what can I – have to hide? This has to be a misunderstanding. Eva says the easiest way is for us to go to another room, where she can ask me questions and the interview can be videoed.

But the reading of my rights has jolted me into caution. Perhaps the simple truth will not be enough to save me. This could even get to court, for god's sake. Then I would no doubt have to engage a lawyer, who would tell me I was naïve to make a statement alone, disoriented from shock, disadvantaged by my law-abiding history and way out of my depth. Luckily I've recently been listening to a *Stuff You Should Know* podcast about police interrogation, which said around eighty percent of people interrogated by the US police foolishly waive their right to a lawyer. This is usually because they are worried that insisting on legal advice would make them look guilty. So I tell Eva I want a lawyer after all. She hands me a well-pawed A4 laminated card with the contact details of around twenty lawyers. Draketown being a small community, I know some names from court cases in the Draketown Post newspaper, but really I have no idea. It's like picking horses when you're a once-only punter who knows nothing about form or track conditions. We skeptics don't even have lucky numbers.

I suggest she pick one for me. "I can't do that," she says. Procedures. We phone number seven on the card, but it's Sunday, so all we get is an answer phone. I try two more numbers at random, but no response. I tell Eva I'll go home, gather my thoughts and get back in touch with her.

"Verity?" says Angela. "Verity Rigby? John's Verity? But that's ridiculous! You haven't even met her."

"Well, I know I haven't sexually assaulted her, but are you sure we haven't met?"

"One hundred percent," she says. "I'm surprised she even knows your name." So I was right: reality and I are perfect strangers to Verity.

The non-event was in Houwhanga, and it must have been a long time ago that it didn't happen. Verity is in her mid- to late thirties now, and Eva's card mentioned "child protection". How far back does the lie reach? We spend the next couple of hours ransacking our memories, thinking of all the times we have been to Houwhanga or Verity's father and stepmother have been here in Draketown. We can't think of an occasion when either of us met her. Angela has always kept a diary and taken some photos, and she spends a lot of her spare time over the next day rummaging through boxes of old notebooks down in the study, unearthing half-buried memories in text and pictures. This afternoon, I find myself saying "Bitch! Bitch!" under my breath.

What have we done to deserve this cuckoo in our empty nest? As I sit, puzzled but fuming, I feel in the mood for some old-fashioned rock music, played loud. The very first track, *Strange Days* by the Doors, is eerily apt:

Strange days have found us
Strange days have tracked us down
They're going to destroy
Our casual joys

Nothing could be stranger than this new reality. Tracked us down. Lain in wait. An unseen predator has ambushed our measured contentment. I keep sifting for reasons why she has done this. People shocked by a cancer diagnosis may wonder "Why me?" I assume this isn't a real question at all, but a desperate protest at the cruelty of fate. After all, no malevolent god has wished this sickness upon them. But my question is a real one: someone I wouldn't recognise if I bumped into her in the street has consciously chosen to accuse me by name of a sexual assault which I could not have committed. I feel violated. Abused. And as for the police, how did they allow this to get so far? Anyone who makes a complaint of sexual assault needs to be treated sensitively and have the allegation taken beyond the front counter, but how much further should this one have got before some facts stopped it in its tracks? It's a small but fatal step from the very reasonable "Listen to the complainant" to the outrageous "Believe the victim."

Yet in one respect I already know that *Why?* is irrelevant. Although I have never met her, I know a little of her history, and this allegation tells me more about what is happening between her ears. I also smell a bigger and craftier rat: someone saner than her has probably encouraged her in this lethal fantasy.

It's like 9/11. When I watched the horror enfolding after the impact of the first plane, I was shocked and confused, as most people were. But by the time we saw the impact on the other tower, we knew it was terrorist attack and had a fair idea who was behind it. As soon as I heard the name of this complainant, I thought "sexual abuse counsellor". I already know something about this recovered memory malarkey. She (almost certainly she) may be the main villain here. A vulnerable woman with unfulfilled aspirations finds comfort with an attentive counsellor who knows how to give her clients the impression she values them. She probably does, in her own way, and is convinced that the therapy she gives them is what they really need. To the client, the counsellor is an articulate and educated authority figure who gently but assertively commands respect. The counsellor tells the client that her problems are not her fault, but have an external cause which probably can be traced. Would she perhaps like to enrol for some more sessions, so that the ugly event which has prevented her from finding contentment can be unearthed? It would be an enlightening story, probably even an exciting adventure – a therapeutic voyage to The Truth about herself. It does cost at least $70 a session (or perhaps much more), but how can we put a price on something so valuable? In any case, there's a very good chance the cause will be sexual abuse, in which case the state picks up the tab…but, sadly, not if the despair stems from something else.

So in one sense the *Why?* can be answered…unless my assumption about a counsellor is dead wrong, of course. It could be, but I'm angry and not sure who I should aim my anger at, so *likely* will have to stand in for *definite.* But, counsellor or not, Verity is clearly convinced this actually happened, so the question remains *Why me?* Of all the people who might play a role in her fantasy, why am I the one she has chosen? I never stop asking myself this question, because I never manage to answer it. Did she just take my name at random from her father's address book? Has she identified me by sight? If so, how?

A friend tells me that Verity deserves some compassion, but "her counsellor deserves none." I never hold much doubt that the second statement is true. As for Verity herself, compassion isn't my immediate response. In the coming months, every morning I rediscover the dark Verity cloud when I wake up. My anger varies wildly, sometimes from one hour to the next. I can spit "Bitch!" seven times in quick succession, one for each of the stairs when I pound up from our hallway to the bedroom. The rhythm works best when I put the stress – and the heaviest footfall – on the fifth syllable:

bitch bitch bitch bitch BITCH bitch bitch. This fury is my default mood, and it stains everything I do. But at times I feel much more charitable, and Verity becomes a lost and lonely soul who needs pity. I sometimes wonder where all these lonely people come from. Where do they all belong? When I pity her, the untruth is not a lie but a sad delusion, and this commitment to ruining my life becomes a singular fault. She may have outstanding virtues I'm unaware of. For all I know she may volunteer every weekend at a soup kitchen and fund a kid's schooling in Zambia. If she were driving in her car, and she saw me sprawled on the road after coming off my bike, would she not stop and take me, a perfect stranger, to the hospital? However, something I learn from her ex-husband in April will lock in that anger, and I learn that another person's delusion that infuriates and endangers you may as well be called a lie.

While Angela traces our Houwhanga visits, I feel an urge to tell people who can help me, and those close to me who need to know. I call my friend Charles, who worked for a time as court officer. He is shocked and concerned, urges me not to worry but nonetheless to treat it seriously. Since the law usually delivers the best justice to those with deep pockets, the best thing to do is to contact a switched-on lawyer, pay what seems a lot of money considering that you have done nothing wrong, and nip the stupid thing in the bud. He suggests Dwight B, a lawyer who he assures me is as good as any in the business. I phone the guy. As it's Sunday, I get no reply. I leave a message on his answer phone.

I also call George, co-director at the school where I am working mornings. I am contracted to teach a class of twelve students for a ten-week exam course, and I am nearly halfway through it. George needs to know, in case the pressure of being stalked by a deranged woman affects my classroom performance. He is dumbfounded, but offers sympathy and support. As it happens, I doubt if the Verity horror ever does upset my teaching, and I'm confident none of my students ever gets the feeling anything is wrong. At least on the outside, I stay in control almost all the time, mainly because of Angela's unwavering support.

This outrage renders us powerless in so many ways; Verity and the police, unseen though they are, have got us in a full nelson. But one thing we must strive to do is regulate our own responses and refuse to let this thing beat us.

I have a compulsion to find things out. Verity has elbowed her way into our lives, and has suddenly become far too important to remain a mere abstraction. What does she look like? Is she in a relationship? Does she work at what normal people would call a job, or is victimhood her sole occupation? Does she even still live here in Draketown? I look in the phone book, but she isn't there. That may just mean she doesn't have a landline, or maybe she has an unlisted number – probably a good idea if you tell this sort of lie. I see that her mother is still listed, and at the same address as before. I can remember John visiting there once when he came to Draketown years ago.

Meanwhile, my efficient wife has looked through photos, diary entries and even letters, and chronicled all our trips to Houwhanga. Here is what she's uncovered (N.B. The *I* refers to me, not her):

> In late December 1991, we did indeed see John and Gloria. We even stayed in their house in Houwhanga and drove their car. This is because we arranged a house and car exchange for about ten days in the summer school holidays – necessary because John and I were both high school teachers. We drove with our infant son in our white Honda to Picton, left the car there, and crossed to Wellington on the ferry. There we met them, after their drive down from Houwhanga. We may all have had lunch together in Wellington – we can't remember. But I do know that Angela and I took their yellow Mitsubishi Lancer and house keys and both couples continued to each other's houses. No sign of Verity and her sister, both of whom must have been with their mother here in Draketown, as normal.
>
> We next visited Houwhanga in December 1997. At the time my mother was terminally ill with melanoma and had been staying with us for several weeks. We assumed she still had some time to go, and my brother Keith came up from Christchurch to look after her and give us some time off, so we went for a North Island break. Our timing turned out to be way off. Mum died the day after we left.
>
> The last time we went to Houwhanga was in January 2008. We visited John and Gloria, this time staying for a full week. On more than one night, John and I argued spiritedly about US foreign policy until the small hours.

February 2

I get a call back from Dwight B, the lawyer. He tells me that I have the right to remain silent, so I don't have to talk to the police at all. However, he agrees with Charles that the best thing for me to do long-term is to agree to make a statement with a lawyer present. If – heaven forbid – the nonsense ends up in court, a jury will look favourably on me if it appears I was keen to assert my innocence openly and comply with the "investigation" from the outset. He says that if I engage him as my courtroom lawyer, it is better if he does not accompany me to the police interview, so he will set up a colleague, Monty, to go with me. Something to do with tactics. Courtroom, jury, "investigation", lawyer, trial? My God, is this real or have I stumbled into a novel? If so, I hope it's like one of those murder mysteries, with a final scene in which everyone sits in a circle in an opulent drawing room waiting for Poirot to reveal the truth and expose everyone's motives. But it's looking more like Kafka than Christie.

So it is arranged for me to front up to Eva at the Draketown police station on Tuesday, February 10 at 1:30 p.m. I'm almost looking forward to it, because I'm confident that if I just present the facts, the whole thing will be over. This is New Zealand, not North Korea. Dwight suggests I come to his office half an hour early, so that I can meet Monty and all three of us can plan our interview strategy.

We have decided not to let my uncle (to whom I am very close) into the loop, because he feels things deeply, and this would upset him too much. Once it's all over I'll tell him about it as a distasteful episode of historic interest only. But I keep informing other family members and close friends, by phone and email. A common reaction is very similar to what I said to Eva when she first hit me with the allegation: "This sounds like a joke....but I suspect it isn't." Angela thinks I'm drawing the circle too wide, and maybe she's right. But I value the support of people I know and like, and the more the better, up to a point. If I see one of them in the street, and he or she asks, "How's it going?" we both know the question isn't rhetorical, and I can reveal the latest news, if there is any. Mud is supposed to stick, but they will surely believe me. I never met the woman, for god's sake, so how could they think I've done anything? Most people I tell encourage me to stay upbeat. It's worrying how many people urge me not to worry.

I email my sister Carol in New South Wales and phone my brother Keith in Christchurch. He is famously succinct and perceptive in his assessment of people. He says, "The moll needs a lead pill." I put off phoning our son. All kids want to believe that they were conceived immaculately, and the merest suggestion of anything sexual by their parents is something they cannot contemplate without wincing. This is an allegation of debauchery by his father with a girl who at the time of the non-offence was more than ten years younger than he is now. What right does a stranger like Verity have to make us suffer this conversation?

But it goes better than I imagine. His response is measured (did we teach him that?) and mature. He doesn't even seem all that surprised, and says, "Yes, I've known a couple of girls who could pull something like that." What? So worldly-wise, so street-smart. That's not from me. He asks if I have thought about hiring a private detective to find out more about her. It would be cheaper than a lawyer and could be useful. What has our kid been doing?

I mention in an email to friends and family that I want to confront this Verity; I want to look her in the eye (after introducing myself, of course) and challenge her to repeat the allegation to my face. Both my cousin Jackie on the Gold Coast and my friend Ted offer the same response, almost to the word: that she would be perfectly capable of repeating the accusation to my face, because she is a True Believer. Yes, they're probably right.

I start to pace. I want to do something.

February 3

I have a preliminary meeting with lawyer Dwight. I give him a printout of my summary of the facts so far. He expresses sympathy that I've been landed in this mess. He says that the system is flawed, no question about it, but that it's the best system there is. I'm not so sure about this. As I ponder what may lie in front of me, I'm thinking that Islamic sharia law has a lot going for it. Sure, hands get lopped off from time to time, but almost certainly not mine in this sort of case.

He phones Eva while I'm in his office, and he learns that it was indeed an alleged event from her childhood in Houwhanga. Eva also reveals that many men have been accused, and that John, Verity's father, is one of them. My god.

February 5

The Draketown Post reports that two Frenchmen holidaying to the west of here have filed a false complaint that they were robbed. Police say that "a large number of police, dog handlers and detectives" were assigned to the case. The false complainants have been arrested, and a spokesperson for the police says that they will be prosecuted. Detective Sergeant Arthur G says, "We take all matters of this nature very seriously... genuine victims ultimately miss out when our resources are diverted in this way to what turned out to be a complete waste of police time." It's encouraging to see the police taking no nonsense and setting what may be a useful precedent.

February 7

My suspicions about Verity's motivation shift to money. In New Zealand it has been possible to stash away a stack of cash by claiming you were a sexual abuse victim – or even the parents of one, if the victim was a child. In the notorious Christchurch

Civic Crèche case in the early 1990s, parents of the "abused" children received at least $10,000 each, and some collected more because they could claim for multiple incidents. People got paid even if no one was convicted. Why would anyone assume such a system isn't open to exploitation?

I suspect the rules may have changed, so that is something I must look into. I know that the number of free counselling sessions to which sexual abuse claimants were entitled was scaled back a couple of years ago, because there was quite a controversy about it in the media. Some letters to the editor suggested that anyone who questioned the funding for counselling was no better than an abuser. Yet when counsellors were being paid generously for each session, both victims and "victims" tended to recover rather slowly from their trauma.

February 8

We visit our close friend Mary and tell her the news. Her jaw drops, of course. She expresses horror at the combination of awful outcomes: jail, ruined reputation and financial loss. She asks how much it's likely to cost, and we say that depends on how far it goes. The cheapest may be a grand or two, but if it goes to court it could run into tens of thousands – with no way to get any back. She says she's just spent $700 on dental treatment for her ageing female fox terrier, and that makes us feel a little better about the likely cost. Pets' teeth, clutch repairs, roof scaffolding, false rape complaints – they're all just financial bombs that can drop on any one of us from time to time. The difference is that Mary chose her bitch and has probably derived some pleasure from her.

February 10

My big day. The anticipation, the rituals, the solemn oaths – it's like a wedding without the food and the love. I arrive at Dwight's chambers at 1 p.m. Both lawyers are already up to speed with all the facts of the allegation: who's who, who was where and when, what couldn't have been done to whom, and why not. Dwight says that this is a file which has probably lain on Eva's desk for months. Poor Verity! How she must have suffered, waiting all that time for the cogs of justice to start whirring. He says Eva has likely been distracted by more pressing cases, and its complexity has made her put this one off. So I was right: as I was innocently going about my routines – eating my breakfast, watching a movie, trimming the lawn edges, writing reports for work – this allegator has been lying in wait, ready to slink up, seize me by the throat and drown me in a death roll.

I have brought a slip of paper with a summary of dates and places, ready to produce it in the interview. They tell me to keep it to myself, because it would be a tactical error to reveal too many facts in the interview. I should keep them for – heaven forbid – the courtroom, because the police may change tack in response to what I reveal. What? Aren't they also after the truth? I am starting to learn just how much my naive optimism makes me a lamb that's slipped into the alligator pond, and how often an action which seems instinctive and honest could actually turn me into lunch.

They tell me that in the interview I must suppress any outrage or exasperation I feel as an innocent man who has no place being accused of such a thing – whatever it is. I must keep a lid on my emotions. I need to stay dispassionate, to answer the questions simply and truthfully. No ego games. I must not try to outwit the interviewer, to belittle her, browbeat her or be sarcastic. Above all, I must be careful not to pretend I trust all my memories of forgettable events from two decades ago. Any jury will accept that it is reasonable to forget some details. If I claim to be certain about something trivial which I innocently contradict in court, a slick prosecution lawyer may try to paint me as unreliable.

I must not agree to the interview being filmed. Gestures and mannerisms in a filmed statement tend to work against a defendant in court, and it's all disadvantage that the jury in effect gets to compare two performances – the filmed one and the courtroom one. I must insist on my right to low-tech question and answer, with the interviewer making notes. Monty warns me that the interviewer will not like this. When I request it, she will look me in the eye and appeal to my sense of macho independence. She will stress that it is my decision, and that I should not be coerced by anyone else.

Monty and I walk the short stretch to the police station. It takes a while for Eva to be summoned, but finally, there she is, uniformed and as business-like as the first time. She escorts us to an interview room deep inside the blue sanctum, and she assumes that I will consent to being filmed. "No," I say, I want notes to be taken. She looks me in the eye and says that I should not be railroaded into a time-consuming and inefficient method. "Call me old fashioned," I say, "but I don't want to be filmed." To her obvious chagrin, we get under way. She questions me and makes notes. Monty sits on my right.

At the outset she just repeats that an accusation of a sexual nature has been made against me by Verity Rigby; the specifics come later. As we get further into the guts of the interview, I'm surprised and delighted at my restraint and outward calm. At times Eva seems faintly frustrated and hamstrung. She taps her pen on the desk. She almost seems to be thinking, "I've got nothing on this guy. Where can I go from here?"

When she asks if I've ever owned a yellow car, I say "No," but then I remember clearly that John's car, the one we used when we swapped houses and cars, was a yellow Mitsubishi Lancer. Would it be a tactical mistake to tell Eva this, or a tactical mistake *not* to tell her? I shift in my chair and tell Eva I need a break to talk to Monty alone. She is polite about this, and leaves the room for a few minutes. Monty tells me I should let her know about the yellow car, and when she returns I do so.

Then the devastating little monosyllable "raped" whacks me like an Exocet, and I flounder. My god, raped? Much more than a grope behind the bike sheds, and immeasurably worse than translucent curtains. A whole group of men, sometimes in a group, recruited and egged on by her father. A paedophile ring, then. In a group! The enormity of the lie, the depravity of its suggestion makes me want to protest "What is this crap? The bitch is a liar!" but I recover and utter a flat "No." I have to keep a lid on my exasperation, but the facts of time and place are screaming and this detective seems as deaf as a post.

After it's finished, I learn one extra benefit of the tedious speak-and-write method: much to my surprise, I get a copy of the text, signed by both parties. An unexpected gold mine. There's not even any suggestion that it is confidential, so anyone can pore over it, ponder its significance, read between its lines, fume at its outrageousness. Monty politely tells Eva that I am entitled to know when a decision will be made about whether to prosecute. Eva says only that "it is a very complex case", that other men have to be interviewed, and suggests a couple of months. I ask Eva whether I can contact John and talk to him about this. She says she would prefer it if I didn't. I already knew that poor John is in the frame as well, but now I learn there are others I presumably haven't met. I know immediately that this issue of whether and how to make contact with John is going to play a huge role from here on.

Monty tells me I did very well. He says my performance was "measured". Yes, I say, I am measured – far too measured to rape anyone, let alone an under-aged girl. Monty's judgment is encouraging, but the word "raped" resonates like a knell, and it's terrifying to contemplate two months of kicking my heels. We walk back to Dwight's chambers for a debrief. He calls the case against me "thin", but says it would be a mistake to assume the police won't prosecute. I agree with this, because naïve optimism can lead to despair when things don't work out. A pessimist treats any happy outcome as a bonus worth celebrating.

Both lawyers advise me not to get too hung up on places and dates, so that a future jury won't see me as a guilty man striving to prove his innocence. They even suggest it would be a good idea not to show the interview transcript to Angela, because we will find it hard to resist checking details to get our story straight. But they concede that real people in the real world can be too emotional to do what is good legal strategy.

Dwight bids me farewell with the words that in any other context would seem unfriendly: "I hope we never meet again." And we don't.

Here is the interview text:

Q: How did you meet John Rigby?

A: I met him through my wife, as his second wife is the traditional best friend of my wife.

Q: When was that?

A: I'm not sure, but probably around 1989.

Q: What were the circumstances?

A: As I remember, it was at the Anakiwa outdoor centre. John and his new wife were already there. I can't be sure, but he may have been instructing. My wife and I drove there to meet them. At that stage his wife and mine were already friends. His wife is called Gloria; my wife is Angela.

We became quite good friends and had long discussions about politics, religion and other subjects.

I wasn't really into outdoor pursuits myself.

Q: Are you still friends today?

A: Yes, but because of the distance we don't see each other.

Q: After that first meeting, how often would you see them?

A: Not often. The next meeting was almost certainly 1991. I think this because in 1991 Angela and I went to stay at their place. I'm pretty sure it was the end of 1991 anyway.

The circumstances of this were that we exchanged houses to stay in. I believe John was living at HOAC* then, and we were living in Draketown.

Q: Have you ever lived in the North Island?

A: Yes.

Q: What were the circumstances?

A: I lived in Houwhanga from April to June 1974. Houwhanga Girls' High School needed a German language teacher urgently. I was still in Christchurch then, doing the last of my teacher training, and they released me early. I taught for two months, then went back to Christchurch.

Q: Have you lived in the North Island at any other time?

A: I think in 1973 I was in Lower Hutt, at Hutt Valley High School as a trainee teacher for two months.

Q: Where did you live in Houwhanga in 1974?

A: I can't remember the street, but I remember the family. It was the Ziffel family. He taught at the high school. I can't remember his first name, but his wife was Betty-Sue.

Q: Can you describe the house for me?

A: No I can't.

Q: Who lived there when you did?

A: Only the Ziffels. I can't remember if they had children.

Q: Did you have access to a car?

A: No, because I flew up.

Q: Did the Ziffels have a car?

A: I can't remember. I do remember it was quite close to the girls' school.

Q: When you were at Houwhanga, did you have much to do with John Rigby?

A: I didn't know him then.

Q: When John was at HOAC did you ever visit him?

A: I don't think so, no.

Q: Did you ever see the Ziffels again?

A: No.

Q: Did you become friends with any other people in Houwhanga at that time?

A: No.

Q: Did you ever go back to Houwhanga at all?

A: Yes, Angela and I did a trip around the North Island in 1997 and visited Houwhanga. When we did that, the house we stayed at was John's own house at HOAC.

Q: Have you ever owned a yellow car, brown seats, a sedan model?

A: No, I have never owned a yellow car.

Q: Around 20-25 years ago, 1990 to 1995, can you remember what cars you had then?

A: I believe around that time I had a white 1978 Honda Accord. My wife and I shared the same car.

I would like to add that John's car that I drove in Houwhanga was a yellow Mitsubishi Lancer sedan.

Q: What was the HOAC house like?

A: It was part of an outdoor education complex, so it was in large grounds. It had something like a confidence course and a creek nearby. The house itself was old and wooden.

Q: The Skeptics Society, what is your involvement?

A: I am now a member. I believe John is also but I don't know when he joined. We haven't talked about it.

Q: Have you met any of John's other associates?

A: Not that I can remember, no.

Q: Have you ever met his daughter, Verity?

A: Almost certainly not; if I did I can't recall.

Q: Have you any recollection of Verity going to Westchester High School, near Houwhanga, and staying with John for about a term?

A: I have a vague recollection of it, that is all.

I would like to add that when we stayed at John's place it was December 1991 to January 1992, and it was the school holidays.

Q: Did John Rigby ever talk to you about working at Mt Ruapehu on the ski patrol?

A: I have a vague recollection of that, but that's all. We didn't have any discussions about his time there.

Q: Did he ever talk to you about his wife and family?

A: Yes, he did, as he would visit them down in Draketown. He stated they had wacky beliefs. I can't remember examples, but I think astrology and that sort of thing.

He mentioned this in reference to his ex-wife and Verity, but not his other daughter. He did seem proud of his other daughter.

Q: Did he ever have conversations about why they separated?

A: No.

Q: Did he talk about Verity much to you?

A: Not really. I just got the impression she was difficult, that her life was mixed up and unhappy.

Q: Have you ever heard of a man called Lance Boyle?

A: No, I don't know the name.

Q: Has John ever visited you here in Draketown?

A: Yes. I'm not sure when. It was probably about four occasions.

Q: Do you know where he stayed when here?

A: On some occasions he stayed with us.

Q: On the other ones?

A: I'm not sure. On one occasion he may have stayed in a hostel.

Q: Do you recall him knowing anyone in Orange?

A: No I don't.

Q: On the occasions he came to Draketown, did he bring his wife?

A: On one occasion, I think. I think she may also have come down once by herself.

Q: Verity is alleging that between 1990 and 1995 you picked her up from Westchester High School and took her to a house nearby, and raped her. Is that true?

A: No.

Q: Have you ever picked Verity up from Westchester High School or any high school?

A: No.

Q: Have you ever had any sexual contact with Verity at any stage?

A: No.

Q: Have you ever talked to John Rigby about Verity, and about sexual conduct with Verity?

A: No.

Q: Are you aware of John Rigby ever having sex with Verity, or giving her to anyone to have sex with?

A: No.

Q: Verity states that there is a group of men that associated with her father that had sex with her in a group and separately. Is that something you know anything about?

A: No.

Q: Does it surprise you that Verity has said this about her father?

A: I know one of the times he came to see us, she had made a similar type of allegation. I don't know what extent her allegation had gone to, but he was upset about it. He talked to my wife about it.

I have read this statement, and it is true, and I acknowledge that it is an offence to make a statement that is false.

*Houwhanga Outdoor Activity Centre.

And so it is done. As I drive home, thoughts and fears buzz around in my brain. How did it get so far? They surely have no case, and what is asserted without evidence deserves to be dismissed with no evidence. I have so many questions about the questions. Perhaps some of them are purposely irrelevant, and it's police policy to unsettle the interviewee by making him wonder why they are asked. Why did she ask me to describe the Ziffel house, when I stayed there before Verity was born? And why the question about the car in 1974? I wonder why it mattered that John and I have been members of New Zealand Skeptics. Given that Verity and her mother are not very selective about what they believe, has Verity decided to target those men among her father's friends who might question those beliefs she cherishes? Who is Lance Boyle? And who is this other person who lives in Orange, a small town maybe thirty minutes' drive from Draketown?

I seize upon things that might be called encouraging. I craved more questions about the ski patrol. Let her lie centre on perverted skiers, because if ever there were a surface I seek to avoid, for purposes of paedophilia or simply moving from A to B, it is snow. Everyone in my circle knows that I regard snow as something useful only for calendar photos. The only time I went skiing, I ended up in a twisted and shivering heap. Snow could prove my innocence.

I wonder about Eva's final question. Was she throwing me a bone? Could it have been an opportunity for me to draw attention to Verity's dubious credibility?

The yellow car is specific, but why is it just "a yellow car", and not "Dad's car"? This suggests I must have procured another yellow car from someone, in a city where her father and stepmother were the only people I knew. The house is also a puzzle, for similar reasons. She knew the house where her father and stepmother lived, because she had stayed with them for a term. However, if the rapists' lair were this one, she would surely say "my father's house". The time envelope is what perplexes me most: some time between 1990 and 1995. I presume this means just once. The strong suggestion is that it happened after I picked her up from Westchester, where she spent just a term. So why does the period of the accusation cover five years? What's more, Angela knows for a fact that Verity spent 1993, her third and apparently final year, at our local high school here in Draketown (not the one I was teaching at). So, even if the accusation is broader than that one term, why does it not just cover 1991 and 1992? It hardly seems credible that she would have forgotten where she went to school and when.

In any case, narrow or broad, the allegation is transparent nonsense. The only time I was in Houwhanga between 1990 and 1995 was for ten or so days in the summer school holidays at the end of 1991, as Angela's earlier records testify. So how could I have picked her up from school? I'm astounded that someone who has such poor memory of actual events can fool the police when she makes them up.

Over the whole five years of her allegation, I was living here in Draketown and teaching full-time at Redwater College. To rape her in or around Houwhanga would take a whole lot of subterfuge and, frankly, rather more effort than it was worth. I would have to take a day off from school by pretending to be sick. Then I would fly from Draketown to Houwhanga, a journey that would require a stopover in Wellington. Arriving at Houwhanga airport, I would have to rent, borrow or steal a car from somewhere and drive to a school I didn't know, pick up a girl I had never met, and take her to a house near the school. Whose house would it be, if not her father's? How would I find a convenient house, under such time pressure, in a city where I had no acquaintances apart from her father and stepmother? Having found such an elusive venue, there I would hastily rape her, and the whole transport rigmarole would have to be repeated in reverse. Angela had no work over the vast period of the allegation, because she was a stay-at-home mum looking after our son. I would have to arrive home in time for her not to know I had left...unless, of course, she was in cahoots with me in my paedophilic exploits. Such a dutiful wife! So if Verity had a grain of brain she would have accused me of raping her in Draketown, where both of us at least lived. All things considered, her lie is so inexpertly crafted that no rational person would consider it credible. Lucky for her the police are the only people she has to convince.

There is also the expense. Domestic flights in New Zealand can cost a fortune, especially off the main routes and not booked months in advance. In court I could call any number of local character witnesses who would say under oath, "Impossible. The PJ I know is far too tight-fisted to spend all that money for the sake of a few minutes' doubtful pleasure." If I craved something extra-marital, why not get a local lady from the "escorts" column in the newspaper? Mary said that this accusation is not just offensive to me: it is a slur on the desirability of certain hardworking Draketown women.

When Monty and I were waiting for Eva at the police station, he reminded me of how vulnerable a law-abiding man can be if the law hits him square in the face like this. He is easy game, because he doesn't know the tricks that are second nature to seasoned criminals. So now I do my best to think like the legal tactician I am not. In court, what would be my best defence? It would have to be singular, because a scattershot approach might look desperate and incriminating. It would be tantamount to saying to the jury, "...and if you don't like that explanation, how about this one?" When I was a high school teacher, I was always suspicious of pupils who offered more than one excuse for not producing their homework: "My dad's long-lost cousin turned up out of the blue and we had to listen to his story about whale-watching in Slovakia, and also I did it but the cousin spilt red wine on it...and my scrofula was acting up again."

So what must be my singular defence? I think of the character witnesses I could call on. They could testify to my frugality, as I wrote before, but also perhaps to my probity. But wait – plenty of convicted perverts have been respectable men, even pillars of their communities, so no one will buy that one. Nor should they. Any prosecution lawyer worth his salt will point out that outwardly decent men can use their position to manipulate, and if they are caught out they can assemble troops of equally respected colleagues who will shake their heads in outrage at any suggestion of impropriety. No, respectability counts for nothing and time and place count for everything: over the whole broad period of her allegation, it simply is not tenable to believe that I could have gone to Houwhanga and raped her. Fast end of tall story.

As I think about the absurdity of her allegation, I'm confused. On the one hand, I am encouraged that the whole thing must appear ridiculous to anyone who gives it even a moment's lucid thought. But on the other hand, I wonder why the "investigation" has even come as far as this, given that her claim is so outrageous. I feel like screaming to Eva, "Check the places and times! It's insane!" But that would be intuitive and sensible, and I have begun to learn that if common sense ever plays a role in dealings with police and lawyers, it is a very occasional one. What prevails is a fixed procedure, a kind of remote posturing by prosecution and defence, like rival bull musk oxen sizing each other up. I start to wonder whether Verity's claims would have been given so much credence if they had involved anything except sexual abuse; if I had allegedly robbed her, would such a story have flown as far as this one?

I arrive home and tell Angela the sordid details. We are in a daze, pondering the absurdity that a perverse action I didn't do on an undetermined day two decades ago to a woman I never met can have such power to transform our real lives.

And we think about John. Maddening and depressing though it is for us, for him it must be worse. He has no geographical defence, because he can hardly claim he hasn't met or been alone with his own daughter. He must also feel guilty that she is the one who has pointed the finger at his friends – at least three of them. Worst of all, he has in effect lost one of his two daughters. All those years of love and solicitude have produced no legacy of value – only this rancour. He's the alleged ringleader, so we assume that he must have been interviewed as well, and that he is aching to talk to us.

We want to contact him right now, but we are afraid to because it is surely possible for the police to trace our calls. Four or more paedophiles – this is a big case with huge stakes for the accused, and surely a lot of pressure on the police as well to get a result. We mustn't give the impression to the police and a future jury that John and I are trying to cook up a story.

But in a way not ringing John is unrealistic and plain stupid. Angela and Gloria are old friends, still in occasional contact. If Gloria happened to ring Angela out of the blue and knew nothing about this, what would Angela talk to her about – new wallpaper in the guest room? How her tomatoes are really struggling in this dry weather?

Angela and I also have questions which go beyond the interview. We know that Verity lived here in Draketown when she was a teenager, but where does she live now? If there is a trial, where will it be held – Draketown? Auckland? Stockholm? I've already looked in the Draketown phone book, and she isn't there, though her mother is. If her mother hasn't moved, the chances are Verity is still here too. I must find her.

I now realise that this is becoming the battle of – and some ways for – our lives. But if Verity wants a fight she'll get it. If she's out to get me, it's surely fair that I'm out to get her. Today she isn't deluded; today she's a liar. She has every right to believe what she wants. She even has the right to be certain about what is false, and to share that certainty with her counsellor, her family and friends. But as soon as she takes that false certainty to the police station and implicates me by name in a horrible crime, she has become the only criminal. I find myself pacing up and down again. Verity is turning me from a be-er into a doer – but what exactly can I do? Well, at the very least I can try to find things out.

February 12

I go to the offices of the Accident Compensation Corporation, the government department which would bankroll any claims Verity might put in for a lump sum payout. I have to pretend to be a victim of historic sexual abuse in order to get to talk to anyone. The Draketown office is small, and the woman interviewing me tells me their sexual abuse point woman is away, and discreetly hands me a card with the number of the "sensitive claims" division of the head office in Wellington. When I get home I call them, but they say my first step is to go to the police with any claim. Any application for payment would be further down the track. The ACC website has no information about payouts, so I am forced to shelve this whole area of enquiry.

February 14

I send an email to Felicity Goodyear-Smith, the Auckland doctor who is the New Zealand authority on false memory cases. She phones me and offers support. She suggests I make online contact with the national group of similar victims. She says my situation is far more common than most people assume. I pace some more.

This nonsense will probably not go to prosecution. However, if it does, I have decided I will defend myself. They say a man who defends himself has a fool as a client, but a fanciful little syllogism plays over in my mind. The prosecution case is surely so feeble that even if my defence lawyer were, for example, a ring-tailed lemur, any jury would still acquit me. Now, surely I can present a better defence than even the most articulate ring-tailed lemur. So acquittal is the only possible outcome. This can be achieved in two ways: either I will be acquitted and we will have to pay a lawyer thousands of dollars (perhaps even tens of thousands) or I can be acquitted and we will not pay a cent. Only a fool would choose the former.

February 16

Payout time. This thing is like a mugging: not only has Verity whacked us over the head from behind, she has also robbed us. We get a joint bill from Dwight and Monty for services so far – very prompt. Think of a figure and add a zero. Guilty people get better value.

All the more reason, then, to defend myself. I mention my intention to Charles, my friend with court connections. Does he think this is a good idea? The full, unedited text of his response: "No." My cousin Jackie also scolds me for what she says is a foolhardy notion. I may have to rethink that irrevocable decision.

I do my first cycle sleuthing. I bike past the home of Verity's mother, which is less than fifty metres off the main road into town, on a quiet side street. I see what appears to be a visitor's car up the driveway. Could be interesting. I make a mental note of the make, model and registration number.

February 18

Verity has become almost the only topic at home. Angela insists that we must free ourselves of her control over our emotions; that if we let her saturate our lives, she has in fact quietly won without even needing her dishonest day in court. We agree to implement VFDs – Verity-free days – from Monday to Friday every week. This means that, barring something life-changing such as a phone call from Dwight telling us that the police have dropped the charges because Verity has returned to her home planet, we will speak no more of her or her allegation. We decide that extending it to cover the weekend would just be unrealistic. We cannot ignore the allegator in the room.

Maybe forty people are in the Verity loop now, if I include those far enough away that we are only in email contact. As for the ones I talk to, the way they refer to my accusation is revealing. They say "the accusation against you,", "the false assault allegation", or offer that ultimate euphemism, silence: "How is it with the, er…?" Some are taken aback when I say, "Oh, you mean the paedophile rape accusation?" But I see no reason for sugar coating. It's just one of a whole catalogue of horrible things I've never done. I've read that some genuine rape victims have given up their right to be anonymous, for something like the same reason. What have they and I done to be ashamed of?

I watch the Youtube TED talk on false memory by psychologist Elizabeth Loftus, one of the most prominent researchers in the field.

Loftus opens with a rape case made tragic because of mistaken memory. It concerned a young man called Steve Titus, who was falsely accused of rape because he looked like the offender, and his car looked like the offender's car. When the rape victim was shown his image in a series of photos, she said, "He's the closest." Later, in court, this became "I'm absolutely positive that's the man." He was convicted and jailed but eventually cleared after another man, a persistent rapist, was charged. However, the experience embittered the innocent accused. His fiancée walked out on him and he lost his job and all his savings. He took a lawsuit against the police but died, aged 35, of a stress-induced heart attack just before the case came to court.

Loftus points out that we often assume our memories are like recording devices – almost like a hard disk, from which events can be extracted when we need them. But they are really nothing of the kind. She mentions experiments in which false perceptions, which later turned into memories, were quite easily planted into the minds of subjects. Memory, far from being an objective recorder of events, is a constructive and subjective mechanism which is easily buffeted by the misinformation – deliberate and incidental – which is everywhere. Loftus refers to research where experimenters convinced the subjects that they had suffered horrifying experiences when they were very young.

The 1990s saw the start of a new wave of specific and sinister false memories. She says

> Some patients were going into therapy with one problem – maybe they had depression, [or] an eating disorder – and they were coming out of therapy with a different problem.

Many of these patients came to believe that some time in the distant past they had endured brutal and often bizarre mistreatment. She adds that most of these cases involved a particular form of psychotherapy, often incorporating dream interpretation, exposure to false information, hypnosis or imagination therapy.

When Loftus initially released her findings, she found herself in the firing line of "repressed memory therapists, who found themselves under attack." Letter-writing campaigns were started against her, and at one point she needed a police guard at her lectures. After she wrote the article *Who Abused Jane Doe?* for the Skeptical Inquirer magazine, she had to endure a lawsuit from the woman whose bizarre sexual abuse claims against her own mother Loftus had questioned.

Loftus concludes by confirming how important memory can be in defining our very essence. But she warns that

> Just because somebody tells you something and they tell it with confidence, just because they say it with lots of detail, just because they express emotion when they say it, it doesn't mean that it really happened. We can't reliably distinguish true memories from false memories. We need independent corroboration.

Like my DNA in a yellow car in Houwhanga. That should do it.

In a column in the Guardian on November 25 2010, Chris French mentions an incident which backs up what Loftus says. Australian psychologist Donald Thomson was amazed to learn that he was a suspect in a rape case, because he matched the description the victim gave. His alibi got him off the hook: when the rape happened, he was doing a live TV interview on the unreliability of eyewitness testimony. The victim had watched this interview before the rape and "had confused her memory of him with that of the rapist."

February 21

I register online with menz.org, a New Zealand support group for men, including victims of false sexual abuse claims. It says this sort of thing is much more common than most people realise, and it's assisted by counsellors who have become skilled at helping complainants make their allegations stick. The site contains a section on what to do if a Verity fixes you in her crosshairs. Beware of refuting accusations too specifically in a police interview, because the police may later change their approach and catch you off guard. I already know this by now, of course. Damned if you refute, and damned if you don't refute. The site also says you may need help, because of anger, bitterness and helplessness. Check all of those, but especially the first and last. You may have trouble sleeping. Check that one too.

I also read some New Zealand case studies, such as the man who was accused of abusing his three daughters when they were very young. They claimed they had suppressed the memories but the horror returned under therapy. He was convicted and sent to jail, but was later acquitted on appeal. The man was found innocent, but it cost him $117,000 in legal fees. His daughters were found to have made false statements but they were not prosecuted, and the $10,000 each they had been awarded was unaffected by the result of the trial. After his acquittal, $10,000 of the father's legal bills were remitted in compensation. Very generous.

The site gives advice for men in this sort of pickle. A lot of it is really scary, not least the range of sentences for sexual violation: from six years at the lower end right up to twenty years. The police monitor the site, and screenshots of postings by members have even been shown in court. It says that the accuser will read your statement, but you won't read hers. Can this really be true? It also contains information like this:

> If you are innocent of all charges, consider very carefully before you agree to a plea bargain. You may be put under pressure to decide to plead guilty to a much lesser charge in exchange for having more

> serious charges dropped and receiving a non-custodial sentence (ie you avoid going to jail). Once you have pleaded guilty to even minor offences, you are a convicted sex offender and this has potential implications with respect to your life in the future including your employment and place of residence.

So there goes any compromise plan I might have had to deny raping a girl I have never met, and replace it with the lesser admission of not groping her behind imaginary bike sheds....or in a yellow car I've never owned.

I also read this:

> ...if you give...the police information proving that the alleged events could not have happened...those allegations get dropped and are replaced by others which you might have more difficulty defending.

What sort of outrageous excuse for justice is this? I have made a statement to police which I have signed as a true record, after a warning that not telling the truth would be an offence. Hasn't Verity done the same? This seems to imply that after seeing my statement she can just protest that at the time she made her statement, the stress of having to recall the horror of her violation made her get some details wrong. The fragile little poppet can then wail, "Actually…sob...I think maybe it was in...*sniff*... in Draketown in 1994," and anything I've done to prove it couldn't have happened in Houwhanga in 1991 just goes down the toilet. Mere allegation has now replaced corroboration, and women's intuition stands in for evidence. If even some of this is true, I may as well buy a one-way ticket to Pyongyang tomorrow.

Of course, the sort of people who make postings on sites like this may have their own unbalanced agenda. But even if this claim is far-fetched, there appears little doubt that in sexual cases the presumption of innocence has been lost: the onus has shifted to the accused person to prove he didn't do it. What makes this worse is that the accusation against me is historic. I have been accused of a grotesque crime from two decades ago with no forensic traces. So how can I reasonably be expected to provide an alibi? Normal rules about evidence don't apply.

I am angry. I pace again. This woman is certainly getting me off the couch.

We are still burning to know if John has been interviewed. Surely he must have been – he was our recruiter, for god's sake. I suggest that Angela ring Gloria. I can go to a friend's house who can later testify if necessary that I was with her and couldn't have played a part in the conversation. But Angela still thinks it's too risky, so it doesn't happen.

Later, Angela is washing the dishes and I am drying. I tell her I have registered with a website that offers help to victims of such false allegations. She asks if I gave my real name, and I say, "Sure. Why not?" She says I shouldn't trust them. I almost never get angry. A former teaching colleague said if I'd been any more laid back they would have had to water me twice a day. But I feel myself reddening and I shout at her. All the absurdity of this accusation and what it is doing to our lives bubbles over, and I run into the hallway, crying with rage and bitterness. I throw the fish slice at the wall, and it separates neatly into two. I return to the kitchen and we are reconciled after more tears and my apology. I retrieve the two parts of the fish slice, which are easily re-assembled with a simple but effective push-lock mechanism. It takes a false rape accusation to allow ordinary suburban dwellers to understand how cleverly such everyday objects are put together.

February 22

My internet research takes me to the website of the Australian False Memory Association. All the stories there are sad, terrifying or both. The underlying assumption behind all these prosecutions seems to be that alleged abusers must be guilty, and that they are always to be prosecuted because children are never dishonest or deluded, and they must be protected. An abused child has more to lose than a prosecuted innocent abuser. Providing evidence that might corroborate the abuse claim is unimportant. Guilty because accused.

I read the article by Chris Taylor about a Queensland man who was prosecuted because a thirty-year-old woman visited a psychologist and "remembered" being raped by him when she lived in his household as a young girl. These were mere impressions from the murky past, and of course they lacked any corroborating evidence. Despite this, he was convicted and sentenced to six years. He spent several months in jail, where the other inmates picked on him because, as a sex abuser, he was "lowest of the low – a rock spider." He was finally absolved of any guilt, and released after several months behind bars, but he remains justifiably angry that the police pursued the matter in the first place. His legal battle has left him "emotionally and financially drained." The cost of legal fees for his four trials came to $150,000. The article adds that a new report to the International Commission of Jurists has urged an investigation into the largely discredited repressed-memory syndrome, claiming at least thirteen men are serving prison terms in Queensland because of similar allegations.

The article is accompanied by a rather touching photo of the falsely accused man with two females unselfconsciously hugging him: his wife on one side and his stepdaughter on the other.

The man's lawyer said he found it disturbing that the case had to go to the Supreme Court four times. The president of the Australian False Memory Association said it was "irresponsible and dangerous for Queensland's justice system to rely on repressed memory evidence...up to twenty years old." The article adds that a report by the British Royal College of Psychiatrists in 1997 revealed that not one case of recovered memory has ever been proven to be true. We tend to remember, not to repress, painful memories. As Elizabeth Loftus points out in her 2002 Skeptical Inquirer article, *Who Abused Jane Doe,*

> ...people who have survived concentration camps, systematic torture by despotic political regimes, and repeated rapes – from the victims of Serbian "ethnic cleansing" to the Korean "comfort women" of World War II – do not forget. They remember, painfully, to this day.

Another expert in the field of memory, Professor Richard McNally of Harvard University, confirms that "People, including sexual abuse victims, are more likely to remember traumatic events." He adds that many genuine sexual abuse victims are incredulous that some people claim to have forgotten them.

What this man in Queensland had to endure was unbelievable, but not as unbelievable as the fact that he harbours no ill-feeling towards the accuser at all; he just hopes that she will get proper psychological help. He says, however, "I blame the psychologists. We need to flush some of them out."

Yes. All we really need to do is stop paying them. As for the other matter of his accuser, I wish I could feel as forgiving towards my Verity as he is towards his, but most of the time I just can't. It's not the way I am. In any case, if everyone were as forgiving as this guy, we would no longer call people like him remarkable. That's my excuse to go on loathing.

February 23-25

I follow up the thread of presumption of innocence, which I wrote about three days ago. The particular problems courts have in dealing with rape and other sexual cases go back a long way. In the seventeenth century English chief justice Matthew Hale said that rape "is an accusation easily to be made and hard to be proved, and harder to be defended by the party accused." American judges read some paraphrase of this "Hale warning" to juries until the 1980s.

I have long been aware of a shift towards believing the complainant in sex abuse cases even without the kind of corroborating evidence which Hale would have considered essential. Back in the early 1980s I briefly went out with a woman who was very committed to women's rights. I need to preface what follows with a warning that, unlike Verity, I concede that my recollections of what happened three decades ago are not fully reliable. However, I think I have it right. One conversation I had with this woman was on the issue of sexual assault. Perhaps it came up because a case was in the news at the time; I can't remember. In effect, she said the woman must be believed, because otherwise a man can always get away with denial, since sexual crimes are almost by definition private. Men being men, they will claim whatever sexual licence they can. And also, why would a woman lie? I conceded that her first point may be true for a small number of men, but abandoning the presumption of innocence sets a very dangerous precedent. She saw this presumption as just a ruse by the males who pull all the strings in society. But it isn't a conspiracy, I said. It's just in the nature of such a private crime that guilt is hard to prove. As for lying, we know that people lie, for all sorts of complex reasons – not just men, but people. It was beyond my wildest imaginings that what I said in that disagreement would become as relevant as it did on February 1 this year.

I decide to do some research on false rape complaints. How common are they? Estimates are all over the scale, depending on the agenda (and usually gender) of the person doing the research. Myths abound, and even myths about myths. The problem starts with definitions. It's not surprising that campaigners for men and for women squabble so much about false rape when it's hard agreeing on a definition of rape itself. Comparing national figures confirms this. For example, in 2010 Sweden had the second-highest number of reported rapes in the world. Proportional to population this was more than three times the number of its neighbour Norway, and thirty times the number in India. Mongolia reported no rapes at all in that year. Of course, this is partly about reporting rates, cultural attitudes and police procedures, but the main reason for the discrepancy between Sweden and other developed countries was its well-publicised legislation in 2005 which broadened the legal definition of rape.

The notion of false rape is therefore doomed to be even more contentious. Bloomberg columnist Megan McArdle calls it "the war of bad statistics". Women's groups often say that not enough actual rapes are prosecuted because of the common myth that women lie about rape. This claim strikes me as a straw man, rather like when creationists ask, "You mean all this just came about by chance?" Granted, plenty of women and girls in stories tell untruths about rape and sexual abuse, from the Bible through *To Kill a Mockingbird* right up to *Dexter and Atonement.* Yet I see no evidence that many people assume real women who allege rape are making it up. On the contrary, the impression I have is that these days most people ask, "Why would she be lying?" which implies the more specific rhetorical question, "Why would she want to put herself through the trauma of a trial if what she claimed were untrue?" Many men say that this assumed veracity is in fact the myth, and that innocent males are prosecuted because of it. The only reliable answer is that no one can possibly know how common false accusations are, because in almost every case no corroborating evidence exists, and the event usually comes down to the hazy issue of consent. Police procedure after a rape report sometimes says more about the prejudices of investigators than about the facts of the case itself. All we know is that no researcher bold enough to settle on a definite percentage can really be trusted.

Unsurprisingly, anti-rape campaigners say false claims are very low. They mean that *successful prosecutions* of false rape complaints are very low. The problem is that, just as it is hard to get a successful prosecution for rape, because there are usually no witnesses and the truth is mired in doubt, it is hard to get a successful prosecution for a false complaint. It works both ways. But the low rate of convictions for false complaints cannot be used as evidence that they are rare, any more than the low rate of convictions for rape accusations can be used as evidence that rape is rare. If we have scant statistics in both fields, how can those statistics tell all of one story but none of the other?

Women's groups usually quote the figure of false complaints at two percent, and they seem to have convinced other influential people that it must be held as gospel. For example, Women Against Rape reported on its UK website in 2013 that the chief crown prosecutor for London said "Studies have indicated that only two percent of all reported rapes are false, which is slightly less than false reporting in all other crimes." Any statement that starts "Studies have indicated…" should raise red flags. What studies? How were they conducted? How were the terms defined? Have other studies indicated anything very different? The last question is not rhetorical. Wendy McElroy noted on *independent.org* on May 2 2006 that legal scholar Michelle Anderson of Villanova University Law School reported, "No study has ever been published which sets forth an evidentiary basis for the two percent false rape complaint thesis."

The two-percent factoid appears to originate from Susan Brownmiller's 1975 book *Against Our Will: Men, Women and Rape.* Brownmiller quoted from a speech by judge Lawrence H. Cooke, who claimed in a speech to New York lawyers that female police officers found just two percent of all rape complaints were false – about the same proportion as for other crimes. No researcher has managed to track down any description of the methodology used to arrive at this figure, or any evidence that the research – if indeed there was any valid research – was peer reviewed.

Even agreeing on what makes a false complaint is tricky. If a rape definitely occurred but the victim identifies the wrong offender, should that be included? Almost certainly not. What about cases where the complainant truly believed a rape occurred, but either nothing at all happened (perhaps she was mentally disturbed) or there was a sexual encounter but the circumstances did not suggest rape? Cooke's estimate appears to have been based only on those complaints which are eventually retracted. Clearly, many false complaints do not fall into this category. The reverse is also true, as women's groups and police have pointed out: recanted accusations are not necessarily false. A genuine victim may retract her allegation for a variety of reasons. Here are just three: she may not want to relive the experience in a court case; she may know the offender and her affection for him overrides her original feeling of violation; she may not be convinced that a jury will reject the offender's claim of consent, especially if he has higher social status than she has.

In America, a report by the National Center for the Prosecution of Violence against Women (NCPVAW) makes this comment:

> It is...impossible to determine that a sexual assault did not happen based on sympathy for the suspect, because he seems sincerely outraged and upset by the charges, he has a credible story, or he appears to be a responsible citizen who does not meet our personal assumptions about who is likely to be a rapist.

So actual rapists can be outwardly respectable, can offer a convincing counter-story and can easily feign outrage and innocence. I'm sure they can, but some men in this category aren't putting it on; these are the very things that define his innocence. I have come to know this for a fact.

Each rape is unique, and so is each lie about rape. However, there are patterns. The NCPVAW report makes a useful distinction between false accusations and false reports. Not every report of rape involves an accusation directed at an identifiable perpetrator. In genuine cases, this is usually because the rapist is a stranger. In false reports, it may be because the "victim" is a disturbed woman who wants attention but is not malicious, and therefore has no desire to get an innocent man into a heap of trouble. In other cases involving false reports but no accusation, the lie may be for a very different reason. She may need to cover up for an affair, for example. A teenage girl may be desperate not to reveal to her conservative parents that she is sexually active. In all such false reports, the alleged perpetrator is likely to be the clichéd hooded man of medium height who came and went in the night. NCPVAW suggests that most false rape stories are reports rather than accusations.

This is no comfort for the police, because rape reports – real and fake – must consume a lot of their time. In the UK, for example, forty percent of all prosecutions are for sexual crimes. Neither is it any comfort to me in my predicament. If Verity had read it, she may have dropped the accusation and contented herself with a mere report. Or maybe not; "our" case is very different. The usual false rape cases NCPVAW deals with are responses to sudden and recent events which prompt responses – some spontaneous, some considered – from the women involved. Verity's historic delusions have to pick out the shape of a perpetrator through the mists of time.

On the other side is what, sadly, may have to be called the male analysis of false rape numbers. This implies that the only qualifications for being a victim of a false complaint are to be male and alive. The most quoted study was done by Eugene Kanin of Purdue University in 1994. Kanin pointed out that historically women were too seldom believed or treated seriously when they complained of rape or sexual assault. The dismissive attitude of investigating officers, often male, stemmed from the prevailing view of women as irrational or hysterical (a word even derived from the Greek word for womb).

Girls mattered even less than women. A female friend of mine recently told me that back in the 1960s, when she was a young girl growing up in a provincial New Zealand town, some pervert exposed himself to her sister. The perpetrator was easy to trace and their father pressed for a prosecution, but the police treated the matter as too trivial to proceed with. Later my friend was herself subjected to the same indecency from the same man, and their father thought there was no point petitioning the police again. The pervert probably went on to offend with impunity.

Some men even assumed that many women falsely complained of rape because they secretly wanted to be raped. Such assumptions went beyond general belief; they were enshrined in laws based on dubious psychology. In 1938 an American Bar Association committee recommended that all rape complainants should be subjected to a psychiatric examination to determine their truthfulness. The blatant sexism in such assumptions guaranteed that when the pendulum swung, it swung clear to the opposite extreme. Kanin wrote that these days, "Some feminists virtually deny the existence of false rape accusations and believe the concept itself constitutes discriminatory harassment toward women." This appears to be based on the obligation to assess all men according to the worst men, and all women according to the best women.

Kanin's study covered the years 1978-1987 and centred on a small Midwestern city in which "agency policy forbids police policy to use their discretion in deciding whether to officially acknowledge a rape complaint, regardless how suspect that complaint may be." The police labelled complaints as false only if the complainant withdrew the charge and admitted it was false. Kanin produced very different results from Brownmiller. The study found that, according to this definition, 41% (45 out of

109 cases) were classed as false. It broadly grouped the motives for the false complaints into three kinds: obtaining revenge, seeking attention and providing an alibi.

The conclusions in Kanin's study were commendably tentative. For example, the writers were cautious about broadening their findings in one city to others that may have had different cultures or police policies. The study has drawn some other criticism, especially from women's groups. For example, they claim that when a woman recants, it does not mean a rape did not happen. Perhaps the woman had no desire to endure a second violation in the courtroom. That is a fair objection in some cases, but almost certainly a minority, especially since the protocol of the police agency was to inform the false complainant that she would be charged and could be liable to a fine or even imprisonment.

Kanin's estimate may have been too high, but the two percent figure is certainly far too low. What I have read from women's groups such as Women Against Rape suggests a vicious circle of reasoning about false complaints. As women supposedly almost never lie about sexual violation, begin with the assumption that false reports are so rare that, in effect, they should be discounted. Therefore assume the guilt of all men accused of rape, and prosecute them. Assume the innocence of all women suspected of false complaints, and do not prosecute them. This drastically lowers – ideally to zero – the number of women who are convicted of false accusations, and that number is used to justify the claim that false reports are rare...and so the circle continues.

The tweet "Believe the victim", sent by some campaigners against sexual violence, betrays a facile and terrifying certainty that rape reports are necessarily true. In a superficial way it's indisputable, of course. If we know that a complainant is a victim, then by definition we must believe her. But to assume that all complainants are telling the truth is denying the necessity of due process. With such hashtag justice there is no such thing as the wrong man, but I suppose "Believe the complainant until and unless her story unravels" isn't quite as catchy, even if it is still shorter than Twitter's 140-character limit.

This sort of tweet is not the only evidence that campaigners treat false complaints as if they simply don't exist. One UK article I stumbled upon in this research featured a photo of an anti-rape protestor carrying a banner that read "Stop prosecuting "false" rape complainants!" If those inverted commas around *false* aren't just sloppy punctuation, they need some comment. On the surface, the demonstrator is suggesting that the police should not prosecute rape complainants whose accusations may appear false but in fact are true. I cannot argue with that, though of course it works backwards from certainty we cannot have. However, the banner appears to imply that no rape complaints are false, which is blatant nonsense.

Let us for a moment accept the discredited two percent figure. This means that even vociferous anti-rape campaigners must concede that a small number of rape complaints are false. Imagine a woman accuses a man she names of rape, and he is taken in, questioned, and charged. However, further police investigation turns the complainant's rape story into Swiss cheese, with scores of reliable witnesses ready to testify that she is lying, and a restaurant receipt revealing that she was happily dining with friends in another town. Her complaint has transformed from "false" to false. I presume the banner-waver would support prosecuting false insurance claimants, so surely this false complainant should also be taken to court…or if not, why not? Perhaps it's because a little male collateral damage is a negligible price to pay in the war against rape. Yet whether false complainants comprise two percent or fifty percent of accusations, if police always want a result, they should prosecute whenever the facts suggest a conviction is likely. Now, where does this leave the banner?

The above example is one I made up, but such cases do happen. Here is a rather different but real one, which anyone can check out at *youtube.com/watch?v=EE8sPzZsWnk*. A taxi driver in Edmonton, Alberta, was accused of sexual assault by four young females who took a ride with him. His taxi had signs that warned passengers that a camera was operating, but maybe these ones were too drunk to notice. When the women entered his taxi outside a bar, they started to smoke, which is illegal. The young women swore at him when he told them to put out their cigarettes. He asked them to pay the $13 fare at the end of the journey, but they refused. When he threatened to call the police, the women told passers-by that the driver had molested them. If it's true that women who make sexual complaints are put through so much doubt that they may as well not bother, no one had told these allegators. Soon after the police arrived, the driver invited them to look at the footage of the exchange, and they quickly said that he wouldn't be charged. The driver was of course ecstatic that his life was not going to be destroyed for the sake of a $13 fare, but he quite rightly wanted to know if the women would be charged for dishonestly accusing him. The police declined, saying there wasn't enough evidence either way.

Not enough evidence either way! It's not often I come across a sexual allegation which is more demonstrably false than Verity's against me, but this is one. How can anyone claim there is no evidence that this complaint was false, and how can anyone claim that the legal odds are stacked against complainants? I presume even the two-percenters can see the injustice here, unless of course they believe that false sexual allegations should *never* be regarded as a crime. Of course, the women were boozed, but if that is never an excuse for rape, it should never be an excuse for a false complaint. What is most disturbing about cases like this is not that false complainants are unlikely to be prosecuted, but rather that they *know* they are unlikely to be prosecuted. These young women showed no apparent fear of consequences at all.

UK politician and novelist Ann Widdecombe wrote in the Daily Express, in reference to a false rape complaint in the news:

> As long as accusers pay no price for lying through their teeth there is no disincentive to fantasists, money-grabbers, vengeance-seekers or those retrospectively embarrassed by their wild behaviour to bring false allegations as readily as they eat breakfast or breathe fresh air.

When Widdecombe mentioned "money-grabbers", she probably had in mind something more serious and premeditated than just avoiding a taxi fare. The fearlessness of these women who lie may be even worse than she suggests. Many men involved in family disputes, especially in the UK, claim that ex-partners routinely throw in a sexual abuse complaint as a matter of course, or threaten to do so in order to negotiate a better deal when the assets – both material and human – are split. I don't know how true this is, but it makes sense. After all, if the breakup was bitter, as these things often are, the aggrieved woman has plenty of motive and no deterrent; she knows no one will prosecute her, so the worst that can happen is that she will not be believed. Why would she not play this game when she knows the only outcomes for her are win or draw?

The two-percenters tend to stress how few actual rapes are prosecuted or even reported, and they insist that this is the only injustice. Their figure for this usually comes out at around five percent. Yet this is surely a dubious claim: it assumes the certainty of rape, where no such certainty exists. Rapists are not investigated; *alleged* rapists are. If a rape is not reported or is reported but not investigated, we do not yet know whether what happened was rape. Maybe the sex was consensual. Maybe no sex even occurred. Maybe (amazing though it may seem) the two never even met. Most other crimes are quite different, because circumstances confirm criminality. When the alarm has been disabled, the ceiling panels removed and the Picasso is missing from its frame, our first question can be "Who committed this crime?" With most rape claims, we must ask a logically prior question: "Was a crime committed?" That's what makes sexual crime such a tortuous area.

With false complaints of rape, all we know is that facts are elusive. Sex can involve powerful emotions and sinister undercurrents, and all sorts of people of either gender can have all sorts of reasons to lie. But neither society nor the law should insist that only the y chromosome carries the lying gene. False rape reports happen, and as the Kanin report says, "Merely to be a rape suspect, even for a day or two, translates into psychological and social trauma." True.

But it is trauma that's worth it, according to Catherine Comins, assistant dean of student life at Vassar College, who seems convinced that no amount of stress can outweigh the benefit of self-analysis. In an article on rape on June 4 2001, Comins had this to say about men falsely accused of rape:

> They have a lot of pain, but it is not a pain that I would necessarily have spared them. I think it ideally initiates a process of self-exploration. 'How do I see women?' 'If I didn't violate her, could I have?' 'Do I have the potential to do to her what they say I did?' Those are good questions.

Only to someone for whom men have no value as people.

February 26

Thursday. Quite a day in two different ways.

I am itching to find out where Verity lives, because I don't know for sure if she's still in Draketown at all. I already looked in the phone book when this thing first blew up, and she wasn't listed. However, Charles has told me that everyone is on the electoral roll. I find the Draketown electoral list in the library and there she is: name, address and occupation. So she is still local. My god – is this good news or bad? It's good that any trial will be local. She's made herself my enemy, and if knowledge is power in some inscrutable way, it must be an advantage that I know something that she and her allies, the police, don't know that I know. What's bad is that I worry that I'll become obsessed with finding out more about her, especially now that I am not teaching and have all this free time. Will I become a sort of stalker? Not exactly me, but I have to *do* something.

So she's probably lived here all these years. Draketown is a small place. I wonder how many times our paths have crossed. Maybe a car that I let pass in front of me at the Frobisher Street traffic lights back in 2002 had her at the wheel, and that woman fiddling for her change and holding me up in the New World supermarket checkout last month was her. But neither of us had any reason to give a second glance: I had never met her, and it would be unfair to expect any woman to remember the faces of all the men who haven't raped her.

Occupation: student. Of what? I wonder. I would bet that it has something to do with sexual abuse counselling, so that she can join the industry and pass on the baton of delusion. But I may be completely wrong, and she's well on the way towards her PhD in astrophysics.

Today I've got the car for a change, so I go out in the early afternoon. I drive up the hill to her listed address. It's quite close to town, but not an area I ever have a reason to visit. The house is at a dead end, on quite a steep street maybe fifty metres above the city. It's on a back section up a long shared driveway, so I can see only a corner of it. I have to walk a few steps up the driveway to see any more. There is no garage, but there is a carport at the end of the driveway, and it has a car in it – the very same car that was in her mother's driveway last week. My god, this must be her. And she's home! What do I do – thump on the door and introduce myself as the stranger whose life she wants to destroy? Far too intuitive, far too human a reaction, of course. Keep a lid on your exasperation. So I drive a little back down the road, sit in the car and wait. Maybe I'll get lucky, but I lack the patience to wait all afternoon. Do police really endure those all-night stake-outs that we see on TV, taking turns to sneak out for pizza and coffee?

No need to be patient, because I do get lucky. After only ten minutes or so I see the car approaching in my rear view mirror, and I take off after it. At the intersection leading onto the main road, she has to stop, and I pull up right behind her. I can't see much, of course – just the head of a woman with a pony tail. She drives down into the city and enters the main car park. A few cars get between us and I lose sight of where she parks, but I know her car's in here somewhere. I cruise around the lines of parked cars, and there it is. It's not a busy time, and plenty of slots are available. I park my own car just a few spaces along, and I stroll past hers, looking through the windscreen at her ticket to see how much parking time she's bought. Not long. I enter a cafe overlooking the park and order a coffee and sandwich. I sit at the window and get ready to turn my snack into a four-course meal. My eyes fasten on her car like drills.

After about twenty minutes, there she is. But she's not leaving yet. She opens the driver's door and gets something from inside, then locks the car again and walks away. I leave the cafe and walk in her direction. We pass each other and she even looks me in the eye briefly. I could follow her, but that really would be stalking, so I call it a day. I feel proud and ashamed of what I've achieved.

So that's her: dumpy, unprepossessing, a little goofy. That's the female I supposedly found so irresistible more than two decades ago that I had no hesitation about making that long commute. We've all changed, but none more than her.

Back home, I tell Angela about my doubtful achievement. Today is supposedly a VFD, so I'm breaking our arrangement, but this is something special. She's mildly interested in the TV sleuth angle of it, but wonders what this sort of thing can achieve. She's right, of course – as usual.

Since we have broken VFD rules anyway, we make another decision. We've endured having no contact with John and Gloria long enough, and will make a move this evening. They're friends, after all. Tonight is the best night, because it's Thursday –

quiz night. I will go as usual, and I will stress to my team mates that it is of crucial importance that they remember that this is February 26, and I was in their company without interruption between 7 and 9 p.m. It is arranged: Angela will ring Gloria during that time, and talk only to her. If John answers the phone, she'll not identify herself and just ask to speak to his wife. Finally, we're doing it.

After the quiz I rush home and ask, "Well? Well?" Angela says that John and Gloria had no idea about any of this. Gloria was devastated, outraged, disbelieving. Yet she knows it must be true; why would friends make this up? She explained to Angela that Verity was always difficult, and things were awkward on the rare occasions when she visited them in Houwhanga. And of course, she made an allegation years ago, but nothing as far-reaching and as horrifying as this. Gloria tells Angela that John and Verity have not been in contact for around six years. The wives talked in some detail for an hour or so, and then Gloria was left with the bitter task of telling her husband the news.

February 28

Gloria wants to contact us again, but is afraid to do so directly. She tracks down the number of Angela's sister, who lives here in Draketown and whom Gloria hardly knows. Gloria rings the sister, and the sister rings Angela. The message is that Angela should go to her sister's at 7 pm to receive a call from Gloria. This is getting too silly. And awkward. None of Angela's family is in the Verity loop, and it will be hard to take a call there away from Angela's sister's three kids. Angela rings Gloria directly. Gloria says that John hasn't slept a wink since this news hit him. The main message is that Gloria has booked a flight to come and stay with us for five days, starting on April 4.

March 2-3

Following my research on false rape accusations last week, I decide to find out more about what happens to women who are caught out. In theory, they can do jail time. In practice, however, penalties are slight – if the liars are prosecuted at all. The UK appears to have the strongest penalties in place. Offenders there can be sentenced to life imprisonment, much to the indignation of women's groups, who say this is a huge disincentive to genuine rape reporting. The common claim that rape is under-reported is difficult to verify; the further claim that the reason for that putative under-reporting is fear of prosecution also needs data to back it up. Perhaps the reason genuine rape victims do not report the event is not what those victims say it is. Some rape campaigners insist that few rapes are properly investigated. That doubtful claim may persuade some real victims not to report, even if it is not true.

What is quite clear is that the indignation in the UK stems from the existence of the law rather than its application, because few women are prosecuted. Rape is supposed to have a very low conviction rate, but it appears certain that the conviction rate for false rape accusations is far lower than that. A 2014 article in the Guardian Online reports that only 109 women were taken to court in the UK in the previous five years for making false sexual accusations. Of those cases, 98 were prosecuted for perverting the course of justice, a very serious charge. The remainder were given the lesser charge of wasting police time. What this means is that a false rape charge, which inevitably causes unspeakable suffering for the victim, usually brings no punishment for the offender.

One UK victim of a transparently false rape complaint points out that the Greater Manchester Police never, under any circumstances, prosecute a false accuser, even though the national legal code provides for such an action. He makes the valid point that this policy discriminates against him as a victim of crime, and he is seeking advice on taking a complaint as far as the European Court of Human Rights. Detective Superintendent Jon Chadwick, head of the Manchester sexual offences unit, confirms that non-prosecution is the GMP policy. This is despite the fact that since the unit opened in 2012, dozens of complaints have turned out to be fabricated. Presumably this means *demonstrably* fabricated; no doubt others would also be false, but doubtful enough for police not to count on a conviction if they were to pursue one. Chadwick explains that the GMP prefers not to prosecute liars because "those making false reports have some sort of vulnerability." Some sort of vulnerability! Many people who set fire to buildings or embezzle from their employers no doubt have some sort of vulnerability as well. Should we never prosecute them either? A contributor on *daftmoo.co.uk* posted the following response to this GMP outrage:

> What would stop a group of people walking into 5 or 10 different Greater Manchester Police stations and each accusing a Greater Manchester MP of rape? Pick random, historical dates, safe in the knowledge that the most you would get is a £90 fine for wasting police time. It would certainly rattle some cages and make the point I want to; that having a carte blanche policy allows women to accuse without any slight fear of impunity (sic).

Such action would be a spectacular way of drawing attention to this GMP policy, which is so contemptible that I am astounded that any police unit can get away with it. Elected UK legislators have deemed a false rape complaint to have repercussions that are so serious that they have attached a life sentence to its most egregious cases. Yet Chadwick's unit has decided never to prosecute this crime, and he has stated this policy publicly. So here is a major crime which a complainant can commit and know she will get away scot-free, even if the evidence is plain that she has committed it – in fact, even if she *admits* she has committed it. Chadwick sees nothing embarrassing about admitting to this policy, which makes me wonder how many other police districts in effect act the same way but keep it quiet.

I assume that one advantage of this approach from the government bean counters' point of view is that no money gets wasted on consultations with mental health experts to figure out how debilitating the complainant's issues are. The police have decided that they will act as judge, jury and psychiatrist, and that any false complainant's mental health absolves her of any responsibility – always. Chadwick, interviewed in an article in the Guardian, says that to work in his unit, "You have to be a people person, not a cold, hard facts person." Aha, so that's the problem. Facts – so emotionless, so unforgiving, so inflexible. The stories people tell are much more absorbing. No one is more touchingly human than the woman who alleges rape. She is by definition a victim, no less so if her story has "discrepancies".

I find the snail-mail address of the GMP and write a letter to Chadwick, in which I politely disagree with him. I include my email address in case he wants to reply. I assume he will write me off as some crank and won't bother, but if he does I'll mention it.

Happily, a small number of liars do face justice of a sort. One false rape case comes from the Daily Mail in the UK. The paper's online edition reports that Michelle Rossiter from Preston (which, luckily for her victim, is outside the Greater Manchester district) was jailed for three years in 2014 after being convicted of perverting the course of justice for making "a series of false claims" in 2010 and 2011 alleging abuse by the same man. What appeared to convince the jury to convict was that she fabricated physical evidence to make some of her claims more credible.

The article quotes Valerie Wise, director of Preston Domestic Violence Service, as saying malicious allegations are rare. She added, "I believe ninety-nine percent of people who make complaints are telling the truth but it is difficult to prove." Indeed it is, so why offer the spurious precision of a percentage in a field which is so contentious?

I manage to track down a Youtube interview with a British man who had his rape conviction overturned after the evidence that the complainant had lied became too overwhelming to ignore (though she still faces no consequences). In the studio there are two interviewer/hosts, one male and one female. Both furrow their brows on cue as they ask the victim to talk about how this has affected him. He mentions everything we would expect: the bitter experience of jail, the ostracism, the loss of earnings, the new fear of intimacy. But he isn't the only guest. Sitting next to him is a (female) criminologist, who waits in respectful silence during his account, but she squirms a little in her seat as if there's something she's just itching to say. When she is finally called upon to comment, she says exactly what the dogma demands: that such incidents are very rare, and that the real tragedy is that they erode the credibility of actual victims. The story may allow a bit part for a man, but the main plot and the theme must be about women.

The Telegraph reports that Jennifer Day was jailed for two years for perverting the course of justice after a false rape complaint which cost the police £4000 and 270 hours. Day had had a relationship with a man she had met on a dating site. She claimed he raped her, but when a neighbour affirmed his version of events, she admitted she had lied. She appealed her sentence, but was unsuccessful. The appeal judge said

> False complaints of rape necessarily impact upon the minds of jurors trying rape cases. Every time a defendant stands trial for rape, defence counsel necessarily point out to the jury that false allegations are made. Allegations such as this drive a nail into the conviction rate.

Perhaps, but that is not all they do. Although it unquestionably matters how the public perceive rape allegations, that is not the main point about a false rape accusation. The main point is that an innocent man may have his life ruined. Yet to Lisa Longstaff, spokesperson for Women Against Rape, this appears to be of little consequence. She called the Day sentence "outrageous" and expressed concern that such a sentence would put women off reporting rapes. Her ire seems guided not by a broad notion of justice but solely by a blind sense of solidarity with women as women. Why not be enraged both by rapes and by false rape accusations? They both happen and they are both illegal. If ninety-nine percent of rape accusations were provably false, some anti-rape campaigners would still intone the old mantra that prosecuting the complainants just reinforces the myth that women lie about rape.

A standout UK case reported by the Daily Mail concerns a young woman called Elizabeth Jones. Her first false complaint was in 2004, when she was just 13. Between 2005 and 2013 she made another eight allegations, but she was still not prosecuted. In 2009 (presumably her tenth complaint) she was given a ten-month detention and a training order – whatever that is. Her eleventh allegation finally got her sent to jail. Her victim was questioned for nine hours before being released without charge. She said she made the complaint because she didn't like him. She was sentenced to sixteen months in jail. The fact that this woman made ten false complaints before she faced jail time hardly suggests police are overzealously pursuing false complainants.

A spokeswoman for the UK Crown Prosecution Service said

> Cases of perverting the course of justice that involve allegedly false rape allegations are serious but rare. They are usually highly complex and sensitive often involving vulnerable parties, so any decision to charge is extremely carefully considered and not taken lightly.

There are those pernicious adjectives yet again: *rare* and *vulnerable*. I also wonder what she is calling rare: false accusations or *prosecutions* for false accusations. They are not at all the same thing. The remark about complexity and sensitivity is also revealing. I accept that in "he said/she said" cases it is usually difficult to say for certain who is telling the truth. In such cases, police should *not* prosecute the accuser even if they strongly suspect she is lying. But in slam-dunks like the Elizabeth Jones case and mine, the police had better have a damned good reason not to prosecute the liar. What is sensitive about it: the fact that she is a "survivor", that she has "issues"... the mere fact that she is female, perhaps? Back on February 5 I made a note of the French tourists who put in a false robbery claim. Would the police change their minds about prosecuting them if they learned the tourists had had difficult lives, or they were mentally unstable?

In another UK case in which a woman was prosecuted for making a false complaint against an innocent man, her lawyer complained about the "vehemence" with which police pursue such women. He said that the police appear to be convinced that anyone who lies to them should suffer severe consequences. This misses the point. When a woman lies about rape but identifies no "perpetrator", misleading the police is indeed the worst thing she has done. When the liar names a man and puts him in the frame, the overriding ethical outrage is not that she has been dishonest with the police. It is a very different matter: that she has threatened to extinguish permanently the happiness of another human being. If the police prosecute such women just because they prefer citizens not to waste their time, then the purpose of laws is reduced to protecting the police rather than the public, and it means the police too are missing the point.

The most polarising recent case in the UK appears to be the tragic one involving a young woman called Eleanor de Freitas. After she accused a man of rape, the victim brought a private suit against her. However, the Crown Prosecution Service took over the prosecution. She killed herself three days before the trial. She had a mental disorder, but according to the Daily Mail her own legal team had "recommended that she was aware of the implications of making a false allegation and was fit to stand trial." Her father was outraged that the CPS proceeded with the prosecution.

A contributor on the website *avoiceformen.com* makes the following analogy based on the de Freitas tragedy:

> For a contrast, consider this hypothetical case. Jack raped Jill. The police let him get away with it, so she brought a private prosecution of rape. The Crown Prosecution Service took over the prosecution. Jack then killed himself three days before his trial. He had bipolar disorder, but a forensic psychiatrist instructed by his own legal team had "recommended that he was aware of the implications of rape and was fit to stand trial." His mother was '"still astonished" that the CPS had decided to prosecute him.

The contributor points out that we are likely to have some compassion for de Freitas and for her father, but none for Jack or her mother. The underlying reason is a visceral conviction that rape is more heinous and more damaging than a false accusation of rape, but he implies that our sympathy may sometimes be misplaced. I think he's right.

What makes this a fascinating case is that the circumstances are far from clear-cut. The police involved in the original investigation remained convinced that de Freitas should not have been charged, and they were reluctant to have anything to do with her prosecution. However, the director of public prosecutions defended the action, saying the evidence against de Freitas was strong, and that the mental state of de Freitas did not outweigh the responsibility of pursuing such a serious case.

I am particularly interested that the police took over the burden of prosecution from the accused man when they saw that they had a case against the accuser which they could win. I wonder why they would not just let a private prosecution run, so that they don't have to pay a penny towards the huge cost. It's very enlightened of them to perform their civic duty so selflessly. It doesn't often happen.

It is encouraging that New Zealand police do sometimes prosecute false complainants, though seldom, and apparently only for wasting police time rather than the more appropriate and more serious charge of perverting the course of justice. In 2005, officers at the Hornby police station in Christchurch had to struggle with a spate of false complaints. One woman was prosecuted after twenty police spent over $15,000 worth of police time on one woman's alleged abduction and assault. She was sentenced to 150 hours' community work.

On November 8 2008 Christchurch police charged 21-year-old Alyshia Clyne with making a false charge of rape. She alleged that an unidentified man raped her in an alleyway while she was out drinking with friends. The police cordoned off parts of the central city, causing disruption to nearby businesses, while ten officers investigated.

Video surveillance cameras and a statement from her friend quickly showed her story was nonsense. Judge Brian Callaghan said, "I am troubled by the number of false complaints." Her name was originally suppressed, because her lawyer said there were "medical and mental health issues" that needed to be explored. There always are. She was sentenced to 75 hours' community work.

Three cases from the USA warrant some detail. The first shows that the complaint itself has become the evidence. In 2012 in Virginia, Johnathan Montgomery was released from jail four years into a sentence of almost eight years for molesting Elizabeth Paige Coast when she was ten and he was fourteen. The two had been childhood friends. Coast made up the allegations after her parents caught her looking at pornographic websites in 2007, when she was seventeen. She offered the story of prior sexual abuse to explain her behaviour and evade any reprimand or punishment. It is a measure of how far the onus of proof has shifted towards the male that the trial judge simply took her word against his, and he was convicted despite the absence of any corroborating evidence. Montgomery expressed understandable relief at being absolved and released, but said he could not forgive his accuser. Coast was charged with perjury and was sentenced to two months in jail. She was to be locked up for weekends only. Outrageously, Montgomery was kept in jail for a time even after his accuser was charged, and was only given a "conditional pardon". For at least thirteen months after his release, he remained an official sex offender, not allowed to go near schools or parks. He also had to meet regularly with a probation officer and could not leave town without permission.

Was justice finally served here? Barely. Her sentence was light compared to his, and around ninety percent of informal voters on the website of the local newspaper thought her sentence was unfair – presumably too light. However, she did also have to pay $90,000 in restitution. Her lie wasn't detected; the truth emerged after her conscience got the better of her and she owned up to it, and she deserves some credit for showing such courage – eventually. She said that it started as a small lie that just got out of control.

However, justice is usually much more elusive, as two other US cases show. An innocent man can easily get accused, and a guilty woman can just as easily get excused – or barely punished. In 2013 Colorado woman Katherine Bennett said that Justin Toth kidnapped, drugged and raped her at knife point. Toth was arrested but the case was soon dropped when holes appeared in her story. This exoneration was too late to stop him from being fired, and he struggled to find work after this nightmare. Bennett was convicted of lying to police and tampering with evidence, both of which are felony offences, and a CBS report before her sentencing made much of the nine years' jail she could have faced. Her parents begged for a light sentence so she could get psychiatric help. Something certainly worked, because she was given just thirty-two days in jail and probation for five years.

Ben Radford on the *Center for Inquiry* website reports that in 2013 Robin Levitski, a student at Clarke University in Iowa, accused a man of abducting her from a social event at knife point and sexually assaulting her. However, the credibility of her story soon unravelled in the eyes of the police investigators. The accused man had date-stamped photos of their sexual encounter which showed not only that it was almost certainly consensual, but that it happened on a different date from when she claimed. Levitski's smart key card showed she had been on campus at the time of the alleged assault. A friend of Levitski said that she saw the complainant leave the event quite willingly with the accused.

Keeping what they knew close to their chests to begin with, the police interviewed Levitski again, and pointed out that her charges could result in a man going to jail for life. Did she think this would be a fair punishment? She replied that life might be too long, but that he should do "several years". Radford is understandably shocked at what he calls the complainant's "utter indifference" to the fate of the blameless man she had recently dated. Levitski kept to her story even after the counter-evidence was presented. After half an hour of further questioning, she admitted that she made the story up to explain away the raunchy images that her grandmother had found on her mobile phone.

Radford comments:

> This case is fascinating and offers insight into the rarely-discussed dynamics of a demonstrably false report of abduction and sexual assault. This is not a case in which the circumstances are ambiguous, or authorities concluded that there was insufficient evidence to establish the accused person's guilt. This is an open-and-shut case in which all of the evidence, including the alleged victim's statements, clearly demonstrate that the accusation was false.

Another slam-dunk, then. But for making an accusation that could have put an innocent man away for life, Levitski was sentenced to probation and a US$315 fine plus court costs. Radford implies this is far too light a charge in the circumstances, and says that such cases happen "far more often than most people realise."

So, when and if the Draketown police find out that my case broadly resembles Levitski's, what will they do with Verity? I think I know already.

Part Two

March 4-5

Have I ever thought John and maybe others really are guilty? Maybe he really did lead a paedophile ring, and I'm just the poor sap whose name Verity got wrong. A friend in the V-loop puts this to me today, and he isn't the first one. It's a fair and troubling question. The answer is yes, the idea has crossed my mind. I am ashamed that I've thought this about a friend, but I've had plenty of disturbing thoughts since strange days tracked us down. It's all about mathematics. Of course, I am one hundred percent certain that I am squeaky clean, but it would be irrational to apply the same certainty to John and the other accused. However, I regard as so unlikely that in effect I rule it out.

First, if this accusation is true, why didn't he also molest Jennifer, his younger daughter? She seems to be happy and well adjusted, and as far as I know has never made any such accusation. It seems logical that when the older victim wised up, a paedophile father would move on to her kid sister. Secondly, Verity has no credibility for me. This gives me an advantage over other people who know about the case. Everyone else must have at least a shadow of doubt about my innocence: my friends, my relations. Even Angela cannot be one hundred percent certain – though she is probably 99.9%. Of course, the police appear to be far less convinced. But I know that Verity's allegation against me is untrue, and in a sense that gives me a special insight into her. Why should I believe her when she makes precisely the same accusation about anyone else?

Thirdly, I wonder about the incidence of father-daughter incest. The notorious

Fritzl case in Austria, in which the father Josef kept his daughter Elisabeth imprisoned as a sex slave for 24 years, is the most awful example in recent years, though a case doesn't have to be as extreme as this to be tragic. So yes, it does happen. However, I suspect that it is not as common as it's sometimes made out to be. The late American skeptic Martin Gardner wrote that "a father capable of raping his four-year-old daughter betrays such psychotic behavior that it is almost impossible for there to be no other records of his mental illness." Gardner probably goes too far, because incestuous fathers could be quite skilled at keeping their depravity from the outside world. However, I find it hard to agree with people who say that what we know is just the tip of the iceberg.

I've been doing a bit of research. In her thorough and insightful book *A City Possessed*, Lynley Hood gives a detailed account of how, starting in the 1970s, some articulate and committed campaigners cherry-picked convenient data about sexual abuse and got all this hysteria on the road. The New Zealand-wide 1988 fundraising Telethon had the theme "one in four", from the assertion that a quarter of girls are molested, many of those by their own fathers. I decided years ago that almost all statistics generally held to be true are patently false, and this is no exception. Almost no one at the time questioned this number, yet even to the casual observer it should have looked suspiciously glib. What does it even mean? Hood says that the figure can be traced to a psychologist and sexual abuse campaigner called Miriam Saphira (formerly Jackson). Her "data" came from a selective reading of research from Kinsey, who had discovered that 24% of women reported at least one sexual contact before fifteen with a male aged at least fifteen and at least five years older than she was. According to Hood, Saphira implied all such cases were sexual abuse, and made no attempt to separate out "incidents" such as non-sexual fondling and accidentally seeing male genitals. Some of the "incidents" were entirely verbal. Hood writes that a more objective reading of Kinsey's findings would indicate that "fewer than one girl in three hundred experienced any sort of genital contact with her own father."

Hood says that Saphira's 1981 book *The Sexual Abuse of Children* was published with assistance from the Mental Health Foundation, and 1500 copies of it were distributed to staff of the Department of Social Welfare. Pseudoscience had become the vogue; worse, it was starting to determine policy. According to Hood, by the late 1980s

> her agonising question ("is she safe with her father?") and her misanthropic answer (that children should be kept away from adult males) had soaked deep into the fabric of New Zealand Society.

Any serious suspicion that John is guilty must be part of this dubious legacy. The other issue about Verity's allegation against John is that it goes further than "mere" incest; it involves a paedophile ring with him as leader and recruiter. This surely reduces the likelihood that he is guilty. How does a man go about enlisting adult friends to rape his under-aged daughter? Are we to believe that this was some sort of male bonding session gone awry? Possible, yes, but I find it very hard to believe without buying into the dubious "tip of the iceberg" assumption. Surely a dissenting friend would report this.

Hysteria about alleged sexual crimes is easily whipped up with figures from questionable sources. In North America a lot of noise has been generated in recent years about what is often called a rape culture in universities. The figure always mentioned in campaigns and written on demonstrators' banners is that one in five female university students have been sexually assaulted in what is sometimes called an epidemic of sexual violence. The ratio has been repeated everywhere, even in official announcements and speeches right up to President Obama. Columnist George F. Will has pointed out that the number became "validated by official repetition." In fact, it has determined policy: in 2011 the US Department of Education's Office of Civil Rights wrote to all American colleges threatening to investigate any of them which did not pursue sexual complaints thoroughly enough. It would withdraw federal funding from those which did not comply.

In December 2014 the US Bureau of Justice released data discrediting the report which yielded the one-in-five figure. According to Christina Hoff Sommers on *The Factual Feminist* Youtube blog, the Bureau's report said that the earlier data was based on an internet study that featured "vaguely worded questions, a low response rate and a non-representative sample." The number offered by the Bureau was one in fifty-three. It also found that, far from a rape culture on campuses, rates of rape and sexual assault were higher for non-students than for students. Some wag posted a comment on Sommers' blog that "5 out of every 4 women will be raped over 300% of the time on 200% of all college campuses, before they even enrol. After they enrol, the numbers triple."

Sommers laments that there is no point trying to debate the statistics, because student activists will just try to shut you up. She spoke on Oberlin campus at Georgetown University on "the need to reform feminism and to correct exaggerated victim statistics." Students, the very group who once loved to spar with people with dissenting beliefs, issued "trigger warnings" based on the claim that what Sommers had to say might cause PTSD. Thirty delicate flowers fled with their therapy dog to a safe space where they could cower from the horror of Sommers' opinions. She had to have armed guards to protect her from the "safe spacers". Some banners proclaimed that "Free speech…does not mean we have to tolerate your misogyny" and "Rape culture is real and you are a participant." Some attended her talk but had taped their mouths over in a symbolic gesture. The campus newspaper denounced the views of Sommers as "harmful", and "not a conversation that students should be having." Really? Are there any conversations that inquisitive and intelligent young people simply should not be having? Or must they be shielded from anything that (as George F. Will incisively put it) violates their entitlement to serenity?

Sommers calls such an over-sensitivity "fainting couch feminism", and she rightly points out that it discredits feminism and women in general. In fact, it turns back the clock to a time when women were considered too delicate to be exposed to unsettling or distressing events or ideas. Freewheeling feminist Camille Paglia has suggested, a little provocatively, that her generation of young women fought for the right to risk being raped. The extremists label Sommers and other women who try to bring some sense to such issues as "gender traitors" or agents of the patriarchy. Men are bad enough, but women who enable men are immeasurably worse.

Why must women be held to be sugar and spice and all things nice, even on occasions when the evidence points to them as villains? Cathy Young reports on Newsday that after the discredited 2014 Rolling Stone story about a gang rape at the University of Virginia, New York Senator Kirsten Gillibrand carped that any criticism of the complainant, referred to as Jackie, amounted to "victim-blaming". In what way was she a victim? Jackie was shown to have made up not just details but the whole thing: the party never happened, friends disagreed with her account, and the man who supposedly set her up for the rape was almost certainly fictitious. She faked emails from a supposed suitor. Earlier in the same year, Jackie had almost certainly made up a story that she was physically assaulted outside campus for her anti-rape stance. Gillibrand stated that punishing the complainant would be "inappropriate".

In an article in National Review on December 6 last year, Tim Cavanaugh took lawyer and Washington Post columnist Zerlina Maxwell to task for continuing to miss the obvious point about the Rolling Stone article – that the story was almost certainly untrue. Maxwell wrote that we should always believe what an accuser says, because the damage done by disbelieving a "survivor" compounds her trauma and is far greater than the damage done by calling someone a rapist.

MSNBC presenter Alex Wagner interviewed two commentators about the Rolling Stone debacle: Ana Marie Cox, contributor to The Daily Beast, and Bill Keller from the Marshall Project, "a non-partisan news organisation covering America's criminal justice system." Nothing that any of the three speakers said showed even a hint of concern for the only real victims: the falsely accused young men. All three lamented the increased numbers of genuinely raped women who would lose even more credibility because of this fake story. Contradicting the plain facts of the very case they were discussing, all three agreed that women tell the truth about rape. Keller said, "The idea that women make this stuff up is a pernicious myth." Cox added

> Anyone who thinks that women out there...are doing false reports of rape needs to ask the woman closest to them in their lives about this. Ask a woman that you know if she would do that, or if she thinks that other women would do that, and you will get the answer "no".

Really? Odd, because I have asked Angela and her answer to the second question wasn't that at all. Yet perhaps there is some truth in it, because I asked some of my male friends whether they would ever rape a woman, and they all said they wouldn't, so now I'm confused. Could it be that some people just don't mean what they say?

Cathy Young regrets the role of the media after the Rolling Stone allegations were exposed as false. She points out that almost no one seemed willing to call the story a lie, a hoax or a fabrication, only that there were "discrepancies" in the complainant's story. What does it take to face the truth when women lie about rape, and what chance does an innocent man have when a woman who has clearly lied suffers no repercussions? Young reasonably points out that "This reluctance to call Jackie's story a false allegation is rooted in political correctness, not fact."

The hype about rape on American campuses has made university a scary place for all young men enlightened enough to know what can happen to them – and for their worried parents. The mothers of three falsely accused students set up a group called FACE (Families Advocating for Campus Equality) to offer support to the families of students suffering under false sexual accusations. They are especially disturbed that internal disciplinary systems subject accused students to the complainant-friendly college evidential test of "preponderance of evidence" rather than extend the due process established over hundreds of years in real courts. The intro page on their website laments that the college kangaroo court system "leaves the havoc of unjustly dismantled lives and ruined futures in its wake." *Dismantled* seems too polite to me, but it would not to US Guardian columnist Jessica Valenti, who dismissed these mothers' concerns by saying "Alternative name for this group: Not My Nigel". I can't remember the last time I heard or read anything so blinkered or so callous.

Female North American college students may be one of the least commonly raped groups of women in the world – possibly even in history. Of course, the expression *rape culture* sometimes appears to mean something other than actual rapes and sexual assaults. It may suggest that some men talk about rape, or make bawdy or misogynistic postings on their Facebook pages. Try telling women in South Sudan or Syria that occasional puerile and boorish thought-rape implies a rape culture.

Bad statistics about the frequency of rape on North American campuses have become so persuasive that many universities now make male students take a course on consent. Yet the default assumption that men are predators is a form of sexual discrimination, and it is beyond reasonable doubt that men doing innocent things – or just taking up space – in the vicinity of children can invite the sort of unfair suspicion that no woman ever suffers. Many men have given up the thought of pursuing certain occupations and leadership roles, such as teaching young children and coaching swimming. In 2013 the Australian TV show Today Tonight ran an item about the indignity suffered by a male passenger on Virgin Blue airways. He was initially placed next to someone else's children on a flight, but a stewardess asked him to move to another seat. She explained that it was the company's policy not to have males sit next to unaccompanied minors. She scouted the rows for an unaccompanied female who wouldn't mind exchanging seats with the man. Virgin declined to be interviewed, but issued a statement claiming the policy was based on customer feedback.

The affected man pointed out that the policy was not just discriminatory but irrational. Since children are more likely to be molested by a male relative than by an unknown male, it would make more statistical sense not to allow children to sit next to their uncles or even fathers. An excellent point.

As an experiment, the show's producers had two adults separately take photos of children at a crowded swimming pool. While the woman snapped away for nearly half an hour no one took any action, but the man who did the same thing attracted such suspicion that after a few minutes another man was asking him what he was up to.

March 10

I come across an encouraging American case. In Minnesota in the 1990s a former patient successfully sued a counsellor for "negligent psychotherapy" and was awarded $2.5 million – at that time the biggest settlement for any such case in US history. Lawyers for the defendant, Dr Diane Humenansky, tried to show that her methods, which included hypnosis, drugs and group pressure, were not sufficient to produce false memories. However, expert witnesses for the prosecution, including Elizabeth Loftus, convinced the jury otherwise. Professor Richard Ofshe, a Pulitzer Prize winner from the University of California, said

> Recovered memory therapy is the worst form of psychiatric quackery in the twentieth century...These reckless and dangerous therapists have destroyed thousands of American families.

Medical school and psychology faculty members from the University of Minnesota said that Humenansky's methods had caused significant harm to the family of the complainant. Judge Bertrand Poritsky agreed with the experts, commenting that the idea that people can repress traumatic memories was not a credible scientific theory and could not be presented to the jury.

It's good news that these rogue counsellors can be held legally responsible, at least in America. The bad news is that this can only happen if the client (in our case Verity) comes to her senses and goes after the real culprit. As in every aspect of this case, I am powerless.

March 13

After ten weeks of teaching mornings, this is my last day. My only work for the next couple of months is part-time examining. I'm not sure if this is good news or bad news for my state of mind. I've enjoyed the work, as always, but Verity has been like an open wound I've had to conceal. Nevertheless, I am convinced that I gave the students no inkling of any problem.

With all this free time coming up, I give some thought to how I am going to cope without going nuts. I need a new rationalisation. I've decided to employ what may be called a "guaranteed advantage" approach. I can explain this with a parallel example. When a New Zealand sports team plays some big international match, naturally I want the Kiwis to win. So what I sometimes do is place small bet on our opponents. That way either result must bring me an advantage: either New Zealand wins – which is obviously good news for patriotic reasons – or it loses, in which case I win some cash.

The stakes are higher in the Verity saga, of course, but I've figured out a rationalisation that may work: a book. From the outset I've been keeping an informal but quite detailed diary of events and reflections and research findings. I'll make it more systematic and thorough from now on. Hopefully the police will withdraw the charges and I'll be in the clear some time soon. That's the best news possible. But the longer the sorry saga goes on, the more interesting the story. With a bit of luck it may be published, and at least some people will then learn about the injustice of this kind of case. I've even decided on a working title: *The Verity Chronicles*. The book would be most publishable if I end up being wrongly convicted, spend ten years inside, lose our house paying for failed legal appeals and get maimed in a brawl in the prison exercise yard...which shows that if you pursue such rationalisations beyond a certain threshold they become somewhat less comforting.

March 16

If the police were to call off the hounds tomorrow, that would be the end of *The Verity Chronicles*. But I have become convinced that even the story up to this point just has to be told. A newspaper article would do it. The injustice and absurdity of it must be exposed, for the sake of others after me. I bike to the office of the Draketown Post newspaper and have a brief meeting with a senior reporter whom I ask for by name. I haven't met him before but I have read his articles. He has the virtues of being mature, reputable and male.

I outline my situation and ask him if he would be interested in running a story eventually; that is, after the police have made the decision not to prosecute...assuming that is the decision they make. He shows some initial interest, but his ears really prick up when I say that I don't want to be anonymous. "Are you really sure about that?" he asks. He is genuinely concerned about mud sticking to me. I reply that I have thought long and hard about the issue of anonymity, and I've decided that it's time someone stuck his head out from behind the tree. Mud sticking to a man emerging from behind a tree – this woman has even got me mixing my metaphors.

In my case, I tell him, this isn't as courageous as it may first seem. The accusation against me is different from most historic sexual abuse cases. Take poor John, for example. He is the complainant's father, so he can hardly claim the two of them were never alone together. This means that the allegation gets reduced to "he said vs she said", and a nagging doubt may persist in the minds of a jury and the public, even if he is tried and acquitted. The whole point about the allegation against me, the whole basis of my defence, is that she and I never met. If a newspaper article stresses this aspect, only a reader who reads no further than the headline can have any lingering doubt. The reporter confirms his interest, and he suggests I contact him when the time is right.

To my shame, I lose control briefly and become blubbery in front of this stranger. Please don't let him think it's self-pity, I think. When I get home I email him and apologise for losing composure. I assure him I am coping better than that reaction suggests. His prompt reply says it's okay – he understands.

After I leave the newspaper office I am in a petulant mood, angry at myself for losing my cool, and angry at Verity because...just because. Walking back to my bike, I pass a shop that sells souvenirs and knick-knacks right in the city centre. It has a blackboard outside with a corny "thought for the day" written on it. In the past I've never paid it much attention, but today's one is "Truth is more important than facts", and I am in no mood to stroll past and leave it unchallenged. It is this baseless idea of "personal truth" that props up the poisonous stupidity of Verity and probably her counsellor: if you think you may have been sexually abused, you were. It is your personal conviction, a part of what defines you as a woman and a "survivor". Well, let my response to such nonsense be a part of what defines me as a skeptical man.

I go inside and approach a woman straightening T-shirts on a rack. She looks older than the only other woman in the shop, so I presume she is the manageress and in charge of the daily pop philosophy board outside. As politely as I can manage, I point out that the statement outside is baloney. There is no such thing as personal truth, and what does not correspond to facts cannot be called truth. If it were otherwise, we wouldn't have the word *belief* in the language. We also have a useful word for a belief which is wrong; we call it a *mistake*. She and her assistant exchange amused glances. She makes a noise like a blocked drain and mutters something desultory about opinions and identity. She assures me that the message will be different tomorrow. Yes, I know that; it always is.

As I cycle home I give some more thought to anonymity and the "mud sticking" notion. Yes, losing your reputation in this way is a terrible thing, because no one is more despised than a sex abuser. My geographical defence is one advantage, but I have another. For most people whose reputations have been sullied in this way, it affects their future employment prospects. When they are turned down for that job or promotion, they will always suspect that the lingering suspicion played some role. And in many cases, no doubt it will have. But I am sixty-two and not far away from retirement. My background is in education, but I do little actual teaching any more. I have already told George, co-director at the school, about the accusation, and he is a sensible guy who supports me. My other work is more remote: it involves examining candidates I never see.

If ever there has been a false rape allegation designed to see the light of day, this is the one. More than other cases, it has no shady issues of "an open mind" or "a balanced view". It offers no debate about the seriousness of a verifiable event, or about the depth and the permanence of the victim's suffering afterwards. Almost anyone can see that there was no event. How much mud can stick?

March 17

I bike in to the Rape Crisis Centre, which doubles as the Draketown Women's Refuge. I want to find out whatever I can about the mindset of the opposition – for that is what they have become. *Enemy* would be too strong, because of course they mainly do thankless work with real victims. I want to ask a counsellor there what she knows about false rape complaints: how many she is aware of from her experience, and what reasons a woman would have to make up such a story. I confess I have another agenda. There is just a chance that Verity has made contact here, and they may know her case. I won't use her name, of course, but when I describe the circumstances the counsellor may put two and two together. When I ask provocatively, "What do you know about having such women prosecuted? I have been the victim of a lie about rape, and if the police don't prosecute her, I will," maybe – just maybe – she will contact Verity again and encourage her to drop the charges. It's a chance in a hundred, because Verity may not even have filed her delusions through these premises. Actually, it's one in thirty-two. That's the number of government-accredited sexual abuse counselling establishments in Draketown.

I arrive at the start of the day, before any staff are there, though someone must have opened the place because there are a couple of women in the waiting room. I browse through the brochures and posters. One says "Rape is about power, not sex."

I soon realise I've made a faux pas. A client says, "You shouldn't even be in here. No men allowed." Oops, of course. Fair enough, I guess. I go and wait outside the door. As women enter I ask, "Are you a counsellor here?" I eventually corner one and ask what she knows about false rape claims. She is polite enough but looks at me as if I've strayed from the set of *Alien*. I give her a sixty-second rundown of my predicament. She no doubt wonders why I would tell a stranger about this. She says she can give me a few minutes, but she has clients to see inside. I guess they have appointments, and they are her real business. I'm just a very tricky curve ball.

It's raining, and we stand talking over the beat of heavy drops on the iron veranda. What she says isn't surprising. She says that such occasions are very rare. I don't argue the point on this, or anything else she says, but I do say that it doesn't matter if false reports make up fifty percent or one percent. All that matters to me is that this is one of them. I would stress that I am a person – not just a statistical blip – but I don't think of that at the time. She says she is an experienced counsellor, but she won't be drawn on the question of whether she has dealt with any false complaints. Instead she speaks hypothetically: a woman who does this may be mentally ill, may be seeking revenge, or may just crave attention. I say that discouraging, revealing and even prosecuting false complaints may benefit everyone, including those actual victims she has to deal with. She agrees, but more half-heartedly than I expect. No sign of anything like fury at those liars who can allegedly make the suffering of real victims so much worse. Can there be no such thing as the wrong man? Are rapists everywhere, and does she see her job as a game of whack-a-mole in which every adult breathing male is a legitimate target, and every allegation by a woman should automatically send a man to jail? She says she is sorry, and seems sincere about this, but she really has to go inside, because actual abuse victims are her stock in trade. I point out that my anger at this lie doesn't mean I have no concern for the real victims. I would ask, "Would your feeling of outrage that you have been falsely accused of murder imply that you have no sympathy for real murder victims?" But that's another smart thing I don't think of at the time, of course. I thank her for allowing me to disrupt her schedule.

This visit was mainly pointless, I guess. I saw no flicker of recognition when I outlined the facts of my case, so it appears poor Verity sought comfort elsewhere. But I think it may have been useful to allow this counsellor to see another side. Every day she no doubt deals with self-defined female victims, most honest and a few deluded, and never gets to talk to a man who has been put in this situation. Men are the unseen perverts and predators, but here I was in living 3D, human and angry. Why would I front up to a place like Rape Crisis if I were anyone but an innocent man outraged by a lie? Let her think about that.

Later my thoughts return to the brochure that said, "Rape is about power, not sex." As I have never committed rape, I can't be sure what motivates a rapist. But it seems a dubious claim to me, for various reasons. The definition of rape has been widened in recent years. This surely makes it harder to assign one underlying motivation to all instances. In a case of what is called date rape, when she's too boozed to utter a coherent No! and he's too far gone to hold back if she does, it seems to me that it is what it looks like: what most people would call a rape, but a rape that has everything to do with primitive lust and little to do with power.

Claiming rape is about power is not so much wrong as meaningless. Any crime can be about power in some circumstances. An arsonist may get a kick from the destructive power he displays. An embezzler usually seeks financial gain. However, she may have been declined promotion and wants to steal from her firm to exert power over her employers as a means of revenge.

The Rape Crisis conviction that rape is about power seems based on an assumption that women know everything about both sexes, and that men know nothing about either sex. One claim sometimes made by many women is that men do not understand the subtleties, the nuances, of female sexuality. Women are more concerned about relationships and atmosphere as a precondition for sex. Men cannot understand such complexities for the simple reason that they are not women. Yet this surely must work both ways. If the sexes are doomed never to properly understand each other's sexuality, how can women, not being men, claim with such certainty that power is always what motivates men to rape? I've never known men to say this. Wouldn't men know what might motivate them to rape better than women do – especially if we are all potential rapists (a claim no more meaningful than the one that defines all women as potential false complainants)?

Rape is too complex a notion for one syllable; we need new charges with new names. No statute of limitations applies to what is called rape, which is why Verity, with the help of a credulous detective and perhaps a compliant counsellor, can hit me with this delusion more than twenty years after it didn't happen. But maybe, with such a broad definition of rape, a statute of limitations should apply only to some cases. "Traditional" rape was enforced sex, usually by a stranger, often associated with violence and with premeditation. We now acknowledge that rape can be subtler in its actions, its intentions, and its degree of coercion. It doesn't require physical force – actual or even suggested – and it often involves someone close to the victim. Spousal rape now has legal standing, and a woman's sexual history can play no role in court. These are all enlightened changes, but it seems wrong to me that when it comes to any statute of limitations, rape is just rape. This means that a woman can hit a man with a rape charge out of the blue after decades, no matter how serious the alleged offence.

If a man did anything wrong all those years ago, what exactly did he do? In definitions as in most other things, we can't have our cake and eat it too. For example, no matter how we define murder, it always involves a body, so we can have no doubt that a terrible crime has been committed, and sooner or later someone should be prosecuted. No statute of limitations should apply. The same cannot be said of all incidents now considered to be rape. If subtler acts of coercive or non-consensual sex are labelled rape, it is no longer tenable to claim that rape is always a horrifying act of violation which will scar the victim for life. Sometimes what we now call rape leaves no emotional scar at all.

Some rape charges now being pressed centre on complex relationships in which it is hard to claim the victim's life has been destroyed. Here is the story of rapist number one. Imagine a man and woman happily living together, but after a time the relationship starts to go sour. During that time, the man comes home one night and pesters the woman for sex. She is really absorbed in her novel and says no, but he persists and she grudgingly complies. Soon after, they split up. After a while they become reconciled, and they once again live in an intimate relationship...but then they split up again amid bitter acrimony when she sees messages from another woman on his phone. The woman decides to make a rape complaint to the police, based on the occasion when he had sex with her when she wasn't really all that keen.

In less enlightened times her complaint would have gone nowhere. In fact, it would have stood so little chance in court that no woman would even bother to take the accusation to the police. Why the delay in reporting? If it was so traumatic, why did she shack up with the rapist again? But according to new definitions of rape and consent, there is no doubt that she was raped and, if a jury believed her factual account, rapist number one would be convicted. The prosecution lawyer would have informed them about "rape myths". The fact that she took a long time to make the complaint does not mean the event was not traumatic, because there are many psychologically complex reasons why real victims may not report immediately. She did indeed live with the accused man after the rape, but these relationships can be extraordinarily complicated. He may have made her so dependent on him that she could no longer contemplate life without him.

Yes, all these things may be true. But they may just be a line that the prosecution can sell to the jury in order to get a chance of a rape conviction, in line with police policy to boost clearance rates for sexual crimes. That one occasion of coerced sex was probably just distasteful, rather than traumatic, and her real reasons to press the rape charge were anger and revenge. We must not be so naïve as to assume that a woman who detests her ex strongly enough would never pretend to have been emotionally scarred by a sexual encounter which she merely disliked. In fact, if she felt bitter enough, why wouldn't she make a rape complaint if she knows she'll be believed? In a case like this, those questions we used to ask – why the delay, and why the continued relationship? – are precisely the ones we should ask, because they may be the key to understanding her real motive and the degree of suffering she has endured. Yet the balance has shifted so far in favour of complainants that even asking such questions evokes outrage. It is seen as blaming the victim and perpetuating rape myths. Keeping the faith involves believing that what is now defined as rape is traumatic by definition, and the number of women who might make such an accusation for dishonest or sinister reasons is known: zero.

Rape isn't always so bad, which must mean that my saying rape isn't so bad isn't so bad. If we define rape as broadly as the law does now, it may inflict no lasting harm at all. Yet the stigma of the word still evokes all the shock of its older, narrower definition. If rapist number one in the preceding account were convicted, he would forever be labelled a rapist, and that label would condemn him to the same opprobrium as another fictional rapist, whom we'll label number two: a deviant who lurked in alleyway, stalked an unknown eight-year-old and raped her at knife point in her bedroom in the middle of the night. Some rapes are much more repugnant than others. But to the public, most of whom have no reason to follow changes in laws of consent, a rapist is just a rapist.

On the website *liberateyourself.co.uk*, an anonymous columnist rails against people crass enough to make jokes about rape. Her headline addresses the article "To all those men who don't think the rape jokes are a problem." She insists she is far too moderate to suggest that all men are rapists. Her line is that even enlightened men who she concedes would never rape anyone have missed something: that the one group of people who do believe all men are rapists are rapists themselves. They just think other men don't get caught. She means that when rapists hear other men make jokes about rape, it just confirms to them that all males regard rape as normal behaviour. If you hear the joke and don't protest about it, you are part of the rape problem. "That rapist who was in the group with you, that rapist thought you were on his side," she says. "He felt validated."

I need to make three comments about this. First, I'm not convinced that actual rapists do think all men are rapists. However, I'll let that go because I've never asked them. Also, since there are different sorts of rapists, as I've just explained, I'm not even sure what sort I should ask. Secondly, it is just silly for me to be held responsible for any of the ways a listener may misinterpret my silence. It is even sillier to be held responsible for any actions other people make based on what my silence was supposed to mean. Thirdly, what kind of rape was he – or were we – joking about? If it resembled in any way the action of rapist number two, above, I am sure all the men I know would glower at the comedian in shock. If the rape were more like the action of rapist number one, I would say it's just as open to humour as burglary, minor assault or even jaywalking.

UK television presenter Judy Finnigan has incurred the wrath of thousands with her comments about whether professional footballer Ched Evans should get his former job back after his release from prison after doing time for rape. Finnigan said that Evans' victim did not receive any "bodily harm", and that the rape occurred in a hotel room after the victim had drunk too much. Finnegan was thus a double heretic: she implied that some rapes are worse than others and that a drunk woman bears at least some responsibility. Purple with fury, thousands of the twitterati called her comments "sick" and "disgusting". Sadly, Finnegan apologised, saying

> I absolutely wasn't suggesting that rape is anything other than an horrendous crime and, as I said on the programme, I was in no way attempting to minimise the terrible ordeal that any woman suffers as a result.

Her apology has it wrong. What legally constitutes rape is not always horrendous at all, and the fairest initial response after learning a man is a convicted rapist is to ask "What kind?" That is, where on the broad rape continuum did his crime fall? Was he like rapist number one, rapist number two or (most likely) somewhere in between?

Who suffers more anguish: the disgruntled ex-wife, victim of rapist number one, or a man who has been falsely accused of rape? I may be biased, but I know my answer. When rape is defined the way it is now, it simply is no longer valid to claim that it always ruins or permanently degrades a woman's quality of life. However, *every* false accusation of rape is, by its very nature, concerned with subjugating, humiliating and ultimately destroying a man. It will certainly succeed if the man is convicted. Even if the man is acquitted it may still cost him his reputation, his job, his savings and probably his marriage.

March 18

What determines the statute of time limitations for an offence must be its seriousness. For example, I accept that no statute should apply to rape of minors. If what Verity is alleging were true, it would be reasonable that police should go ahead and prosecute. My objection is not that her allegation is from so long ago, but rather that it is so clearly false that the police should have seen through it. Yet it doesn't work in reverse. Just like some instances of rape, a false rape accusation is a terrible offence with far-reaching and devastating consequences, and it is surely reasonable that it should not be bound by any statute of limitations. Imagine I am wrongly convicted and jailed, then the police in 2035 were to obtain conclusive proof that Verity's 2015 accusation had been a pack of lies. I assume there would be no legal basis to prosecute her. Why this double standard on how long after a terrible crime a prosecution can be brought?

Rape – like other crimes – may sometimes be about power, but the consequences of a false rape complaint are *always* about power, whether intentional or not. I concede that when the woman is genuinely deluded, her actions may be neither malicious nor even conscious. However, their effects are inescapably powerful. Destruction (in arson, for example) and disempowerment (in a false rape accusation) are easy ways to make a difference. I cannot be sure what has been going through Verity's brain, but these lies or delusions appear to be a way to gain control, a way to matter in an otherwise unrewarding and inconsequential life. And matter they certainly do, especially to the middle-aged males whose subtle but pervasive socio-sexual control she and possibly her counsellor may hold responsible for her "issues". This humble woman's reach has become almost unimaginably vast, over time, over place and over humanity. Her fantasies, not from last night but from two decades ago, have come to define the lives of a whole group of unfortunate people all over the country. The law, whose very purpose is to support the disadvantaged, has empowered her and made us weak.

Women who deny the prevalence or the effects of false rape complaints imply that only men can play the power game. Slate columnist Cathy Young challenges them with this:

> To recognise that some women accuse a man of rape is not anti-female, any more than recognising that some men rape women is anti-male. There is power in a charge as uniquely damaging as rape, and women are no less likely than men to abuse the power they have.

Angela finds it amazing that some women downplay the incidence or the potential damage of false rape complaints. She has been forced into a better position than almost any woman to comment, of course. She wonders how one of these "two-percenters" would react if, for example, her brother stumbled into the path of one of these women and a false accusation became more than just a statistically improbable abstraction. I remind her that the Verity case shows it's not necessary to come anywhere near them.

Some rape activists may claim that when we examine the root causes of the unhappiness of so many women, what we see is the effects of a male-dominated society. According to this philosophy, even if Verity's truth is different from other people's, by definition she is a victim and I am an oppressor, so isn't it a profound contribution to universal justice if the police accept her personal truth? Male dominance in our patriarchal society constantly subjects all females to societal and symbolic rape. This is the real issue, and the fact that one or two men may have their lives ruined by false reports is just a distraction.

Or perhaps they make no such claim, and I'm just putting stupid words in their mouths.

March 19

I need to see my GP on another matter, and I decide that he is another person who needs to be brought into the V-loop. Maybe dwelling on this allegation will affect my health down the track. I break the news to him, and he is all ears. He is dumbfounded. He takes my blood pressure as a benchmark. Perfectly normal: not just 62-years-old normal, but normal normal. He asks me how I am coping, and I tell him I'm getting by most of the time, but I'm losing a lot of sleep. Now that I'm not teaching I can catch up to some extent by getting naps during the day, though it isn't the same. I tell him I even go through short stages of euphoria. He says he is no psychiatrist, but he assumes this is the mind's way of compensating for times of helplessness and despair. Neither of us talks of depression, because that might lead down the road of medication, which both of us want to avoid. He's been my doctor ever since I came to Draketown, and he knows not only *that* I will cope, but *how* I will cope. He sees I'm too angry to top myself. He suggests that I should keep active, and I assure him that's what I'm doing. I mention cycling and tennis, but I don't admit to the pacing... and certainly not to running up the stairs to my *bitch!* rhythm.

He wants to know more about the accusation. One problem with my story is that it's hard to make it short and still persuade the listener I'm innocent. When I tell anyone I have to say, "I haven't even met the complainant." The listener's natural response is then to ask why she has chosen me, and I have to outline the relationships.

The doctor may have patients in the waiting room dying of beriberi, and I don't want to delay him. But he genuinely wants to know more, so I give him the main points. I have brought him an envelope with the same edited version of the police interview that features in this diary, and I hand it over, saying, "You may want to have a look at this in your own time. Read and destroy."

My GP knows how the game works. He says that this is probably all about "recovered memory", dredged up by a sexual abuse counsellor, and it has happened because of pressure from activists to have sexual complainants believed, no matter how outrageous or tenuous their claims may be. He calls it the sexual abuse industry.

He says, "The mental health consequences of a case like this are huge. So many people are affected." Very true. I have been reading on the website of the Australian False Memory Association about the ripple effect of a similar case there. It estimated that between 42 and 90 lives in six extended families were touched – some of course potentially ruined – by the accusations of one person (or the encouragement of one deviant counsellor).

The financial repercussions alone are vast. Take Verity's allegations. Wasting police time in what Eva keeps insisting is "a complex case" is just the beginning. Taxpayers have forked out god knows how much for her counsellor. I have spent a small fortune on a lawyer so far – just for a couple of hours. It's an amount I used to regard as a lot of money, but against a case of this scale, it is small change. If the case comes to court, there is the cost of a trial, including the personal lawyers' fees for myself and the other poor defendants. Imagine that Verity's delusions are believed, and she achieves what she would call justice: we are convicted. There appear to be at least four accused. I have heard that it costs $100,000 a year to keep someone in prison. Four people locked up for maybe ten years equals four million dollars. On top of that, Verity has seen to it that those four people can contribute nothing to the wealth of the nation by using their productive skills during their incarceration...except by painting fence railings or sewing mailbags or whatever busywork prisoners do these days.

So when it is over and she is satisfied that justice has been done, I would whimper (or would I scream?) from my cell: "Do you matter enough now?" Poor disempowered Verity, Verity the incest survivor and rape victim, has at last made quite a mark.

Biking home from the doctor's, I get to the top of the very steep path at the south end of Standard Street. Usually I get off and walk, but today I'm angry enough to kick it into low and summon the do-or-die power to pedal the final two revolutions before the crest with a puffy *Biiitch! Biiitch!* Phew, got there. How did I ever manage without her?

March 20

I work out that Verity's house is visible from a point near town on the busy main road, near Draketown Hospital. The house is there up on the hill, quite a long way off. I can see the carport outside, but it's so distant that it's not easy to pick out whether the car's there. I need binoculars to tell for sure, so when I bike to town I sometimes stop, get the binoculars out of my backpack and see if she's home. I want to get an idea of her movements. The electoral roll labelled her as a student. If she isn't now, does she work? If so, when and where? I try to keep my observation short, because there I am standing at the side of the main road peering through binoculars at the distant hill. Draketown's a small place. What if someone I know drives past and sees me doing this?

March 22

I write to Novopay, the central education pay office in Wellington, to request a copy of my records from 1990 to 1995. I want to find out what days I took off sick over the period of the allegation, to cut down the possible Houwhanga rape days. I think I used to take an average of about one day off a year, so there's a good chance I taught here every working day she was attending Westchester. This should be useful if it comes to court – as long as Verity cannot just change location and time willy-nilly on her sworn statement. If she can just say, "Actually, I'm pretty sure now it was Draketown in 1997," all pay records will be useless, of course. But what can I do?

March 23

More cycle sleuthing. On the way to town during the morning rush hour I stop at that point on the main road where I can see her house up on the hill in the distance. No waiting needed – even without binoculars the light's good enough today for me to pick out two ant-like figures filing out from the house to the car. She's on the move. There's only one street she's likely to take if she's driving down into town, and it joins the road I'm on about a half kilometre further on. I remount and pedal as furiously as a sixty-two-year old can. This is a western, and I'm heading her off at the pass. The timing is perfect: there she is right in front of me, so I slot in behind. But a man is driving. I can see a bald head on the driver's side, and that must be her in the front passenger seat. So she has a partner, or maybe even a new husband. Then the car stops and the driver gets out. He's a beefy man, and one of those people it's hard to put an age to, but he looks much older than she is. He heads into an office, presumably his work. Verity gets out briefly to fetch something out of the back seat for him, then she gets in again on the driver's side, takes the wheel and drives off. I start to chase but my legs have given out and I can't keep up. How I long to be sixty-one again!

I rest for a minute, then I go back to the beefy man's place of work – if that's what it is. Then I realise that I'm not sure which of the many doorways in this densely-packed road he went into. One of the premises is a gym of sorts, and I go inside and look at two clients puffing and blowing on cycling machines, but neither matches. I peer as discreetly as I can through windows of other businesses, but no luck. Then I see him come out of a doorway and walk up the street, so I tail him at a safe distance. He walks into a coffee shop and I follow him. It's early morning but there are quite a few customers. I am right after him in the line, so I get a good look. Smartish casual clothes, no tie. No wedding ring either, though that may not mean much. He's quite chatty with the barista, so maybe he's a regular here. It sells fair trade coffee, so he's obviously a man with profound ethical awareness. He sits down with his coffee. The only free table is right next to him. I sit there and pretend to read the supplied newspaper. He must have arranged a meeting, because another man comes and sits next to him. I have to change my position so that I can hear with my right – my tinnitus-free ear. Did that move look suspicious? They didn't seem to notice. Even on my right I can't make out much, but the snatches I pick up seem to be about financial matters – things like profit predictions, hiring policies. I decide he must have some sort of influential position, not just from the topic of conversation, but also because he is obviously free to take time out from work so early in the day and go to a cafe.

On the way home, I feel proud enough to think I deserve a Corvette – or at least four wheels – rather than this bike.

I tell Angela about my beefy man find. Of course, she's interested, but I can tell she still doesn't like this sleuthing. I think she has the feeling I'm becoming obsessed, though she doesn't say it.

It may be stupid and pointless, but here's the way I look at it. When I bring selected people into the V-loop, their usual reaction is something like, "How awful. I really don't know how I would react if something like that hit me over the head." *They don't know how they would react.* They seem to be implying that they would do something desperate or irrational or at least out of character. What forms could this take? Some may hit the bottle, or fight bitterly with their wives from morning till night. The most vulnerable may slit their wrists, the most vengeful may go to Verity's house and slit hers, and the most deranged may go postal and take out everyone they can at the Draketown police station. In the catalogue of irrational reactions a victim of a false rape complaint might descend to, most would be more destructive than biking around town with binoculars in a backpack. Strange days bring strange ways. Verity's getting my mind a little frazzled, but my conscience is clear.

March 25

At the front desk of the free legal advice centre, I am required to give details of my case, including the name of any person I am in dispute with. This makes me nervous, because I'm scared that revealing Verity's name may be breaking the law. Still, it would be worrying if I knew the law better than they do, so I go ahead. Finally I get in to talk to Josephine, who is very pleasant. She is even a lapsed member of New Zealand Skeptics ("I must get round to joining up again") with plenty of sympathy for me in my situation, though her position requires her to remain detached, of course. Either she has little doubt of my innocence or she is very polite. She says this is a horrible thing, and more common than people assume. I tell her that if the police call off the charges, the first thing I want to do is go back to them, ask if they are going to prosecute Verity, and tell the reporter at the Draketown Post to go ahead and write a story on the case. She is horrified, and warns me that "there is no statute of limitations on rape." If I go to the media, the police may decide to prosecute me after all. This puzzles me. If they drop the charges against me because they can see them for what they are and don't like their odds of a conviction, what will be their new reason to go after me: pure spite? Maybe so. It could be that Eva or her superior despise unassuming middle-class men who don't just curl up and die.

She refers me to Lionel C at The Men's Room, a place that helps men with all kinds of problems particular to them.

March 26

Today is my appointment with Lionel. I arrive a little early, and the place appears deserted. I sit and look around. Clearly an environment for men: hardly any pictures or decorations, not even of Harley Davidsons. A woman's touch wouldn't be out of place here, but maybe they're no more welcome than men are at Rape Crisis. Then Lionel appears, and he takes me into another room for a chat. He's the kind of guy whose easy-going manner makes me open up. I tell him the story. He nods knowingly. He knows about women playing the "survivor" game. I get the impression from his comments that there is a covert gender war going on. He says that his usual business is dealing with custody battles and child support payments, and he says that men get a raw deal in this field and in so many other legal disputes. When cases come to court, women find it easier to gain sympathy from juries and judges. If they are convicted, their sentences are usually lighter than sentences for men who have committed equivalent crimes.

He has also dealt with false accusations like the one against me, which he says are more common than people assume. So many people in the know tell me this. He tells me about the sexual abuse industry that forms the sinister background to this kind of claim, and how difficult it has become for innocent men to clear themselves, because the onus of proof has shifted onto them. Police policy has changed for a variety of reasons. In the past they were accused of not treating reports of rape and sexual assaults seriously enough, and they are desperate to change this image. In the famous case of Louise Nicholas (see Wikipedia), they were the actual rapists. More women are now in senior positions in the police and have introduced new procedures and expectations. As for the rank-and-file officers, they just do what they are told to do. If a falsely accused man cannot take the pressure and commits suicide, no matter – he must have been guilty. I tell him I'm not inclined to give Verity any chance to spit on my grave.

He concedes he isn't a counsellor, and as I'm leaving he asks if I want to see one. No, I say; I'm not convinced that a cuppa and a chat with someone who happens to have a five-year degree in counselling is any more helpful than a cuppa and a chat with him. Besides, it was probably a counsellor who helped get me into this hole.

March 31

On the way into town I do a little detour past her mother's house. Her car is in the driveway, and there are the two of them in the front yard, chatting and pointing at something. Some plants, maybe. What right do they have to act so normally?

I read an article in The Independent about false accusations made against teachers in the UK. In a survey of over 600 teachers, 22 percent claimed to have been victims of false allegations by pupils. The trend is so dispiriting, even for those who haven't been hit yet, that many have lost the will to carry on.

It's interesting that comments are open for the article. The figures look doubtful even to me, but no one has questioned them. This implies that people accept that children will make false complaints, so why does the myth persist that they are rare among adults?

April 3

I email memory researcher Elizabeth Loftus in Seattle with an outline of my case. She replies immediately, offers her sympathy and adds, "Sadly you're part of an unfortunate epidemic." She advises me to get up to speed with all the latest information and with similar cases to mine. From what she says, they shouldn't be too hard to find.

April 4

Gloria arrives. I've been counting the days till her visit. Surely she has brought information that will help us all. We learn that she and John have told no one, not even family. They are afraid that blabbing will get me into more trouble, because they assume I have broken the law by getting Angela to tell her to tell John. Angela and I are astonished. We try to convince her not to worry about us, and that Eva's comment was only a preference, but Gloria seems to think that there may be some law that we don't know about. We say we doubt it. More important, we tell her that we've found it very comforting to let selected people know, and recommend the same for her and John. She still seems unconvinced.

She says that she and John are both worried that the Verity saga will affect the friendship between them and us. A fair point to bring up, but there's no danger of that. There's certainly no reason to blame her at all for this nonsense, and as for John, I long ago learnt that children can turn out badly despite the noblest efforts of their parents.

Gloria gives us some more details about Verity. She took her parents' split harder than Jennifer, even though Verity is older. She refused to accept that her father really wanted to break from her mother. She was convinced he was just going through some sort of mid-life crisis and all would revert to the way it had been. This makes me think that maybe her false accusation is not aimed at me so much as us; that is, Angela and me, because Angela and Gloria are friends, and this would be a way of taking out her spite. Certainly extreme, but nothing about this case falls short of extreme.

We learn that when she was a teenager, Verity attended school only spasmodically, because she had ME (also called chronic fatigue syndrome). Hers was that particularly debilitating strain which is so hard to treat: the one that goes into remission every Friday, only to recur in its most virulent form each Monday morning. Her mother had the same condition. Gloria reminds us that Verity was once married to a man called Benito, and the match yielded a daughter, Edda, who would be about thirteen now. We had vague memories of this. The marriage split up after a short time. After Gloria leaves I'll see if I can track this Benito down.

She also tells us that Verity's younger sister Jennifer hasn't been in contact with her father for a few years, and doesn't answer any letters or emails from him. Her last message said something about not contacting her again because of *what he's done.* My god – Verity must have poisoned Jennifer's perception of their father.

We also learn something of Lance Boyle, the man mentioned in my interview who is presumably a co-accused. Gloria doesn't know him, but John has told her he was a neighbour years ago, when he and Charlotte lived in a remote part of the North Island and the girls were very young. John says Lance was a little rough around the edges, a pot smoker and maybe even dealer, but he is dumbfounded that Verity has accused him of this. It is very odd, even for what Verity uses as logic. She appears to imply that her father procured rapists to violate her repeatedly in two different locations and in two different periods in her life. Such appalling luck with men! The question is either "How easy is it to recruit paedophiles?" or "How easy is it to convince police investigators that it's easy to recruit paedophiles?"

Gloria gets into the spirit of our new lives so completely that she even starts calling Verity *Verity*, instead of her real name. I tell her we can even see her house, and a short time later there we all are, standing on the main road and passing the binoculars around. This almost seems normal behaviour now.

Tonight we watch the DVD of *A Shot in the Dark*. A little classic comedy does us all some good.

April 7

Justice delayed can be justice denied. Is someone actually working on this case file, or is it just lying in a dark place to mature, like a fine wine? With Gloria still here and with her and Angela listening in the background, I nervously ring Eva to give her a gentle nudge, to see if I can find out why it's taking so long for common sense to prevail. I always prefer to talk face to face, so I suggest I come in and see her. She shows no interest, "unless you want to tell me something new." Does she expect a confession? No chance of a meeting then, so I have to ask her over the phone. Are there any developments? Why has John, the supposed ringleader, not even been interviewed yet? I tell her the wait is intolerable. She says, "Peter, I have to investigate" in a tone that reminds me of my mother telling me that she just had to disinfect my grazed knee. But I see no evidence that she is investigating at all. She repeats that it is a complex case, and files from different parts of the North Island haven't been sent yet. I ask if this means there are even more than three suspects. No answer, so maybe there are. If so, this may be good news: more lies may mean less credibility and perhaps more chance of inconsistencies in Verity's allegations. Who else raped the poor woman: the Dalai Lama? Yosemite Sam? Some retired plumber in North Carolina?

I ask why, if the case is so complex, it cannot be part of police procedure not to interview anyone until all can be interviewed. In that way, the first (apparently me in this case) doesn't have to wait an unbearably long time. Even over the phone, I can almost see her rolling her eyes as she says, "We don't operate that way." Well, why not? I wonder. If normal police procedure caused undue stress on a complainant like Verity, would a brusque "We don't operate that way" be a suitable response, or would her complaint lead to solemn conferences and revised manuals? Eva's answers to my questions display a catalogue of contempt. She says I should just wait, and why am

I trying to hurry things up? She asks if I have something to hide. Why am I nervous about the outcome, if I have done nothing wrong? If I am innocent, I should have faith in the police and in the justice system, and just get on with my life.

What? What? Am I really hearing this? Is she seriously suggesting that guilt can be the only reason an accused person may be worried when an allegation like this is poised over his head? Am I not entitled to preserve my natural pessimism? I protest that there are people who have experience of helping men in my position and assure me that I should not be so naive as to trust those very institutions to deliver a just result. Having already practised her callousness and naivety, she turns to condescension: "Peter, you are listening to the wrong people. You must learn to think for yourself." Yes, my friends tell me that all the time. I end by saying that I am not sure how much it matters to her, but this episode has poisoned any trust I used to have in the police. At that point she says that there's no purpose in talking any more. Finally we agree on something.

Let's get some perspective here. A couple of years ago I had to send our subwoofer in to be fixed. After about six weeks nothing had happened, so I phoned the service centre which was dealing with it. I was connected to the technician on the case, who said he had found it a tricky job, and he had to wait for some parts to come from England. However, he conceded that was no excuse for them not to let us know what was going on, and he apologised profusely. So what we have here is an electronics engineer humbly apologising for the fact that we have to put up with our stereo system being unable to reproduce notes below 45 hertz, but when I ask Eva what is happening with an accusation that could put me in jail for years, cost us tens of thousands of dollars and make me a social outcast, she just asks me dismissively what the problem is. Unbelievable.

Later, while driving in the countryside, Angela, Gloria and I are stopped at a random police checkpoint. The young policeman checks my licence and sees I am not boozed. He hands back my licence, smiles and expresses a mock-profound hope that I will enjoy the rest of my day. Procedural courtesy is so well learnt at the police college. Perhaps future training will extend to courtesy that matters.

On the phone this evening, Mary says to me, "The police aren't stupid. They'll see through Verity's lies." She may be right, but if it isn't stupidity, what is it: procrastination? Myopia? Irrationality? Disorganisation? Pure vindictiveness, perhaps? Something certainly is amiss. One of the scariest explanations for me is laziness. Perhaps it's just too much bother for the police to do even the bare bones of a proper investigation required to see that this isn't the usual "he said/she said". This may mean that they just have the contradictory claims of Verity and myself swirling round inside their heads, and don't go to the trouble to check the simple facts that matter. In a meeting to decide whether to prosecute, all they can say is, "Well, she seems convinced that he raped her, but he came through the interview looking like an innocent man. This is a tricky one, so the fairest thing we can do is let it go to trial and have the jury decide his fate. Of course, we could look more carefully at the facts, but…nah, they may get in the way of our procedure." It would be so easy for them to consider this fair, but it isn't. For us, a trial is a disaster, no matter how it turns out.

Let's turn this around. Imagine the police finally do weigh up the facts and learn not just that Verity's allegation may not be true, not just that her story is unlikely to sway a jury, but that it *cannot* be true. Do they prosecute her? "Well, it's hard to say whether she was being vindictive or whether she's just a disturbed woman. This is a tricky one, so the fairest thing we can do is let it go to trial and have the jury decide her fate." Not a chance. They will regard my trial as serving the broader public interest, but not *her* trial.

Of course, I'm not really anti-police. It's just that, like anybody else, I'm swayed by the particular dealings I have with people or institutions. Right now the slogan on the side of New Zealand police cars – "safer communities together" – seems more trite than usual. Eva's expressionless face has become the face of the whole police force. I don't even know if she is really handling this, but she's the only one I see. She uses the first person singular all the time, but I think her rank is detective constable. Is there some puppeteer of higher rank pulling strings somewhere out of my sight? Is Eva a victim too? Maybe she knows cases like this just waste her time, and after a couple of drinks at police happy hour on Friday she declaims against the stupid system that compels her to pursue them, but come Monday she puts on her uniform again and has to play the game. Perhaps she has little chance of promotion if she doesn't play it convincingly. But I doubt if she's just a time-server. I have no way of knowing for sure, but when she suggested that maybe I was guilty her voice rang with the commitment of a true believer.

I think some more about Eva's comment that "it's a complex case." On the surface of it, this may seem a reasonable explanation for the delay, but it isn't at all. It's just a smug reply to fob me off, issued by a detective who cannot find a needle in a box full of needles. I have no way of seeing into the police "investigation", and this opacity allows them to evade, to delay, to obfuscate, even (as far as I know) to lie. *Complexity* is a complex word. In what specific way is this case complex? Is it legally complex, logically complex, psychologically complex, forensically complex, chronologically complex, geographically complex? Are the accused being "investigated" as an integrated group or as individual offenders? If the former, why hasn't the supposed head pervert even been interviewed yet? If the latter, why haven't the police looked at the details of where Verity and I were during the period of the allegation and concluded that the woman has not told the truth? My *individual* case isn't complex at all.

I also give more thought to Eva's comment "I have to investigate." This sounds perfectly reasonable, but it has its limits. I suspect that with any alleged crime other than a sexual one, an accusation as far-fetched and tenuous as this one would have been dismissed even before it got to the stage of an interview with the alleged offender. If what Eva calls investigation does not assess the time and the place of the accusation as its very first step, then what does it do? "I have to investigate" in these circumstances seems to mean either of two things. It may mean she has to get me into the frame and she's having trouble making me fit, or it may just be a procedural statement designed to counter bad publicity the police have sometimes received about not pursuing sexual complaints thoroughly enough. It seems to mean, "If we're not seen to go after this one, however weird it seems, we'll have women's groups or the media on our backs." Police can gain kudos from claiming that they have boosted their sexual abuse clearance rates, but I would be astounded if they had a category for false sexual accusation clearance rates. I can't imagine Eva receiving a commendation for putting away a criminal like Verity, with her district superintendent saying, "Well done, Detective Braun. This woman has caused untold misery to many innocent victims, and you've done the public a great service by getting her sent down." Have we – Angela and I, and all the other falsely accused and their families – become victims of a police image makeover? Individual police officers can show physical courage in the front line, when they break up a fight or face down a deranged gunman. Breaking the terrible news of a fatal accident to the victim's parents takes a different kind of mettle. However, the reluctance of one woman in blue to clear me of this unfounded accusation shows pure moral cowardice.

The police seem to define some words differently. When trainees graduate from police college, they must be given standard-issue Bluespeak dictionaries along with their caps and badges. They certainly don't use the Concise Oxford, which has separate entries for *prosecute* and *persecute,* and for *suspect* and *perpetrator.* It also has this definition of *investigate:*

> v. carry out a systematic or formal inquiry into (an incident or allegation) so as to establish the truth.

What the police ultimately seek is not the truth but a conviction – a "result". According to this definition, what Eva is doing in my case seems not so much a flawed investigation as no investigation at all. All this time and heartache are going on a non-investigation of a non-event. It is clear that in historic sexual cases the police prosecute for the same reason that dogs lick their nether bits: just because they can.

April 8

We take Gloria to the airport in the morning. Her visit has brought all of us some comfort, and we are sad to see her go.

Angela and I switch on the *I Am Innocent* episode on TV about a man who was convicted and imprisoned for a rape that he clearly didn't do. After a few minutes, Angela timidly asks, "You okay to watch this?" and I say we'll see how it goes. The case was similar to mine in the sense that the police had tunnel vision. They just had the guy in the frame and wanted a result. Another non-investigation. His original lawyer was too slack to pick up that the police had not allowed a corroborating witness to take the stand. Watching it makes me morose (not depressed – I refuse to take medication) and angry, because Eva seems to be thinking the same way. This case was different from mine in the sense that a rape clearly did take place, so the innocent guy who went to prison certainly wasn't the only victim. A guilty man is walking free. The innocent man was awarded a cash settlement and received a belated apology, but it clearly changed him – and other people's perception of him – in a way that nothing will ever compensate for. One thing that certainly didn't change was the way police conduct their investigations.

April 9

I have my second meeting with Lionel at The Men's Room. No special reason, just an update to a knowledgeable person with an attentive ear. I tell him that there's no progress in my case, and he is amazed that John hasn't been approached yet. I suggest that maybe the reason the police haven't questioned John is that they're playing a tactical game: maybe they're waiting for one of us to break cover and do something that will betray our guilt. "No," he says firmly. "All the police know is procedure." They just do what they're instructed to do, and attributing subtle tactics to them is giving them far too much credit. "Treat them as stupid and slow," he says. I mustn't mistake lethargy for strategy. Yes, I see that now. When you control all the big guns, when you have the whole system on your side, tactics and nuances play no role. Neither does speed. Just plod along following your forefinger through the lines of the manual and chances are you'll get a result. This is scary, because my "case" requires a real investigator to see beyond standard guidelines. Procedure has its uses but also has its limitations. It wasn't procedure that persuaded Captain Chesley Sullenberger to pitch his Airbus A320 into the Hudson River.

Lionel also tells me that he's a little surprised the police haven't wanted to look at my computer. This hasn't occurred to me, but he says it makes sense: child protection team, rape of a minor. My reaction is to think they should go ahead. In fact, I would welcome it. The only problem is that my computer is indispensable for the examining work I do. Who compensates me for the loss of income? It isn't just the direct financial loss. I work on private contract, and I have always tried hard to establish myself as an examiner who does the work quickly and efficiently. How do I explain to my employers in Wellington why I don't have my computer, and what good will must I lose with them because I'm unaccountably out of action for who knows how long? I could borrow someone else's computer, but setting up the necessary software is such a hassle that I'd rather not think about it. And maybe if the police take your computer they prohibit you from using the internet at all. In that case I can't do my main work.

I'm ashamed that I break down for a short time and get blubbery, as I did with the reporter. I apologise, but he says it's okay – it's normal, and he doesn't know how he would cope if it happened to him.

Lionel brings up two new angles: maybe I should consider seeing my Member of Parliament, and going to the Independent Police Conduct Authority. I make a mental note of these suggestions. I also tell him that keeping a diary helps me cope, and that perhaps the whole saga will get published one day. He agrees that writing can be therapeutic, and he says that other men frustrated by the way the system has treated them have had the same intention. He suggests that before I commit to publication I should give careful thought to my exact purpose, or purposes, in doing so. Yes, I say, I've already done that, and I have a whole list of purposes – which may be the same as no purpose at all. Most important, I want to show as many people as possible that false rape accusations happen, and perhaps telling my story can help in some small way to swing the onus of proof back onto the prosecution, where it belongs. Secondly, I want people to see how police have mishandled this case. Ideally, I would like to see Verity prosecuted, because such a precedent would bring long-term benefit in the future, not only for wrongly accused men, but perhaps also for genuinely abused women. However, I don't think anything I write can help to get her prosecuted. I suspect she will evade liability for her whole life. Finally, I find the writing process cathartic. It's my booze.

Lionel wishes me well with my diary, but he warns me not to take the loss of reputation too lightly. He adds something I hadn't really thought of – some people will say, "Of course, the reason he went into teaching was to groom victims." I guess this is like some deviants becoming priests or scout leaders, or pyromaniacs joining the fire service. He also says that none of the other men who said they would tell their stories actually followed through to publication. There it is, of course. There is the reason the public has no idea how common such false charges are: they don't get into the news. Convictions make the headlines because they are sensational and strengthen the notion that rapists and paedophiles are everywhere. This results in a general belief that rape complainants are always telling the truth, which boosts the chances that juries will convict in other cases. Acquittals get no publicity because a man is so blindsided by the accusation and the resulting process that he spends all his energy and money just on freeing himself of the horror of it. If it finally ends in justice he has no fight left, and of course he still wants to keep a low profile. He has no motivation to expose the system by writing about it or by bringing a prosecution against his accuser. I'm determined to prove to Lionel that I will do one of these things – or both. Someone has to.

April 10

I find Benito, Verity's ex-husband. Like Verity herself, he isn't in the phone book, but where would I be without the electoral roll? There he is, with his address, so I turn up at his door. What a find! I introduce myself (Christian name only) and explain what's going on. He says, "That must be a tricky situation for you." Well yes, just a little. I ask if he knew about her accusations against me and others. He says, "Hmm, so she's still pursuing that. She mentioned it a long time ago, but I didn't know if she was carrying on with it. She hasn't talked about it for a long time." Accusing a group of innocent men of paedophilia may as well have been an Italian cooking class which she was once thinking of joining but decided she didn't have the time.

He says he still has frequent contact with her, as they share custody of their daughter Edda, now in her early teens. He and Verity are back on fairly good terms. He concedes that Verity has her faults (well yes, just a few), and she has struggled through life, but he is pleased that she's getting some stability now that she's with Heinrich, her new partner. He's a professional guy with some standing in society and occupation. An accountant, in fact. Aha, so this is the beefy man.

This revelation, that the accusation means almost nothing to her, is the most outrageous, the most infuriating news I've heard since the saga began. The ostensible purpose of this whole case, and any others like it, is that a woman's life has been permanently blighted by the actions of a group of debauched men, and they must be brought to justice. So who's feeling the stress? Who's behaving as if life will never be the same again – Verity or the suspects?

But when I think about it, her indifference makes sense, because all the consequences are on one side. The repercussions for me, John and the other innocents are devastating, and can be divided into incarceration, reputation and remuneration.

In the first, any of the accused men can go to jail for maybe ten years. In theory, she can be prosecuted for bringing a false accusation (Crimes Act section 115), conspiring to defeat justice (section 116) or at least wasting police time. However, the police almost certainly won't bother, because they know that anti-rape activists will cry foul or some counsellor may sign a piece of paper testifying that she is a vulnerable and directionless "survivor" who can't be held responsible for her own actions. I (or another accused) could bring a private suit against her, but we'll have to pay for it, and the result will likely still be an acquittal because of the alleged mental state of the poor woman.

In the second, she can take no flak because the law will guarantee that she will remain anonymous, no matter whether we are cleared, charged, convicted or acquitted.

In the third, the police pay all the costs of her case against us, but of course we must pay for our own defence, and get no recompense if it's found to be a pack of lies. So why should any of it matter to her?

It can be hard to distinguish between a lie and a sincerely held delusion. But this news makes Verity's untruth seem more like a lie – or a delusion so infuriating that it's the next best thing. So these life-altering horrors, so vicious and so perverted, such a betrayal of trust by the man whose natural role should have been to protect her, play such a minor role in her life that she has filed the allegation away in a back room of what passes for her mind. I am furious.

Benito, singing like a bird, confirms what I have suspected: for years Verity has gone to a counsellor. He also says that when the marriage split up there was a dispute over Edda. Verity accused him of sexually abusing the kid in order to get sole custody. It caused him so much despair that he turned to alcohol and drugs. For months he was allowed to have no contact with the girl, and was worried that he might be barred from ever seeing her again, but when it came to court the judge threw out her accusations in short order, seeing them for what they were, and joint custody was granted. Of course, she faced no consequences for making these false allegations.

How amazing that Benito has become friendly with Verity again. He tells me that he's an easy-going and forgiving person, and I can see he's right. He says, "I've learnt that holding a grudge makes you sick." That's probably right too. All this forgiveness, all this understanding. I think again of the Queensland guy who was actually jailed after a false memory accusation, but forgave his accuser and hoped that she would get the psychological help she needed. These are better men than I am. But if Verity cannot forgive me for what I haven't done to her, I find it hard to forgive her for what she *has* done to me. I didn't want to play this game, and I'm the player who can't just ask to be dealt out. She can. If I am forced to play, those are the rules. If I'm in, I'm in to win. It's very interesting that she's played this game before, with Benito. She's learnt that the possible outcomes are a win or a draw. That's why she wants to play again.

I tell Benito that Verity had better watch out, because I've done my research and I know what crimes she can be prosecuted for. I even quote chapter and verse. Will he tell her about this meeting? Probably, and it's comforting to think that she may feel some heat for a change. On the other hand, she will probably know that any private prosecution threat is just a bluff, and that the police themselves won't go for her. After all, nothing happened to her when she lied about Benito abusing their daughter, so she's learnt that abuse is a card she can play with no disadvantage.

Benito tells me that one reason for his forgiveness is that he has no doubt that Verity was sexually abused way back in her past. "But," I protest, "she accused you of molesting your daughter, and you know that isn't true. Doesn't that mean she has no credibility in your eyes when she accuses others?"

The phone interrupts us, and I realise it's her. It's Verity! My god. The enemy, the predator – so close. A conversation follows for two minutes or so. I can hear what he says, of course. I can even hear her voice jangling through the receiver, but I can't make out her words. He says he's sorry, but he can't take Edda in the weekend. His car has broken down....No, he can't borrow a car from anybody...Well, he's sorry if he gave the impression it was up to him...That would be great...He owes her one.

I'm trapped in the lives of people I have nothing in common with. It's like I'm a part of their fractured family. I want to scream, "Get me out of here – I've been put into the wrong life! Please just let me go back to how things were."

The phone conversation ends, and he just says, "That was her."

He comes back to Verity's credibility. He replies that he has no doubt the abuse was real, because she has described it to him, and it was so detailed that she couldn't have made it up. She even remembered the colour of the jacket that the abuser was wearing, and she remembered that she had a sore hip after the ordeal.

I shake my head at him. "But wait," I say. "Even false memories can have convincing detail. The detail and the sincerity are no proof that it actually happened." I want to hold him by the lapels and scream full in his face. This is the essence of the whole sad story. It's all about detail. False and fatal detail will destroy us.

He is unmoved. "Where there's smoke there's fire." Such an incomparably stupid idiom. The logically prior question has to be, "Is what looks like smoke really smoke, or something billowy and spectacular but fake, like dry ice?" I don't think of this response at the time, of course. Not that there would be any point, because his certainty is a statement of faith. *Dry Ice* – now there's a better title.

He tells me that she was upset that Verity's younger sister Jennifer for a long time didn't believe her accounts. Aha! We knew from Gloria's earlier comments that Jennifer no longer wanted contact with John, but this seems to confirm that the sensible one was eventually won over by her sister's graphic detail. This is good and bad news. If Jennifer once was skeptical, maybe she can be made skeptical again. That could help us all in court. But if not, how awful for John that even if Verity's delusions don't send him to jail, they will cost him not just one of his daughters, but both.

He adds, "Then there's Verity's nymphomania."

"What?"

"She was always all over me. Couldn't get enough of it. That's got to come from somewhere. What made her so sexualised? It must have been sexual abuse."

This is so irrational that it knocks me back. I stammer, "B-but some women are just like that. No one knows why." At least, I don't think so. I could have added that I hadn't met many. Where were these willing babes when I was nineteen?

I see he has a computer, and I write the search term "Elizabeth Loftus TED false memory" on a scrap of paper. I say, "Have a look at this. She gives a good case for doubting what people say they remember." He says he will, but he won't, of course. That's not how religions work.

I glance at my watch and say, "Sorry, I have to go. I'm late to meet my wife in town." I want to stay, because this has been really useful, and he isn't holding back. I'd love to milk this one meeting for all it's worth. I'd like to see him again, but I can't, because talking to him is the riskiest sleuthing I've done. I'm scared the police will find out, and this meeting won't please Dwight if my case goes to court.

As I bike into town to meet Angela, I think about doubt. In a way, this whole thing is about doubt. Why are so many people so intolerably certain about things which should be doubted? Certainty can be such a pernicious and destructive thing. Verity and Benito are as certain of their fantasy as I am of facts: not *my* facts, just facts. Gloria said that there are two sides to every story, and it's tragic that Verity and apparently Charlotte don't see our side. But this story has only one side: we didn't rape her. What other side can there be? Truth is more important than facts? Baloney. It's bad enough that an unknown woman is seeking to destroy me, but what makes it worse is that she is seeking to destroy me with a lie.

After this meeting, I think yet again about Eva's claim that she is investigating. The geographical disconnect between accuser and accused should be enough to throw the case out, but now I learn about Verity's historic false claim against her ex. Well, does Eva's "investigation" consider Verity's court history? If I, a semi-retired English teacher and incompetent cycle gumshoe, can find out about it, why can't Eva?

I'm choking in fake smoke. Does Eva live by this silly proverb as well? Is it what motivates her in her pursuit of perverts? I wonder what courses Eva has had to attend to get into the "child protection team". Maybe she had to pass a course in which the textbook was written by someone who promotes the dogma that complainants are entitled to their "personal truth": that if they think they were abused, they were. So their perception of reality has shaped their actions. I wonder how much sympathy a real rapist would garner if he used the defence "I have had a difficult life, low self-esteem and no luck with women. Rape was my way of feeling I had some control."

April 16

My research on the history of "recovered memory" in sexual abuse cases all tends to lead in one direction: the 1988 American book *The Courage to Heal* by Ellen Bass and Laura Davis, and I take it out from the central library. This copy proudly proclaims itself as the "Twentieth Anniversary Edition", so clearly it's been quite a seller. It even has an accompanying workbook. A *workbook!* If ever I am fortunate enough to gain compensation for everything this allegation has put us through, my itemised claim would have to include emotional damage from having to read parts of this book – the pseudoscience, the pure misandry, the anti-family vitriol, the fourth-rate poetry.

The Courage to Heal outlines symptoms of suppressed sexual abuse from decades earlier. The authors do not admit that most of these symptoms are general enough to have had any number of other causes, if indeed such symptoms point to anything at all except a general malaise. If a weepy "survivor" doesn't remember any sinister event, it doesn't mean it didn't happen; on the contrary, it confirms that it did, because she must have suppressed it. Historic sexual abuse therefore cannot be falsified; it is necessarily true. If the "survivor" remembers it, it happened, and if she doesn't remember it, it happened. Anyone seeking corroboration is in denial. Abuse by fathers is an undeniable explanation for all the problems any woman has, will have, has had, or imagines she has.

Robert Shaeffer's scathing 1994 review of the book concludes in this way:

> We miss the big picture if we imagine *The Courage to Heal* as some sort of irrational singularity that just happened to have done a lot of harm. For the simple fact is that *The Courage to Heal* is merely one of a large number of such books for "survivors"...Few if any books, in the entire canon of "Women's Studies", expresses the slightest degree of doubt in the validity of so-called "recovered memories," or the slightest degree of remorse for the suffering of innocent men falsely accused thereby...The harm caused by *The Courage to Heal* and similar books is not that of honest error in scholarship, but rather represents a form of sexual and ideological warfare. The harm it has caused is not

> accidental, but rather one that is celebrated with a degree of malicious glee.

The writers had no qualifications in psychiatry or psychology, and the book is all the more damaging because it uses simple language that can appeal to lay readers. It continues to be widely recommended in sexual abuse circles. I know that it is still on the reading list for New Zealand rape crisis groups, and it is even a required text for some university courses in the UK. I don't know if Verity's counsellor has read it, but she probably read something inspired by the faith it promotes.

This is one of the most damaging holy books. Its spirit has contaminated the thinking of countless campaigners in what has become the sexual abuse industry. This is most clearly seen in the perception that almost any disturbing or even slightly unusual feature in a child's behaviour is to be attributed to abuse. One of the most revealing incidents revealed by Lynley Hood in *A City Possessed*, her book on the Christchurch Civic Crèche case, concerns the testimony in court by Karen Zelas, a prominent and respected "expert" on sexual abuse of children. Zelas claimed that most abused children "either deny or fail to disclose abuse" when it happens, and "initially deny abuse" when asked about it later. She said any combination of the following can demonstrate abuse:

> Headaches, sexual knowledge, unhappiness, nightmares, night terrors, toileting problems, tantrums, delayed disclosures, sleeping problems, anxiety, fear of men, aggression, hyperactivity, denial, avoidance behaviour, sexualised behaviours, nausea, red bottoms, separation anxiety, stomach aches, progressive disclosures, vomiting, gagging, fussiness

No doubt they can, but they can also show all sorts of other conditions…or no condition at all beyond being human and young. The confident and eloquent Dr Zelas was probably used to worshipful listeners hanging on her every word, and never had to field tricky questions from articulate people outside the faith. Defence lawyer Rob Harrison asked Dr Zelas this very pertinent, very necessary question designed to test whether her assumptions about sexual abuse were falsifiable:

> What behaviours in young children are *inconsistent* [my italics] with the child who has been sexually abused?

Zelas replied, "I haven't thought about that."

The pop psychology from books like *The Courage to Heal* has given us this automatic assumption of sexual abuse. The bungling response by Zelas shows us that whatever we call this assumption, it isn't science. A scientist would reject the assumption that a possible cause of any observed behaviour is a necessary cause. Yet there has been a movement in the abuse industry to stifle any explanation other than sexual abuse when a young child wets the bed or is afraid of weird Uncle Alastair. To these people, sexual abuse is necessarily true.

When Michael Jackson was accused of sexual abuse back in 2005, one of his accusers from an alleged incident years earlier admitted that he had initially denied that Jackson had ever touched him. Unfortunately, the sexual abuse industry doesn't do this sort of denial. David Feige from *slate.com* wrote that Dr Anthony Urquiza, who had been called as an "expert" witness for the prosecution, told the court about a condition he called "child sexual abuse accommodation syndrome", or CSAAS. This is the tendency for genuine victims to deny that the abuse happened, as a way of coping with the trauma.

Feige points out the absurdity of accepting such a syndrome in court. He writes that

> not reporting abuse is...consistent with suffering from child sexual abuse accommodation syndrome. So is bad behavior, trouble in school, the failure to tell an accurate story, and even the recantation of the entire allegation of abuse. In other words, every criterion usually used by the defense to discredit a witness is actually transubstantiated into evidence that is perfectly consistent with abuse. And here's the genius: Not exhibiting these signs of CSAAS doesn't mean a child wasn't abused—just that he or she didn't get the syndrome. In other words, a noncredible witness is suffering from the syndrome, but a credible one is merely a credible witness who was legitimately abused. CSAAS is a prosecutorial silver bullet and a fabricator's best friend. Every mistake you make is consistent with it; every mistake you don't make further confirms your credibility.

Feige adds that with this sort of syndrome testimony, "Up is down, falsehood is truth, and there is an excuse for everything." We can thank our lucky stars that Verity hasn't denied that she was abused. Then I would *really* be in trouble.

Once you join the sisterhood of sexual victims, details can change as long as they do not interfere with the defining and indisputable fact of abuse. Even the identity of the perpetrator may not matter. Here are some comments on the subject from *Notes of a Fringe Watcher*, by Martin Gardner:

> Paul McHugh, a psychiatrist at Johns Hopkins University, in "Psychiatric Misadventures" (American Scholar, Fall 1992), writes about a woman who under therapy came to believe she had been sexually assaulted by an uncle. She recalled the exact date. Her disbelieving mother discovered that at that time her brother was in military service in Korea. Did this alter the woman's belief? Not much. "I see, Mother," she said. "Yes. Well let me think. If your dates are right, I suppose it must have been Dad."

April 17

I track down Cedric L, an acquaintance who used to be a policeman. I don't know him very well, but it may be useful to get him in the V-loop. His first response when I tell him the fix I'm in is to say that he was having a conversation just two weeks ago with an old friend of his, visiting from out of town, who is also facing historic sexual abuse allegations. He says this is more common than most people assume. He shakes his head in horror as I outline the scale of my predicament. He also confirms that any false complainant has a whole deck of "get out of jail free" cards, even though the law has provision to prosecute her. I tell him that the investigating officer assured me that if I'm not just shrugging this off, it means I must have something to hide. I assume all police in Draketown know each other. "Eva B?" he asks. I nod.

I put to him one question I've been burning to ask: is it really possible for the police to keep this file open indefinitely, if they are convinced that one day they will find the source of what smells like smoke? Yes, he says, it's possible. Damn! No, I can't live with that. After a certain time – a few more months, a year maybe, I don't know – I'll just have to stop finding things out and actually do something. Eventually this inaction just turns from an "investigation" into a fixation, into a form of cruelty. And it's all based on vague memories from two decades ago. I tell him that when I have endured all the waiting I can, I will have to blow the gaff and go public – and I won't be anonymous. He nods as if he understands, almost as if to suggest it's about time someone did.

When I phoned Eva to get some news about what was happening with Verity's allegation, she told me that I should just relax and enjoy life, because the system will clear me if I am innocent. This revelation from Cedric puts her callousness in a new light. What Eva would call a happy and just outcome for an innocent man can apparently take one of two forms. Either I don't get prosecuted because police look at the evidence so far collected and don't like their odds of getting a conviction, so they let the case lie – perhaps for ever – while they wait for something or someone to corroborate Verity's lie. Yet this is intolerable, because I will always have this possibility hanging over me that I will be taken from my retirement village when I am ninety-five and be hauled in front of a court. The other way the system can clear me is if I am prosecuted but acquitted. Does Eva consider this just, when it means that I will be named and shamed, endure intolerable stress as I hope for good luck in the jury lottery, and probably have to pay a fortune?

April 18

Angela phones Gloria, who says she and John have at last told a couple who are close to them. These people say that they know someone else in a similar fix. This situation seems to be more common than most people assume, but everyone caught in the trap is desperate to keep it quiet. This guarantees that the only people who know how widespread it is are those few people who have contact with more than one victim: men's counsellors, some lawyers and legal advisors. John and Gloria have also told some family members, and she says they feel much better for having done so. They have also seen a lawyer, who tells them not to tell the ex-wife, or to pre-empt the police by walking into the local police station, or in fact to do anything, because the police don't like "smart-arses" – presumably cycle gumshoes like me. Despite this, John writes letters to ex-wife Charlotte and second daughter Jennifer. Will he get a response?

April 22

I watch another *I Am Innocent* episode on TV. It investigates a case from the North Island which is in some ways similar to mine. The central character is the brother of the complainant. The deranged woman was led down the "recovered memory" path by a dodgy counsellor. In the woman's mind, anyone who doubted that she had been abused by their parents decades earlier became part of "the other", the unbelievers. It fits the pattern. This woman was clearly much further gone than Verity, and needed to be hospitalised because she just couldn't cope. This was clearly a woman who was very ill mentally.

Although the parents were the main victims, the brother himself was investigated. What I find interesting is that he wasn't prosecuted, so the police quickly saw sense. Where are those police officers, and have they thought of transferring down here to Draketown? Most interesting of all is that the charges were dropped, so the guy could have stayed anonymous. Despite this, he had the courage to front up on the show and use his real name. Good luck to him. Enough of this "mud sticks" excuse, true though it may sometimes be. The social and legal pendulum won't shift away from where it is now, with even the most transparently deluded complainant being believed, unless more men have the conviction to do that. Hopefully I will be another – eventually, when I can do so safely. Which isn't really courage, I suppose.

Unlike the woman in this episode, Verity leads an ostensibly normal life, which is why I usually don't have much sympathy for her. I'm not sure Verity is mentally ill at all. You don't have to be crazy to want to see a counsellor. If during your therapy you become convinced of the truth of something false, you are just deluded, not insane. Plenty of sane people are certain that silly things are true, from scientology to the Bermuda triangle and creationism.

April 24

My friend Barry arrives from Christchurch to stay the weekend. He's in the V-loop and I've warned him that there's one subject that dominates in this household. He says he understands and can live with that – or at least put up with it for a couple of days.

April 25

The three of us drive over to Woodstock for the day, and have a wonderful time at the aviation museum just out of town. Not a single mention of what's-her-name.

April 26

Barry and I get to talking about the case. He agrees with me that what the police are doing doesn't seem to be a true investigation. He offers a perceptive angle on this. The way the system appears to work is that I get no chance to present the evidence that can save me; the adversarial game plan requires my lawyer and me to keep it aside to use as a defence weapon in court. But the result of this purely procedural approach is that a case goes to court which the police would surely have thrown out before that stage if I could have given them the information I hold. I assume the police get no kudos from losing a case in court, so it is in their interests almost as much as mine for me to front up to them now and say, "Look at the whens and the *wheres* of this accusation. Look at the complainant's history. It just doesn't add up." Why take a far-fetched case to court? What do even they, the police, gain from this?

This is similar to the point made on the British False Memory Society website by a man who suffered an accusation like mine:

> After your initial interview, it would be helpful and hopefully

constructive to have a second opportunity to be formally interviewed again some days or weeks later. On the basis that you are innocent until proved guilty, you are there to help the Police with their enquiries. They should welcome this. This offer should be cast in stone as part of the formal process. At the second interview, you should be invited to present your list of the witnesses who you want to have interviewed by them. They can probably add things of value to the investigation. That should be a requirement of the process.

April 28

This item appears in the local newspaper:

Child sex charges laid

A Draketown man has been arrested and charged with 14 child sex offences, including the attempted rape of an underage girl.

The 51-year-old man was arrested about 10:45 am on Friday.

Police say the alleged offending happened in the early 1990s.

He has been charged with eight counts of unlawful sexual connection with a female aged 12 to 16, five counts of indecently assaulting a female aged 12 to 16 and attempting to rape a female aged 12 to 16.

He is to appear in the Draketown District Court on May 4.

Multiple charges, but apparently just on one girl, who was a teenager in the early 1990s. Could this be more of Verity's handiwork? It's possible – the same broad span of years and ages. My police interview implied that one of our ring of perverts lived in Orange, which isn't far away. If he is Verity prey, this looks like scary news, because the police have bought into enough of her story to charge him. I decide I just have to go to that hearing on May 4.

The accused will no doubt have name suppression at this early stage, and poor Verity is guaranteed anonymity for ever, of course. If I do find her hand in this, I will have an almost irrepressible urge to tell the defendant or his lawyer that it isn't true, that the woman has no credibility. I will want to plead with his lawyer, "Check the liar's history! She has accused her ex of child abuse on the daughter, but it was thrown out in court. Check the places and times of her accusation against me!" This is information that can save all of us.

May 1

I visit Josephine at the free legal advice centre again. I want to ask two specific questions: how difficult is it to bring a private suit against Verity, and how feasible is it for me to approach either the lawyer or the defendant the following Monday if I learn that this is another Verity case? On the former, she says it may be prohibitively expensive, but she really isn't sure. The problem is that normally it is the police who do all prosecuting, and she knows that they are unwilling to do so when women make false claims like this one. I could spend a king's ransom on a private lawsuit but still not get a conviction. No surprise there. My friend Ted has already warned that when anyone asks a lawyer, "Can you help me with this legal issue?" the answer is unlikely to be *no*. Never ask your barber if you need a haircut.

The latter question shocks her and she warns me that it would be naive and dangerous to interfere in any way in the preliminary court appearance of the other defendant. The police apparently take a keen interest in who attends court sessions. Imagine if this man turns out to be guilty, and I was seen talking to him. She is quite strict and almost mothering. She is also right, of course, but her advice takes any remaining wind out of my sails. In my mind I have so many objections, but they turn into feeble pulses of "But....but...", vaguely felt but not articulated. No point hanging around here. She has answered my legal questions as best she can, and she isn't a counsellor, God bless her.

I leave the office feeling trapped and helpless and desperate. Right now, life is just an unwelcome pulse. I cross the road and sit on something – a fire hydrant, I think. I am close to tears. Before the meeting my stomach was rumbling, but my appetite has gone now. Draketown being a small place, a guy from a rival quiz team waves to me from across the road. He comes over and chats, so I have normality forced upon me. His chosen topic of not-to-be-missed restaurants brings back some appetite, and after he moves on I treat myself to lunch.

But I still pick at the food. I suffer another attack of common sense. I wonder how everyone in the legal system – the police, lawyers, this legal advisor – think a guilty sex offender acts after someone has accused him. I assume that he would probably hide away behind a tree somewhere and quietly hope for a convincing lawyer and, if not a gullible jury, at least a sympathetic judge. That is, the very opposite of what I am doing. It is the affront of a barefaced lie that enrages you and goads you into action. Why should this furious compulsion to do something – to do *anything* – be considered so incriminating?

It is a newly opened Thai restaurant, and I am the only diner there – and only Westerner. A humble and effusive waitress tends to me, all smiles. Some Buddhist monks in full yellow robes are a few tables down. The staff fuss around the monks, and one waiter brings out what looks like a wooden model of a junk-like vessel, more than a metre long. He lays it on a table. Then I see that it is a sort of Asian xylophone, and the waiter plays it gently as incense is burnt and everyone joins in a Buddhist prayer. They harmonise beautifully and the result is quite haunting. Right in the centre of Draketown, between traffic lights and a shop that sells photocopiers, I suddenly feel fused with something exotic and uplifting.

The waitress returns to me and explains that the monks have come from out of town, and the ceremony is to bless the new business. She asks me if I like the food, and I say yes, very much. Will I come back? Perhaps I might like to consider their special night: a buffet on Wednesday. I could bring my friends. Yes, I will do so, and I mean it too.

I have travelled to all kinds of places, but I have always been an unapologetic Westerner. Right now I would relish being an honorary Thai, because Verity seems to embody all that is wrong with the West, and Asian culture seems refreshingly Verity-free. But I suppose these people believe in reincarnation. Maybe they're right. Maybe I raped Verity in a previous life, when we were both black-handed gibbons swinging through the jungle, and this is the memory she has recovered under therapy. Could a Thai court convict me for that?

Of course, huge numbers of women suffer terribly in many Asian cultures at the hands of men. In comparison, what I am going through is like nirvana. My Canadian friend Farzana, who grew up in Pakistan, is in the V-loop. She has told me how ironic it is that where she comes from a woman who actually is raped faces ostracism as tainted goods. If she reports the rape she may be pressured to salvage some respectability by marrying her rapist. She may even be prosecuted for adultery, for heaven's sake. But here in the sophisticated West, a woman can make it up and suffer no consequences.

When I get home I look through some of the brochures that I picked up at the legal advice centre. One is entitled "For Victims of Sexual Violence", so it seems worth a look. It says

> Sometimes it is difficult for the police to find enough evidence to make an arrest or prove the case in court, especially if the crime was reported some time after it happened. This can mean that the case cannot go further; it does not mean you were not believed.

Fair enough as far as it goes, but it should add "...unless your claim is a vicious lie." The terminology is a giveaway. It refers to "the victim" and "the offender" with no sign anywhere of "alleged". The alleged victim is allowed to see the courtroom before the trial in order to get acquainted and comfortable with this alien environment, and to have a "support person" present at the trial. But what if the "offender", who would more fairly be called the accused, also under stress and about to endure a harrowing and threatening experience, also needs this kind of comfort? Are innocent men supposed to be macho enough to tough it out? The alleged victim is guaranteed to have her anonymity preserved, of course. Members of the public are excluded if she gives evidence, and the media cannot report her name. These conditions are perfectly reasonable. But I wonder why a man can have his name revealed publicly at his first court hearing. After all, at this stage he must be assumed to be innocent, and his reputation suffers irreparably just by being named.

Then I read about the financial support Verity is entitled to, and I feel like I've been taking crazy pills. Both she and her chosen support person get paid $100 a day "court attendance fee" over the course of trial. I read this twice. Yes, I got it right. She lies and I tell the truth. She then gets paid to repeat the lie, and I must pay tens of thousands to repeat the truth. I don't even get compensated for two bike tyres and one replacement front spoke.

Something can be so unspeakably outrageous and irrational that your only reaction can be demented laughter. I have gone right through despair and come out the other side. As I sit at my desk reading this, my head collapses onto my forearms and I guffaw uncontrollably. It is the laugh of a man who has been instantly transported through Hades and into Teapot Land. Luckily Angela isn't home, so no one can have me taken away to beat my head on the walls of a rubber room.

Of course, this policy at first appears reasonable if the complainant has genuinely been abused. But I still think it's an outrageous idea. If she has suffered horribly, and is therefore reluctant to front up in the courtroom to relive her experience in a sordid trial that must recall all the details, is a cash payment for attendance meant to overcome that?

Recovering a little, I read further. If I am convicted, Verity and her support person can receive up to $1500 each to travel to any future parole hearing in order to give their views about whether the authorities can take the risk of letting me, a convicted and stubbornly unrepentant paedophile, back into the community. The poor little butterfly can hardly be expected to make the trip alone. Just a sigh now; no one can guffaw for ever.

Tonight we get a call from Gloria. We are getting a little careless – the four of us seem to have abandoned the principle of having a witness who can testify that John and I haven't spoken to each other. However, the point is that we haven't. We may no longer be able to provide witnesses to confirm that during all phone calls I was elsewhere. However, Angela or Gloria can still take the stand and say honestly that John and I never spoke to each other. Oaths matter; it is vital that none of us needs to tell even a minor or undetectable lie. Perjury not discovered is still perjury.

Gloria asks Angela if we have heard anything from the police, but Angela assures her that if anything as important as that had happened, one way or another we would have let them know by now. They have had no response to the letters John sent to Verity's mother and sister. From her account, John is coping worse than I am – he isn't eating or sleeping much. He says that whatever happens, he refuses to go to jail. What does he mean? We're worried about him.

Gloria says that the two of them have disagreements about what to do. Or, more accurately, whether to do something or nothing. He wants to fly down here and confront his ex-wife and even Verity herself, but she insists that he waits and stews, as their lawyer advised. Angela tells her about the local case that may also involve Verity, and about my intention to go to court on Monday to find out what I can.

I've been thinking a bit about that advice the lawyer gave John and Gloria about not being a smart-arse, about leaving it all to them. A cynic might say they stand to profit very nicely from keeping simplicity and common sense out of the process. At six dollars a minute to take control for you, what do they have to gain if the system is more intuitive and transparent?

May 4

I go to court, but learn nothing. The place has lots of little rooms and is busier than Penn Station. Crime seems to be a growth industry. The clerk at the front office can't tell me anything about this case, because the accused's name is suppressed, which prevents the clerk from doing a search.

Most court business seems to be about alcohol, one way or another. I go to one court and watch a judge award liquor licences to grateful applicants and fines to morose drunk drivers. It's less intense but more quietly chaotic than on TV: lawyers and officials are coming and going, and passing notes and documents to each other. I wonder if it really would be such a good idea to defend myself. Apart from anything else, I don't have any documents to pass. Would I bring some manila folders just to look like I belong? I get discreetly thrown out of another court because the only members of the public allowed there are those waiting to be called for jury service. I don't feel at home in this place at all.

I go home and mow the lawns, though they don't really need it. Just a kind of pacing, really.

May 5

A newspaper article tells us that this is rape awareness week, and there will be a stall in the city drawing people's attention to the burgeoning problem. The spokesperson says sexual abuse is on the rise, and "it is not just historic stuff that people are seeking help for." This means that some of it is historic, then. How much? I wonder. She repeats the mantra that rape is not about sexual gratification, but "power, control and manipulation." She also says the complexity of cases is increasing, which puts great demands on staff. This is an interesting claim. Why would complexity be increasing? I would expect that over one hundred cases or one thousand cases, the average complexity of valid cases would remain unchanged. It seems to suggest that the tentacles of a typical "investigation" have to reach out to touch more people, or people less connected with the complainant. Such as people in the complainant's father's address book, perhaps?

May 6

I get news about this week's court case after all, because it's reported in the newspaper. The guy has been named, and he has opted for a jury trial. He's been remanded on bail until July. If this were a case of incest, he probably wouldn't be named because it would reveal the complainant's identity as well. So, if the complainant is unrelated to him, there's still a fair chance that this is a Verity case. I'm burning to contact him and ask the name of the complainant, but I daren't of course.

May 7

I have lunch with a friend who has connections in accounting. I bring him into the V-loop and ask him what he can find out about Heinrich. He says he'll do what he can.

May 8

Friday, and the last day of sexual assault awareness week. I bike into town and track down the stall in the main street. It is manned (?) by three or four women of varying ages. I approach the oldest woman. I stress that I support the awareness she is raising, but ask if she has any statistics on *false* rape complaints. She concedes it does happen, but she doesn't know how often. I have printed out my thoughts on rape and power, as written in my March 17 entry. She says she will read it and pass it on to their leader, but I think she'll toss it after I'm gone. She is polite but looks at me oddly.

When I get home a fat white envelope is stuffed into the letterbox. Christmas! It is my pay records from the head office in Wellington. At last. I rush inside and rip it open. Pages and pages of photocopied salary and attendance tables going back to my teachers' college days. Someone has put some time into this. All kinds of stuff I don't really need, a lot of it so old it is hand-scrawled. If it had gone any further back, it would have been on stone tablets. I flick and flick, and finally....there it is: classroom attendance records from 1991, the year Verity attended Westchester High School between July and December. I had one day off: July 30, which was a Tuesday. Damn damn damn – I'd hoped for no days off. This is the most disappointing Christmas parcel since Auntie Lorna got me a beach shirt instead of the rocket gun she promised.

July – middle of winter. I probably had some kind of cold or flu. Maybe I went to the doctor. I phone him, and he checks his own hand-scrawled records from that year. Nothing that matches July 30. He asks if there is any news on my case, and is amazed that John hasn't been questioned. He calls the whole thing "medieval" and offers to help in any way he can, way beyond just medical matters. I know he means it too.

He reminds me that I had a minor operation to remove a sebaceous cyst at the hospital around about that time, and although the doctor doesn't have a record of that, the hospital itself might. I also had some tests done there on a couple of occasions to try to pinpoint the cause of my chronic mild anaemia. I'll try to find out next week.

My doctor called the Verity outrage "medieval". An interesting point. We have to go back a long way before we strike an era when it was normal to assume the guilt of the innocent without corroboration, or to sacrifice even a small number of innocents for the sake of catching any number of offenders. Such a practice contravenes the spirit of the Magna Carta, and that is eight centuries old. Admittedly, it was largely symbolic and most of its principles were never adopted in practice. Its clause 39 does not specifically mention the presumption of innocence, but many legal scholars have interpreted it in that light.

Blackstone's Formulation that "it is better that ten guilty persons escape than that one innocent person suffer" dates from the 1760s, but the notion it embodies is much older. A similar principle clearly existed in ancient times, and it can even be found in Genesis 18: 23-32:

> Abraham drew near, and said, "Will you consume the righteous with the wicked? What if there are fifty righteous within the city? Will you consume and not spare the place for the sake of the righteous who

> are in it? ...What if ten are found there?" He (the Lord) said, "I will not destroy it for the ten's sake."

John Adams, when defending some British soldiers charged with murder, added this warning about what may happen when Blackstone's Formulation is thoroughly and systematically ignored:

> ...when innocence itself, is brought to the bar and condemned...the subject will exclaim, 'It is immaterial to me whether I behave well or ill, for virtue itself is no security.' And if such a sentiment as this were to take hold in the mind of the subject that would be the end of all security whatsoever.

May 9

Angela gives me a beautiful blue file folder with "Verity Stuff" written neatly on the front, so that I can keep all the accumulating paraphernalia together: newspaper cuttings, printouts, brochures, employment records, business cards. A useful idea, and typical of her efficiency, but it's sad that it's come to this. Verity has become another job.

May 10

Our friend Mary – she with the ageing fox terrier bitch – rings on another matter, but the talk turns to Verity. She tells me she has told a couple of friends (whom I also know) and asks if that was okay. "Sure, no problem," I say. The circle is gradually edging wider, which gives me a thought. Draketown isn't that big a place. What if I told everyone I know about this, and told them to tell everyone they know? After a while the only people unfamiliar with the case would be hermits living up in the hills. Maybe that would be tactically useful. Lionel and others have told me that the police work according to procedure. This means that they think in a formula, based on certain assumptions. Their normal assumption about an historic sexual abuse case is that the accused man will strive to keep all allegations under wraps at all costs, to preserve his reputation. What happens if the accused blabs to all his friends, and they blab to everyone else? If the case is widely known in the community and is generally perceived to be ridiculous, how do the police proceed? Maybe they won't know how to cope with that. But I decide against it. I just don't know enough about tactics in this game I've never played before. One way or another, lots of people are learning about the accusation anyway.

May 12

I phone the hospital to find out my medical records. They tell me I'd better come in and see them, and I do so. They confirm that my operation was in 1994, so that's no good to me. For information about the tests, I have to fill in a consent form to dig into the files, and they'll mail me the results in a week or so.

My accounting friend also gets back to me with his findings about Heinrich. He says he has been involved in some rather shady accountancy dealings, and was once declared bankrupt. Interesting. Does this mean there's a chance Verity may be after money in this enterprise? I have wondered about this for some time, but I always thought it was probably a long shot.

May 14

This morning I get round to reading last night's paper, and there is an article by a young female columnist about the prevalence of sexual abuse on women, and the financial struggle faced by women's refuge centres in the face of funding cuts. She says that sexual abuse is massively underestimated in New Zealand. I write a letter to the editor questioning her figures on abuse. I also ask if the columnist would like to comment on false rape reports, and what penalty she considers would be reasonable for any woman who makes one. The local paper doesn't allow pseudonyms in readers' letters, so I have to give my name. I sit with my finger hovering over the mouse, wondering if this might be a tactical mistake, but finally I send it. I wonder if the writer, or any other readers, will write a response.

May 16

I call my brother Keith and give him an update. There isn't much since I last spoke to him, but I tell him about the parallel case in the newspaper, and how I'm dying to know if it's another of Verity's enhanced memories. He offers to telephone the guy anonymously. I get excited at this, and tell him yes, yes – go for it. Let's *do* something! I'll ring back later to give him the contact details. Then I tell Angela about this, and she looks doubtful. "It might look suspicious if the police find out," she says. I raise my voice at her. This is our worst skirmish since the fish slice hurl. But she's right. We play tennis and all is well again. I phone Keith and tell him I've changed my mind. But one way or another, I'm still determined to find out about that other case.

May 17

Angela phones Gloria again. No news. It's now clear, in case there was ever any doubt, that John's not going to get any response to the letters he wrote to wife and younger daughter. It's now almost six weeks since Eva assured me that John would be interviewed "soon". Does this word also have a unique definition in the Bluespeak dictionary? I am starting to think that if the police keep playing pass the parcel with my file I will have to contact the IPCA (Independent Police Conduct Authority), a suggestion Lionel made in our second meeting. At some point justifiable delay turns into a kind of harassment: passive and detached, but harassment nevertheless. Angela gives Gloria the name of the accused in the other local sex case, and John says he doesn't know him.

I have another thought about the delay in interviewing John. What if the police phone me tomorrow and say (in effect) that they've seen through Verity's lies, and have decided to drop all charges, not only against me but against all the suspects. So the whole thing just fizzles before John makes any official statement – maybe before any of the other co-accused has to do so. It's wonderful news, but it's also terribly sad in another way. It would mean that we never needed to contact him and tell him what has been going on. He would have been none the wiser, and he would have been spared all the rage, the gloom, the sleeplessness. No result of this horror is free of sadness and guilt.

Some sayings have their uses, unlike that dangerous one about smoke and fire. A friend in need certainly is a friend indeed. I decide to widen the circle a little more, and I email my old friend Herb from the deep south. I tell him our lives changed on February 1, and ask him whether he wants the short version or long version. He emails back and opts for long. I respond in the simplest way by sending all of this diary so far. To my surprise, he reads the whole thing and phones in the evening, furious. He wants to help, right now. He wants to fly up here tomorrow, front up at the bitch's door, and demand to know why she's chosen me, of all the people she doesn't know, to dump her delusions on. He asks why I didn't let Keith go right ahead and telephone the guy from the other case. He insists this story has to be told, sooner rather than later, for the benefit of other people further down the track. I should push my way onto some investigative TV show.

I tell him I'd love to do all those things, but they are all far too human and instinctive, too perfectly understandable. He knows this, of course, but he is so full of rage at the injustice that he wants to act. He is adamant that Verity has to face some consequences. Maybe if the police won't take her on and if it's too expensive to bring a private suit alone, get all the accused, including some friends, to share the cost. He says he'll be a contributor, and I know he will do it. He and I don't get together very often these days, but I see I have no better friend. I'm touched by his commitment, by his determination to do something, but I tell him I have learnt that I can't risk doing any of those things. I've already been too much of a smart-arse. Angela is right: having friends thump on the enemy's doors and phone them anonymously are actions which even an inexperienced prosecutor can use to paint me as a guilty man determined to interfere with the process of justice. Imagine if the prosecutor says to me in court, "An anonymous caller telephoned the complainant. Do you know who it was?" One of my two possible answers will incriminate me indirectly, and the other will be perjury. I don't want to be in that position. But I am on the case in the only way I can: keeping this diary. I am as determined as he is to get this bizarre story told – but just not yet, and not in the way he suggests.

Herb says he wants to pitch in with anything: time, money, whatever it takes. He says he wants to do it partly for me, but also for men. For men! Sure, why not? It doesn't sound very PC, but if a female anti-rape campaigner were to proclaim proudly, "I do this for women," would anyone raise an eyebrow?

He tells me he's impressed with my sleuthing so far, considering how circumspect I have to be. But something he says questions the value of what I considered the most useful gem I've found out: Verity's earlier accusation against her ex. Herb says he suspects that may not be allowed in court; information about previous actions she took may be seen as prejudicial, because the jury have to consider this individual case on its merits. Of course, Herb admits he is no lawyer, but I make a mental note that this is something I'll have to ask Charles when he comes back from his current holiday. Maybe – hopefully – it applies only to information about the history of the defendant, not his accuser.

May 20

It's a cool clear Draketown day and I bike into town, over the hill. When the sun is at the right angle I don't need binoculars, and today the glint tells me Verity's car is at home. She seems to lead an easy life – not much sign of any regular job. The same could be said of me, of course, but I'm sixty-two and semi-retired; what's her excuse? I'm not after her today anyway, so I cruise on down the hill into town. I bike past the cafe where I first saw Heinrich, the beefy man...and there he is again sitting at a table inside with two other guys. Does he live here? As I bike past I get just a two-second freeze-frame of him with a sandwich poised to enter his mouth, but that's him all right. How tempting to stop, dismount and go inside. What could I say? I've already tossed some lines around in my head:

> I'm the guy who didn't rape Verity.
> Watch out fella: one day Verity could accuse you as well.
> Tell Verity to watch her back: Crimes Act section 115.

Yes, any of those would do it. Got to keep it short – just blurt the words out loud, crisp and cool, then disappear. Surely he must know about her accusation, so he'll put two and two together and figure out who I am. He'll realise that I'm not just some random crazy man, because I know his partner's name. No doubt later he'll tell her what happened, and maybe she'll feel a bit of heat. She'll wonder how I know, and will hopefully wonder what else I know about her and her life.

But of course I do nothing of the kind. I cycle on to Fresh Choice on Norreys Street and buy some canned sardines that are on special this week. As I stash them into my backpack, a morose feeling comes over me. I am becoming too measured, too restrained, and I sense that I'm entering a long period of limbo. Perhaps all this omega-3 fatty acid will help me get through it.

May 21

My letter to the editor on rape and sexual abuse is published in the Draketown Post.

I email my ex-students Fridolin and Evelyne, a couple from Switzerland. I got very friendly with them when they were out here. Fridolin is a keen tennis player, and he took out temporary membership at the Trent club so that we could play each other. He is a judge's assistant back home, and I was interested to hear whether this kind of false charge happens over there. He replies that, sadly, it does. He'll keep on the lookout for any case that makes the news, and he'll let me know how it plays out in their very different legal system.

May 23

An article on the BBC website reminds me that there is another side, which can be even sadder than what we're going through. A rape victim in the UK is to receive a £20,000 settlement and an official apology after police conceded they did not investigate her rape complaint properly, and actually arrested her for lying about the attack. The complainant had mental health problems and had been in trouble with the police before. Police didn't carry out the thorough forensic tests that would have confirmed the assault. Instead, they charged the complainant with perverting the course of justice.

Any complaint of sexual assault or rape has to be treated seriously, and this young woman's case clearly was mishandled. Yet I find one comment by the complainant's mother revealing. She said, "A woman comes forward and tells the police authority she has been raped: you expect them to do everything they can to put the rapist away." Actually, no. An allegation is not evidence, so what you should expect is that the police will do everything they can to investigate the complaint, to treat the complainant with respect, and to prosecute the *alleged* rapist if appropriate. This statement may just have been careless choice of words when put on the spot, but at face value it does seem to imply that women never lie about rape. And they do.

The difference between this and the Verity delusion is that this British case wasn't historic. Corroborating evidence was there to be found, but the police didn't bother to look for it. "Recovered" memories of supposed events more than twenty years ago, in circumstances which are geographically close to impossible, should be rejected in very short order – certainly long before the four months this has been hanging over us.

An accusation can be shown to be false in either of two ways. One is that the complainant retracts it. The other is that the facts just don't match. Neither of these applies in the British case, but the second applies in Verity's.

What makes the police prosecute, not just in rape cases but in any cases? Throughout the Verity attack, I've often wondered about this. Do they always prosecute any time it's clear someone has broken the law, or do they use their discretion? The police aren't there to make laws but to enforce them. Therefore, the only reason they should prosecute is that they can. All laws are passed to serve the public good, and if the police can pick and choose which lawbreakers to go after, they are bypassing the very purpose of our laws; they are playing God.

The Verity case and this British case, opposite though they are in so many ways, are similar in a sense. In both cases, careless initial investigation put the wrong person in the frame. If Verity is shown not to be telling the truth in this allegation, she has brought a false prosecution. Or perhaps she has perverted the course of justice. Only a lawyer could tell me which, but one way or another she has certainly broken the law. If they do not prosecute her, what reason would they have for not doing so, and what right do they have to let that reason bypass the purpose and spirit of the law? Put another way, if such a law isn't designed to apply in a case like this one, when does it apply, if ever?

In most cases of rape complaints which the police suspect are false, it is quite right for them not to prosecute the accuser. Such cases usually centre on murky "he said/she said" counter-claims, and proving that she lied may be as tricky as proving that he did. But my case is different. If even a cursory police investigation shows that the places and times just don't work out, then the woman has made a false and malicious statement which was designed to put an innocent person away for years. On what basis would the police not prosecute her? Would it perhaps be a firm belief, despite this example to the contrary, that women don't lie about rape? Or perhaps a fear that such a prosecution will cement a perception among vocal women's groups that the police still don't take women's complaints seriously enough? We cannot know how many rape complaints are false. But what we do know is that some are. Now, what should happen to an accuser whose complaint is *demonstrably* false?

Charging Verity is surely in the public interest, because it helps to protect innocent people from such charges in the future. It may lend more credibility to genuine rape victims. Of all the people who should be marching down the main street, waving placards and screaming for liars like Verity to be prosecuted, perhaps those with the clearest reason are groups like Rape Crisis.

May 24

The Draketown Post has an article which shows the lengths police will sometimes go to in order to bring a successful prosecution. It tells the story of Operation Explorer, in which an undercover policeman was placed among local motorcycle gang members to gather evidence of their alleged criminal activity. The police running the operation became concerned that the gang was getting suspicious that the "plant" may have been a cop, so a plan was hatched to boost his credibility in the eyes of the gang by faking his arrest. The police prepared a phony search warrant, and one of them signed it instead of the court registrar. They planted apparently stolen goods, and some ammunition and drugs, in the undercover cop's lockup. They then arrested their own man outside the gang's headquarters. He was charged and even appeared in court before several judges, all of whom assumed it was a genuine case. When the truth became known, the court threw out 116 charges against 18 gang members. The presiding judge said the police actions constituted "grave misconduct, possible criminal offending and misuse of the justice system." He added that their misconduct "was pivotal to the police gathering evidence against the defendants," and that allowing the trial to continue would therefore mean the public would assume the court condoned such police behaviour.

What I find most disturbing is that this misconduct was not down to one rogue officer, but at least three. And this is an institution that Eva tells me I should blindly trust.

May 25

I have lunch with Bruce, a teaching colleague. There are two main topics: religion and (surprise!) the Verity case. We agree that the two have strong similarities. For example, both require True Believers: people who have unshakeable faith in matters which, to say the least, should be doubted. So is Verity's accusation a lie or a delusion? Is she disturbed, or is she wilful? Tough questions, and we can't decide. We can't even decide whether the questions are purely semantic ones, so finally we just shut up and eat.

But later, at home, I start thinking again about Verity's untruths. It seems to me that her claims have to be considered in the plural, because there are many, and they are from different times. The accusation against Lance Boyle comes from when Verity was probably just a toddler. We all have hazy memories of our very early lives. For example, throughout my childhood and even early adulthood I was afraid to go swimming. I always thought this was because when I was very young – perhaps only two – I was swept out to sea at the beach. These days, as an adult, I'm not sure whether that really happened. But even if it didn't, the image (or false memory) of it sufficiently terrified me in my youth that I kept out of the water. I know that as a teenager I had a poor body image and was especially self-conscious about being pale. Perhaps, in my subconscious, the "memory" of this event provided a useful excuse for not stripping off.

Referring this to Verity, it is just possible that she is sincerely convinced that her memory of abuse by Lance Boyle is real, and it serves a similar subconscious purpose. Perhaps; I'm hardly an expert on these things. But it's when I think of her allegations from her teenage years that my sympathy for her evaporates, and not just because these are the accusations that put me in the frame. When I allegedly raped her, she was at least twelve. Now, I know it didn't happen. So what is the explanation: is she mistaken or is she lying? Unlike impressions glimpsed in the half-light of our earliest memories, an actual rape at twelve surely isn't something you can just forget about, then "recover" under therapy, years later. I find it hard to believe there isn't something deliberate, something wilful in this allegation – either by her or by her counsellor.

May 26

A woman from the records office at Draketown Hospital calls to say that I did not undergo any medical tests on July 30 1991. I may be forced to trust the members of the jury. They would have to weigh up the slight possibility that I flew up to Houwhanga on that day and committed rape...but then hopefully reject it as ludicrous.

Then I remember that someone – I forget who – suggested a week or two ago that I should try to find out whether Air New Zealand keeps historic records of passenger flights to provincial cities on ancient turboprops. It's worth a shot.

May 27

I phone Air New Zealand. It's hard to talk to a real person. I listen in a loop three times while a disembodied and metallic alien keeps reading the same three options. For new bookings I should press 1; for flight arrivals and departures, 2; for air points, seating and meals, 3. Nothing to help me there. But I discover that after the alien says "I'm sorry, I didn't get that" the third time, an actual person interrupts. He asks how he can help. I say "I live in Draketown, and I need to prove to the police that I didn't fly to Houwhanga on July 30 1991 and rape a woman. Do you have passenger records that far back?" To his credit, he doesn't seem to think I'm pulling his leg. He says he'll go away and talk to his supervisor. He returns and says he's sorry, but records don't go back that far. Never mind: even making a useless discovery can be useful, in a sense, because it does close an avenue of enquiry.

May 28

I give some more thought to Verity's allegation. Maybe I shouldn't be so sure most people would regard it as unbelievable. Just as I can respond with exasperation, "I couldn't have done it, because I couldn't have gone to Houwhanga," a detached and purely rational observer (Mr Spock, say) may respond, "You are expecting me to reject the idea because it is so absurd. But however I look at it, I can't escape absurdity of one sort or another. The alternative is that she has accused someone she doesn't know of rape. What motive could she possibly have? It's not rational to assume she would hold some sort of grudge against someone she doesn't know. So it's also absurd to believe you didn't do it." Accepting my statement of innocence therefore requires any listener to try to be rational about the irrational. It requires a new, inverted kind of thinking that abandons what we think we know about what motivates people.

When I think of Verity's accusation in this way, I have to re-assess Eva's reason for tapping her pencil in the interview. At the time I thought it might mean she knew I was innocent and she was just going through the motions. But maybe that was too optimistic. Maybe she was thinking "It's too crazy to believe she would accuse someone she hasn't met. This guy must have done it. Now, how can I get him?" That would also explain the delay in clearing me: Eva and her puppeteer may see any contrary evidence as a mere distraction, because a Verity lie would just be too irrational, too weird. Following this line, the only explanation that makes sense is that this guy is a paedophile, and some time – if not next week, then in 2037 – he's going to slip up.

I get an email from cousin Jackie. She's just read this diary up till about a week ago, and she's become convinced that Verity must be bi-polar. I don't really understand things like this. I have the impression that sanity is a singular thing, but there are so many ways to lose it that it really takes a psychiatrist to diagnose any one deluded rape complainant's disorder of choice. Plenty of movies show us even the experts don't always get their diagnoses right. But Jackie tells me that she has encountered quite a few bi-polar people in her time, and she's developed "a bit of a radar" for them. She says they lie "as easily as we butter our toast," which explains why Verity's going about her life as if she's done nothing wrong. Maybe there's something in the old saying that madmen (and presumably women) never go grey.

Jackie's theory interests me enough to check out bipolar disorder on that most scholarly source of information on psychiatric conditions: Wikipedia. Maybe bi-polarism (bi-polarity?) is contagious, and I've caught hers, because for a while it's like I'm checking myself out. It says sufferers have wild mood swings, between depression and euphoria. Sounds a bit like me lately. It adds that they make decisions with little regard for the consequences...tracking Verity to the car park, or standing there in her ex's kitchen listening to tales of her nymphomania. When I skim further down the article, the sub-heading "rapid cycling" catches my eye, and I'm immediately concerned that furious pedalling down the hill from the hospital is a sure sign that the cyclist is bi-polar, but then I notice that it refers to the speed of mood cycles. No, I'm perfectly sane, unless naivety about the insanity of others is itself a kind of insanity. It's easy to convince ourselves we have any condition, because I guess we all have a little bit of any symptom we read about. We Leos are especially susceptible to being deceived in this way – and to being sceptical about astrology. I stay convinced that my brain has just one pole.

The Wikipedia entry contains a suggestion that omega-3 fatty acids may bring some benefit to bi-polar people. Interesting. Maybe I should anonymously send Verity a truckload of sardines.

So is she bi-polar? I can't say, and maybe no one can. I have a rival theory to Jackie's, which I've arrived at after almost four months of deep psychological analysis, admittedly from a distance. She is suffering from PLS: *pernicious lying syndrome*. The only known treatment is prosecution.

May 31

Gloria rings. No news. She mentions something interesting, however. She and John used to have foreign students staying with them. A couple of years ago they had to follow the new procedure of having a police clearance before they could host any more. She was cleared but he wasn't, and so they were not allowed to continue as hosts. No reason was given, which seems very odd. If the reason was anything other than this allegation or something related to it, what else could it be? Yet if it is true, it means that someone who remains in the eyes of the law an innocent man, someone who hasn't even been interviewed, let alone charged, has already become a victim of an allegation he officially knows nothing about.

June 1

Four months today since this thing hit us, and almost two months since Eva's assurance that John will be interviewed "soon".

The menz website has a new link to a report on the annual conference in Cardiff of FACT – Falsely Accused Caregivers and Teachers. It says the UK "is currently experiencing a wave of sex-abuse hysteria." One speaker, barrister Chris Saltrese, specialises in this field and estimates there are now thousands of falsely convicted men in prison in the UK. He says that "The great majority of historical allegations of sexual abuse are fabrications." The main movers are police policy and juicy cash payouts to successful complainants. Another of the speakers was a former teacher and broadcaster who was arrested, waited 672 days for his trial, and then was acquitted by the jury in a matter of minutes. Unsurprisingly, the acquittal has not stopped the charge from affecting his career as a TV presenter. A conference attendee was told by a police officer that police KPIs (key performance indicators) include figures for successful prosecutions for sexual abuse.

June 2

With quite a bit of foreboding, I set the first of two deadlines. If the police haven't contacted me and cleared me by my coming birthday (August 18) I will send a complaint to the Independent Police Conduct Authority. I have discussed this date with Angela, and she agrees that no sixty-three-year-old should put up with this. That will be almost seven months after the allegation first hit us. It worries me because I'm stirring things up – I'm being a smart-arse – and neither Dwight nor the police are going to like it, of course. But it's just right, for god's sake. I can't go running to my lawyer whenever I want to do anything reasonable and justified, anything human. Why does the system have to keep squatting on normal citizens, forcing them to endure the unendurable, maybe for ever?

I wonder what happens when I make such a complaint. How long does it take to be heard? Will Eva and her team be asked any hard questions, or will it just end up in a whitewash in which the Authority says that what I'm going through is quite normal in this sort of "investigation"?

The more important and much scarier deadline is when I throw my arms up in despair and force the issue by going public. That will have to be later. Hopefully I will be cleared before the need for it.

June 4

It is now two weeks since my letter was published in the Draketown Post, and no response has appeared. When I learnt last week that Air New Zealand doesn't keep records from two decades ago, I wrote that sometimes a nil result can be informative. This silence from women's groups tells me a lot. Why was there no attempt to refute my figures? My letter challenged the sexual abuse statistics which underpin the very ethos that spurs them to write angry articles and to set up stalls in the street. If my figures are baseless and can be refuted, where are the outraged responses that prove me wrong with quotes and references? Either none of them read the newspaper or they just make up their data, as I suspected.

I have a close look at the website of Chris Saltrese, the UK lawyer who specialises in defending false abuse victims. One interesting issue he mentions is that the accusers do not have to appear in court. This is to protect them and to ensure they do not have to suffer the indignity and distress of reliving their trauma. The thinking behind this is understandable, but it upsets the legal balance in favour of the prosecution. It means that the complainant's initial statement to police is all the jury has to assess her credibility. In most criminal trials, jury members have the opportunity to compare a complainant's statement to police with their statement under oath, and any discrepancies can be exposed by the defence lawyer under cross-examination and detected by the jury. There is only one way to tell the truth but a hundred ways to lie, so it is difficult for a liar to keep a false story going consistently over many retellings. In sex abuse cases, all the jury members see is the original statement by the complainant – probably filmed. With just one telling, no comparison can be made.

It makes me wonder about Verity's original statement. Was she filmed? How I would love to hear the actual words she used that dragged me into this: that one sentence in which my name was the subject. How did she word it? When she said "Peter Joyce", did she spit the words out with rage or snivel in mock recovered fear? Maybe she stuttered them out because she had to dig deep to remember my name from her father's address book.

Saltrese attacks the common assumption that genuine sex offenders are more likely than other offenders to deny their crimes. He says that research from the 1980s showed that sex offenders are actually more likely to confess than other criminals. This should tell jury members not to be swayed by any prosecution argument that outwardly respectable and dull men – the male, pale and stale like me – are manipulative liars leading double lives. Rather, it should convince them that character witnesses are a legitimate aspect of defence.

The Saltrese site also questions the usual figure trotted out as the proportion of false accusations:

> Official figures for false allegations are misleading. At 2 per cent they only deal with cases that are proven to be false. These tend to be contemporaneous allegations where there is independent evidence to disprove the claim. Most allegations cannot be definitively disproved and rely on one person's word against another's. The rise of historical allegations and prosecutions has exacerbated the risk of wrongful prosecution and conviction. It is easier for a jury to come to a rational verdict when the evidence is fresh and there are circumstantial facts to rely on either way.

A separate article by Saltrese and legal consultant Margaret Jervis at www.insidetime.org makes this disturbing point about what he calls "stale" cases lacking active evidence:

> ...the rate of conviction in historic uncorroborated cases is higher than in contemporaneous claims. In crude terms this suggests that, the further the complaint goes back, the more likely it is that the jury believe the complainant because of, rather than despite, the lack of evidential hurdles to overcome. Strange? You may say so, but in our system, that's a matter for the jury.

Great.

June 5

At times in this diary I've touched on the comparison between being raped and being falsely accused of rape. They are of course very different horrors, and that may cause us to say they shouldn't even be compared. I concede that what I am about to write is a kind of straw man argument, because I'm putting words in the mouths of women who are not here to object, but with that admission I'll carry on. I suspect that if I were talking to a member of Rape Crisis or some other women's group right now, she would be bold enough to make such a comparison; she would say without hesitation that being raped is much worse, and would probably be outraged that I could even suggest that a false accusation could be as bad. She may be exasperated that a man would even pretend to know. But I can respond that she is in no position to make such a claim because she has never been falsely accused. If she were to exchange lives with me for a while she might start to understand how it feels – and I haven't even been charged yet.

In an article on slate.com on October 12 2009, Emily Bazelon and Rachael Larimore quote a man who is well qualified to make the comparison. His girlfriend was raped and, much later and independently, he was falsely accused of rape. He says

> It turns out that her experience of being raped and mine of being falsely accused of rape were very similar. ... One important difference, though, is that when she was violated, she received a great deal of help (medical, legal, psychological). Apart from family and friends, I was on my own. My legal and psychological problems had to be dealt with by me at a time when I couldn't eat, sleep, or think (except, of course, about killing myself).

No two rapes are identical, and neither are two false rape complaints. These complexities must cloud our judgment, but that doesn't mean we can't offer an opinion. After all, in all sorts of matters the law assumes one crime is more damaging than another, which is why the penalty for murder is more severe than the penalty for fraud, for example.

Back on March 17, after I visited the Rape Crisis centre, I recorded some thoughts about how the definition of rape had broadened. I gave examples of sexual incidents which we would now classify as rape, but which surely would be unlikely to destroy a woman's permanent quality of life. I added that a false rape complaint can always destroy a man, even if that is not always the complainant's intention.

There is another difference: time. A rape, horrifying though it often is, has already happened; the worst is over. A woman can begin to recover from it immediately afterwards. Admittedly, in some cases the experience may be so horrifying that recovery is slow and emotionally painful, and retelling the details later in the courtroom may be a distressing experience in itself – but surely not as bad as the actual rape. On the other hand, all the terror of a false rape complaint is yet to come, enforced by an invisible entity constrained by no limits in power, time or money. What cripples you is a fear of what may happen some time later: the trial, the incarceration, the loss of reputation, the financial ruin. On February 10 this year, these were the possibilities coolly and indirectly presented to me by Eva in the interview. And if these things happen, *when* will they happen? It's of no concern to Eva whether it's next week or in thirty years. In effect, she works for Verity.

June 8

I read in the Las Vegas Review-Journal about a case in Michigan in which a serial liar was jailed for making a false complaint, despite having obvious mental problems. At five years, this is the longest sentence I have uncovered. Sara Ylen had pleaded no contest when she was caught out in an earlier scam in which she pretended to be a cancer sufferer and received thousands of dollars from supporters and even got treatment from a hospice service. In her rape claim she said two men, both of whom she knew and identified, burst into her home and violated her. She faked her own injuries and even "carved a vulgarity on her arm," but the men had incontestable alibis. Ylen had accused another man of rape years earlier, and he was sentenced to a minimum of fifteen years. He was released from jail in 2012 after his conviction was finally overturned.

Her lawyer asked for a year in prison, but the judge was unmoved by this request. In sentencing, he said

> This is a tormented and disturbed woman who will go to extraordinary lengths to wreak havoc upon other individuals, potentially subjecting them to life in prison in order to gain sympathy and notoriety for herself.

The lawyer who prosecuted Ylen called the sentence "justice in its best form." I agree. Granted, she was clearly deranged, but the repercussions of her offending were so far-reaching that anything less than several years in jail would be an insult to the two men accused and especially the one jailed. The police officer who appears to have investigated Ylen's second rape allegation said, "My law enforcement side said I should have known better, but I saw her with my heart." Like Eva, she was all heart. Police investigators do need to show heart, but to think with a different organ.

Another prosecution, this time from the UK, resulted in prison for the accuser, but her sentence provoked more controversy than the Ylen case. The Mirror website reported in 2014 that 30-year-old student Rhiannon Brooker falsely accused her boyfriend of raping her so that she would have an excuse for having failed her legal exams. She faked injuries to suggest he had beaten her, and even alleged he had caused her to have a miscarriage by punching her in the stomach. He was held in custody for 36 days before police realised his alibis made her claims untenable. Judge Lambert commented that Brooker was an intelligent woman who "went to significant devious lengths to pervert the course of public justice." She was given three and a half years in prison.

Brooker's lawyer Sarah Elliott said that "every day in prison would be agony" for her client. Elliott said she would suffer because prison would separate her from her new baby, and stressed how much motherhood had changed her. However, the British Solicitor-General considered Brooker's sentence too light, citing "the calculated and repeated nature of the lies told," and lodged an appeal for a longer one. The three appeal court judges rejected any extension. Opposition justice spokesperson Emily Thornberry expressed surprise that the Solicitor-General had lodged an appeal, and said the government's priority ought to be ensuring more rapists are prosecuted. Thornberry said

> Ms Brooker, a mother with a young child, received a custodial sentence of over three years for a non-violent offence...I think the priority of the law officers should be to address the widening gulf between the soaring numbers of rape allegations made to the police and the dwindling number that ever get prosecuted.

Speaking for Women Against Rape, Lisa Longstaff said

> We at WAR are very relieved that the court of appeal took into account her being a young mother of a small child and the terrible impact of prison on both of them.

I find the anger at the appeal disturbing in three ways. First, Opposition spokesperson Thornberry was being disingenuous in drawing attention to the number of rape allegations and rape prosecutions. As I have pointed out before, these figures are always debatable and their implications can be fiddled in all sorts of devious ways. Was she chasing female votes? Secondly, Thornberry drew attention to the fact that Brooker's crime was "non-violent". Yes, a false rape complaint is always non-violent, but so are many other crimes that have devastating effects. Thirdly, it is indeed sad that a mother and baby have to be parted. However, Thornberry and Longstaff's sappy appeal for sympathy because of motherhood should never be used to determine a sentence. Can males use any equivalent?

In all kinds of crimes, female offenders do get a better deal. Sonja Starr at the Michigan Law School did a very thorough analysis of the way male and female defendants were handled. Starr considered not just sentencing itself, but followed each case through from the arrest stage. Christina Hoff Sommers on her Factual Feminist site points out that Starr's research shows "women are significantly more likely than men to avoid charges completely, and they are twice as likely to avoid incarceration if convicted. On average, men receive 63% longer sentences than women arrested for the same crime."

Sommers points out that the sentencing gap between men and women for the same offence is six times as large as the sentencing gap between blacks and whites. She offers no empirically valid explanation for the disparity, only suggestions: that prosecutors and judges may be reluctant to jail mothers, that female offenders are often seen as mentally unstable or as victims of controlling males.

Word of my case is spreading around. I get a call tonight from David, a lawyer friend of Charles. This lawyer has dealt with "quite a few" cases of this kind, including one that ended in the suicide of the accused man. I ask whether he believes the man who killed himself was innocent. "One hundred percent," he says. David says this kind of false accusation is far more common than most people realise, and he is convinced it's such an epidemic that most people in jail for historic sex abuse or rape are probably innocent. It has become a punishment without a crime. He confirms my worst fears about the difficulty of providing an alibi after so many years, and that the police will allow the complainant to shift the goalposts of her original sworn statement in order to foil any alibi a suspect provides.

The legislation change which has helped to make all this possible was alteration to the New Zealand Evidence Act section 23 in 1988. Until then judges were obliged to warn juries that they must not be tempted to convict a defendant on the basis of uncorroborated testimony. Conviction required more than the word of one person: either independent factual evidence or the word of other witnesses. This requirement has always been central to any notion of justice. From 1988 the onus of proof shifted for sexual abuse and rape cases, because the usual absence of witnesses or evidence presumably meant that convictions were difficult to achieve. In these kinds of cases, judges no longer give such warnings, and defendants can be convicted on uncorroborated testimony.

The corollary of this was that more such cases came to court, because the prosecuting police saw that the reduction of the case to "he said vs she said" meant that a jury was much more likely to convict. This was especially true when the complainant could offer a compelling account of her suffering. When so many people with so much power in our system are certain that complainants are always telling the truth, and when the law is changed in such a way to support this certainty, in effect the complaint itself becomes the evidence.

David also confirms that the police can take far too long to make a decision to prosecute or to clear an accused man. One case he mentions took fifteen months from the initial interview. I tell him I will send a complaint to the Independent Police

Conduct Authority in August, and I will go public with a newspaper article after a later deadline which I haven't decided on yet. He says he understands my reasons for doing so, but suggests strongly that I don't take either of those actions without conferring with Dwight first. I'm encouraged that a lawyer can at least hear me announce these intentions without throwing up his arms in horror.

June 10

I've been thinking again about malice and anger, on the one hand, and forgiveness on the other. The man released in the Michigan case called Ylen's sentence "a slap on the wrist," so he wasn't feeling very forgiving. Plenty of people would sympathise with his lack of sympathy, and readers' comments that accompany articles about such cases often make strident calls for the false accuser to serve the same time her victim would be liable to. These calls are usually from men, but not always.

The counter-arguments are partly legal and partly "just" emotional. Insanity has for a long time had legal standing as a way of mitigating a defendant's responsibility, and it's fitting that it should. This means that a woman who makes such a complaint may be disturbed, and she deserves more pity than punishment. The problem is that with false rape complaints which do not clearly involve revenge or malice, no other explanation except mental instability seems possible. Psychology is an inexact science, and it can be very hard to decide whether the mental state of a false complainant should be considered an explanation, a mere excuse, or something in between. It therefore becomes too easy – a matter of mere procedure – to shift the "may be disturbed" to "is disturbed". No other explanation fits, so she must be mentally ill. This means that police will not want to prosecute a false complainant because they know her defence lawyer will convince the judge (or judge and jury) that she is a "sufferer" who mainly deserves pity. The Michigan judge clearly did not think this way.

Coming back to Verity, the way the law ultimately regards her will be different from how I regard her, and this brings me to the "mere" emotional aspect. The law must strive to be objective; that is part of its very purpose. But I am a single human being, vulnerable and fallible, who has been forced to be a protagonist in this case. No matter how logical I like to consider myself, my personal involvement means I cannot – and even should not – be objective. It's odd to dwell on what Verity thinks of me and what I think of her. It's ironic that I consider myself rational and I think of her as emotional, what with her delusions and her apparent paranormal beliefs. Yet in this weird remote conflict we are having, she is apparently cool and indifferent, and I am the one spurred by emotion to do some bizarre and pointless things. The Verity death roll has turned me into the angry and irrational one.

I often think of Benito's justification for forgiving Verity: that holding a grudge just makes you sick. It's true that my anger against her serves no useful purpose. It may make things worse, because anger just generates more anger. I admire Benito for his forgiveness, and I wish I could emulate it. But I've come to learn that we're all emotional creatures, however rational we may consider ourselves. Anger is not all I've been feeling in the past four months, because confusion, raw fear and a kind of hollowness have never been far away. But what we call anger is certainly a part. Some people have told me that she is a sick woman, so any ire towards her isn't only unproductive but also unwarranted. I'm barely a person to her at all, just a pretext, or a spectre she may sometimes glimpse when she occasionally unlocks some remote vault of her brain.

It's true that Verity's allegations probably aren't motivated primarily by malice; she is who she is and just does what she does. But if we tolerate her false accusation on the basis that humans are not fundamentally rational, surely we must extend this tolerance to my anger. I'm emotional as well, and anger is a large part of what I feel. It may not be productive, but it just *is*.

Perhaps it's something else as well. We are so often hamstrung by words – their history, their connotations and associations. *Anger* is just an easy word to use for the way I feel, but it may not quite hit the mark, and the particular feelings I call anger may be different from Benito's, for example. I see I've used the words *anger* or *angry* eleven times in today's entry (twelve if I count *ire*). But maybe the word is just a lazy approximation, and the main emotion that's had me in its clutches for the past four months would be more accurately described as "sustained exasperation" or "an attenuated sense of violation." Now, has any research been done to prove that these specific conditions have damaging long-term effects? Words aside, I feel what I feel. What I do know is that I regard Verity's allegation – perhaps more than Verity herself – as a dangerous adversary, in the same way my dying mother sometimes saw her tumour. A stalking alligator is not malicious, but its prey has to regard it as the enemy.

Part Three

June 11

Since I decided to treat this diary seriously, I've been determined to keep it up to date and to aim at getting it published eventually. Recently I mentioned this to former court clerk Charles, and I said, "Of course, I can't do anything until after either it goes to court or the police call off the investigation." I always assumed this was true; that any publicity would be seen as interference in the legal process that might follow. He surprised me by telling me I may be wrong. After all, I haven't been charged. All I've done is have an allegation conveyed to me, and I have volunteered to make a statement to the police about that allegation. No charge has been laid, and if the police delay in declaring me innocent means that this diary gets published before they get round to charging me, tough legal luck for them and Verity.

So the diary cannot be too early. In fact, I've just learnt that it can actually be too late. If the unthinkable happens, I may not be free to tell my story after it is over. The June 7 episode of Radio New Zealand's *Mediawatch* programme brought home how draconian some new measures are in restricting freedom of speech after a sentence ends. A woman in a high-profile case who was recently released from prison had the following restrictions placed on her by the parole board:

> You are prohibited from initiating any media contact by way of television, radio, print media and social media, including Twitter, Facebook, blogs or contribution to any websites, whether via post

> or anything else. You are required to decline by "No comment" any request from any media whatsoever for interview or for information about yourself, your offending, imprisonment or rehabilitation. You are required to discourage any friends and family from any media contact either on your behalf or their behalf.

I'm not sure how the RNZ reporter got hold of the wording of these restrictions, because presumably the woman was not allowed to tell anyone in the media any details of what she was not allowed to tell the media.

June 12

Back on April 17 I wrote that Cedric, my ex-policeman acquaintance, has a friend who is also facing historic sex abuse charge. Cedric sends me an email saying that his friend now lives here in Draketown, and the two of them are due to meet this evening. Can he mention my case to him? Sure, I say. In fact, I give Cedric my email address and suggest his friend get in touch with me. It may be useful to meet and to compare notes. Cedric tells me that his friend is also desperately waiting for the police to decide whether they will prosecute.

June 14

Gloria rings Angela. There's no news up there, of course. She and John have known about my diary for some time, but I haven't sent them a copy. Gloria says they would like to read it. I've been in two minds about this, but I knew it had to happen. I suspect John has also been doing some research about similar cases, and he also may be able to put me right if I've made any mistakes about the family background and personalities. On the other hand, Verity is still his daughter, and I've written some strong stuff about her. Will he object? Maybe he'll be upset at the fact that some friends of mine, who know about my side of the case but don't know him, think there's a chance he may have something to hide. It may upset him if he sees this as a cross-section of a likely public response in the future if – heaven forbid – this nonsense comes to court.

Despite my misgivings, there's no question that I should send them the diary. Apart from anything else, they have a right to read it. So I tell Angela to tell Gloria I'll email it to them. But she's paranoid about the police intercepting our communication and reading it. Angela's response is that if they will ever know, they know already. So it is sent. I await their response with trepidation. At what precise point between fury and solidarity will John's reaction fall?

June 15

Today is the eight hundredth anniversary of the Magna Carta. Ah, the thirteenth century – how I miss those enlightened times, when concerned people rebelled against the notion that the state prosecutes people just because it can, or because an influential group insists that it must.

June 16

The main article in the Draketown Post today reports that a private litigant may bring a prosecution against the police involved in mishandling Operation Explorer, as mentioned in my May 24 entry. The police themselves had decided that no prosecution of their own officers was warranted. For a private citizen who wasn't involved in the case to bring such a prosecution just seems to be grandstanding, and it would be a pity if this kind of action ended the careers of police officers who may be dedicated professionals with the best intentions.

However, it is amazing that those sworn officers who are supposed to enforce the law on our behalf can be so certain the end justifies the means that they will break the law themselves. I find it hard to believe that they could have so little idea which of their actions are legally acceptable. Don't they learn all this in their training? It's much more likely that they knew the law but were confident they could get away with flouting it. What is also infuriating is that the gang members, who most likely have been up to no good, get away scot-free. Holding the wayward police officers to account for their legal excesses may serve a useful social purpose in helping to prevent others from doing the same.

Indirectly this has a bearing on my case. It shows that even right here in Draketown there are police officers who will go any lengths to get a "result". I am an alleged paedophile. I've mentioned before that there is a chance the police may seize my computers. If police will illegally fake a charge to get a conviction in another case, how do I know they won't plant illicit photos on my hard drive, if Verity's sincere and weepy recollections convince them that I raped her when she was a minor?

June 17

I get a reply from my cousin Kay in Auckland, after emailing her earlier in the week and bringing her into the V-loop. She tells me that that she once had a tenant who claimed she had been abused by her father and brother, and the Accident Compensation Corporation paid all her rent, and even funded her university tuition for a B.A. degree.

June 21

I email my ex-policeman acquaintance Cedric to ask him what he thinks the police are doing in what Eva calls their investigation. He says that when there is no statute of limitations they are in no hurry, especially when the offending is historic and is therefore unlikely to be happening now. How very ethical of them. He says that files will spend a lot of time filling up in-trays, especially if they have to go between cities.

Cedric tells me more about how the police conduct an "investigation". Looking at specifics such as time and place, which I have been insisting are the logically prior aspects to consider, "is something probably done later, after all relevant people have been spoken to." How odd is this? First, it makes no logical sense to do things in this order if the truth is what they are after. Secondly, I know that in this case they haven't spoken to the most relevant person of all – the alleged ringleader. So if they haven't followed the illogical procedure which they normally do, and haven't followed the more logical procedure which a true investigation would suggest, then exactly what have they been doing for five months?

When people in the V-loop ask what's new, and I say "nothing", their normal response is to say that no news is good news. I agree in order to be polite and to change the subject, but it's not true at all. No news is smack in the middle of desirability, right between news that I have been cleared and news that I will be prosecuted. What scares me is that even if the police do not believe this is a credible case they may still send me to trial to dispel any accusation that they have not done their bit in combatting the rape "epidemic".

June 27

Another disagreement with Angela, but nothing that has utensils flying or even raises our voices. My first words in this diary are "Anonymity be damned." From the time the diary became serious I have always preferred to go public and not to hide my name. The reason is that I wanted to do more than save my own hide; I wanted to draw the public's attention to the injustice and the exasperation (not to mention the apparent frequency) of this sort of allegation. An anonymous approach would allow this but would have less force.

I have always thought that Angela supported me in this, but she tells me today that it makes her uneasy. The reason she hasn't told me this before is that she was convinced that I was committed to going ahead and using my real name no matter what she said, so there was no point trying to oppose it. But this really isn't the case. Showing my face and name is a tough decision in a charge like this; as Jackie says, the genie of anonymity can't go back in the bottle. I need to have Angela's full support without any pressure or persuasion. I confess that her dissent in this matter lets me off the hook by giving my natural spinelessness an excuse to prevail, so no anger at her is necessary. This change means that I have now abandoned both my brave original plans: to let my name be known and to defend myself if – heaven forbid – this nonsense comes to court. So it is that procedure wins and normality makes cowards of us all.

June 28

Gloria rings Angela tonight, right on schedule. No news, of course. As for this diary, I am relieved to learn later that both of them support it. Gloria has even suggested some titles, which seems to indicate that they would be happy for it to be published. The only change they suggest, apart from a couple of typos that they picked up, was to replace the fake name of John's second daughter. The name I gave her happens to be her real middle name.

They want to get progressive diary updates, and I am delighted that they're so keen to be involved. Perhaps from now on this will be our diary, and I will just be the scribe. Such collaboration multiplies our strength rather than adds to it. Apart from anything else, it means that if and when John gets interviewed, I'm likely to get hold of the notes and incorporate them. It would be perverse to say I'm looking forward to this interview, but I await it with nervous anticipation. How similar will it be to my own? Will Eva herself fly up to conduct it? Does the fact that John and I are friends affect the way the police will handle it? After all, Eva knows that John and I at least have indirect contact, and she will suspect that I will get to read the transcript.

Angela and Gloria talk for about an hour, and when I walk past from time to time I hear quite a bit of laughter. Angela tells me later that the effect of the Verity delusion has mellowed just a little in Houwhanga. They are sleeping better than before, and Gloria can talk to Angela about other things. Life is gingerly edging its way back in.

July 1

Five months now.

There are two ways into the city from Trent, the suburb where we live. The slightly longer and more scenic way is round the port. The shorter route is over the hill. It is on this more direct route that Verity's house is visible in the distance, and her mother's place is just off it as well. Today I go to town for the first time in quite a while, and I drive round the port. It isn't till I am almost in town that I realise I haven't given any thought to going the other way and seeing where Verity is. A small sign of improvement.

July 2

All my reading today leads me towards the notion of consent. I'm especially interested in means of conveying consent, and whether someone who ends up on a rape charge may genuinely have believed she consented. We cannot assume that all men are equally competent at reading the signs. This is not a trivial matter, because intention is crucial. Rape activists tend to play down the idea of miscommunication, insisting that if a woman makes a rape complaint, it isn't because the alleged rapist didn't perceive her boundaries but chose not to respect them – perhaps even got a sexual kick out of disregarding them. I am convinced they are wrong in most cases.

A Canadian programme to reduce sexual assaults on campus unintentionally offers insight into many sexual incidents labelled as rape, in a way that backs my claim. The US News online edition of June 10 2015 has details of a new programme for female students which has almost halved the number of reported rapes on campus. The trial was conducted among 893 first-year female students between 17 and 24 at two Canadian universities. The students were assigned to one of two groups: the control group given the standard brochure about avoiding sexual assault, and the experimental group assigned to the new, comprehensive sexual assault resistance programme. The programme took a full twelve hours, and it

> taught women how to effectively assess the risk of sexual assault by men they knew, recognize the danger in coercive situations, get past emotional roadblocks to resist unwanted sexual behaviors and practice verbally resisting the behavior or actions. The program also...included several hours bringing all the instruction together in a session on safe sex practices and effective communication about sex.

In short, the programme made sure a "no" was unambiguous. One year later all the women filled out surveys. The number of women who claimed to have been raped in the experimental group was only half those in the control group, and the number from the experimental group who reported attempted rape was only a third of those from the control group.

Clearly this is good news for all women, and for all men except actual rapists. However, the programme reveals something unintended about rape complaints. However we define rape, intention must play a major part. If a man merely misunderstands what a woman communicates to him about consent, surely he has not committed rape, and when the police turn up at his door the next day his shock is not feigned. If half of reported rapes can be prevented by a programme that stresses clearer communication, what it really means is that those reported rapes which are prevented really would have been the result of misunderstandings.

We know that men tend to be the undiscriminating ones who are likely to pester a woman for sex. By contrast, women are usually the "gatekeepers" who confer their favours in a more selective way. What this programme says about the fifty percent of "rapes" that it prevents is only that the women who become "victims" are those who were incapable of rebuffing men who are churlish enough to persist. Being able to resist is a useful skill for a woman to have, as this programme shows. However, no woman who lacks those skills and has sex she later regrets can fairly claim to have been raped. In other words, when a rape defendant's lawyer insists in court that his client was genuinely mistaken about consent, he is likely to be telling the truth.

I also learn that software developers have been getting in on the sex act. The BBC reports the launch of the "We-Consent" smartphone app, which allows willing partners to make a twenty-second film clip in which they give their names and say they give consent for what is about to unfold. The app works only if the camera detects human faces and "both people involved are clearly heard saying *yes*."

Rape Crisis in England and Wales, whose policy appears to be the extinction of the human race, is of course lukewarm about the idea. Spokeswoman Katie Russell commented that "Someone saying yes to sex on camera does not necessarily prove that they have given their consent," and "Consent must fully and freely be given by someone with the capacity to do so." Granted, it is possible that one party has been bullied or perhaps even been forced at knife point, but more subtle intimidation is also possible even if both parties sit down for two hours and write a detailed contract, after which their only cravings will probably be for a sandwich and cuppa.

Ms Russell naturally couldn't pass up the opportunity to repeat the mantra that false rape complaints are no more common than rocking horse manure: "The concept seems to assume...that false accusations of rape are a common problem...[but] they're absolutely not." I'm no more enthusiastic about the app than she is, but obviously for different reasons. I can only shake my head and say, "My god, has it really come to this?" Since marital rape is now recognised in law and many marriages end in acrimony, will part of the safe sex message be that every married man should insist on using such an app every time he has sex with his wife? It's also clear that any cautious man who thinks such an app may help him in court is sadly deluded. What if the woman just says she changed her mind? But the Rape Crisis response implies that, as much as it always insists that valid consent is necessary, no form of consent will ever be sufficient. Further, the response implies that women must own the concept of rape. They must safeguard their right to define rape, and if any woman claims that it has happened, all of us – police and juries and the general public – must believe her. Men are not stakeholders in rape.

But we are, Ms Russell, and we have every right to be outraged – and fearful – if no woman is ever expected to take a measure of responsibility for sex which she later regrets.

July 3

The money motive returns.

Two days ago I was crowing about how relaxed I've become recently about the Verity intrigue. I mentioned that I drove to town without giving any thought to what she was up to. I could have added that most days when I get home I no longer rush to the answer phone to see if I have a call from Dwight giving me the good news that the police have seen sense and cleared me.

I ring the Accident Compensation Corporation and use the Freedom of Information Act to get answers to some of my questions about compensation for sexual abuse. The woman I speak to is uncommonly gracious and patient as I ply her with questions about payment policies.

She says she can't help me with statistics about how much ACC paid out in the past year to sexual abuse claimants, but she gives me an email address to contact for that information.

She does tell me the Corporation will not pay out on anything suffered before 1972, the year of the government Act that established the Corporation. From that time until 1992, lump sums were granted. I knew this, because parents of children allegedly abused in the Christchurch Civic Crèche case each promptly received a payment of at least $10,000 – long before any conviction and in fact before the case even came to court. These days victims are eligible for either a lump sum or ongoing payments, depending on how they are assessed.

Current policy allows ACC to pay claimants for the psychiatric effects of sexual abuse, even for historic cases back to the 1972 threshold. The condition for payment is that the claimant must be able to prove that she has a psychiatric condition which impairs her, and if she qualifies, she will be assessed for the extent of her impairment. The payment is capped at 80 percent, which would give her $133,802. The two dollars seems like a sick joke, tacked on the end of such a vast sum.

No such payment requires a perpetrator to be convicted, as the ACC is not a prosecuting organisation; the "evidence" that the abuse has really taken place rests solely on the analysis by the counsellor or psychiatrist that the claimant is suffering psychiatric impairment consistent with such a cause.

All this suggests that Verity may have already got paid – or perhaps is about to be paid – for her terrible suffering when we came nowhere near her all those years ago. If money is her motive, what would be her most lucrative technique? Mere historic gropes won't do it, because no one would believe that they can cause 80% impairment. However, enduring the horrors of a paedophile ring should be enough, especially if the leader of that ring was the adult male whose shoulder you really needed to lean on. The identity of the other men in the perverted group wouldn't really matter; any friends of her father's would do.

This explanation now strikes me as very tenable, especially when I think about her partner Heinrich being an accountant with bankruptcy and some dodgy deals in his background.

So this morning I'm hopping mad again. To be more accurate, I'm pacing mad. Actually, that's not accurate either, because my emotions are mixed. It's back to the "Bitch! Bitch!" of five months ago, but tempered with a quiet feeling of satisfaction that I may have got an insight into her motive.

I may be completely wrong, but if the truth turns out to be something different, it will be no less far-fetched.

July 8

Of course, sometimes the smoke is real, and so is the fire. A big story overseas this week concerns American comedian Bill Cosby, long after the public started wondering about whether the twenty-five or so women who have accused him of assaulting them were telling the truth. It always did look suspicious, because there were so many apparently unconnected complainants and their stories were so similar. After Associated Press went to court to petition for the release of court documents, a judge decided to unseal testimony which revealed that Cosby admitted procuring drugs to give women he wanted to have sex with. In court, Cosby's lawyer objected to the further question, asking whether he actually gave the Quaalude sedatives to these women. At best this is perverted behaviour, and at worst criminal.

This from Cosby of all people, whose squeaky-clean TV image as Dr Huxtable and whose real-life espousal of decent, family values now make him look the perfect hypocrite. In 2004 he made his "Pound Cake" speech, in which he attacked some African-Americans for neglecting their children, committing a disproportionate number of crimes and lacking personal responsibility.

Today CNN online has a column on Cosby by Sally Kohn, who says of the latest revelations that "this does not sound like sex. It sounds like rape." She may be right, but no one knows until and unless it comes to trial. Her main angle is to take the court of public opinion to task for disbelieving so many women for so long. She points out that the first allegations were made against him back in 2000, and the next wave came in 2005, but almost no one got to know about them. Cosby's immaculate image protected him and condemned the women not to be believed.

Kohn oversteps the mark when she implies that cases like the Cosby one show that a rape culture prevails. In an earlier entry I discredited the notion that there is a rape culture in North American universities, because female students stand less chance of being raped than female non-students. "Rape culture" is then a flawed term when applied to a specific group like students, so Kohn must be trying to apply it to society in general. But in that case what does it mean – that men sometimes rape women? True, sad and sometimes tragic, but no news. If Kohn intends something more specific than that, she should be clearer. Cosby has not even been tried, let alone convicted. If he is guilty, this unusual case is evidence only that an extraordinarily influential person can get away with a lot of nasty things. We knew that as well.

Kohn goes on to say that "patriarchy...is the problem" and that the Cosby case shows that "in the *he said/she* said dynamic around rape we're more inclined to believe the man." Pure nonsense. The Cosby case is a special one, because we have every reason to suspect that there are people who may seek money or a kind of perverse acclaim from discrediting or defaming such a well-known public figure. Our skepticism in such a case does not mean that in most cases we're more inclined to believe the man. My situation seems to suggest quite the opposite.

We also have to be careful about the evidence of multiple accusers. Juries, not to mention the public, tend to be persuaded by numbers, on the basis that "They can't all be lying." In fact, they can, and Tyler Kost knows this. He is the young Arizona man who was prosecuted and held in jail on the testimony of a group of teenage girls whose Facebook posts showed they had almost certainly set him up. Kost's lawyers even discovered that the lead detective in the case had been fired for allegedly lying to internal investigators.

July 10

A weird day, in which I learn some new information and question something I thought I'd found out last week. One step forward, one step back. Or maybe all my steps in the past five months have been sideways, because nothing I find out or think I find out is likely to make any difference in the long run anyway.

When I phoned the head office of the Accident Compensation Corporation on July 3 I was suffering from information overload, so I go to the Draketown office to confirm what I'm unsure of. I speak to the woman who handles what the Corporation calls sensitive claims. I have no reason to give my name, but tell her I have been accused of historic rape of a girl, and I suspect that the complainant may be after money. How does the system operate, and what would she be entitled to? Secretly I am hoping this woman has handled the Verity case, and my questions cause her to doubt any claims she made.

She confirms what I heard over the phone about how the payments work, but one thing she tells me makes me uncertain once again about Verity's motive. She tells me that no perpetrator is necessary for the ACC to pay out. I had assumed that any claimant had to back up her claim by making a specific allegation and lodge a complaint with the police, even though ACC would play no part in any subsequent prosecution. This woman tells me that the sole criterion from the ACC's perspective is that a psychiatric assessment reveals some degree of impairment that stems from sexual abuse. I ask whether it is possible for someone simply to walk in off the street and say that they can't function as a full human being because they were abused by an unknown person thirty years ago. The answer is yes, as long as the examining psychiatrist assesses the impairment as a consequence of sexual abuse. This strikes me as hopelessly naive, given that psychiatry is such an inexact science. I find it hard to believe that all – or even most – of the assessments are correct. But that is beside the point.

What matters is this means if Verity is mainly after money, no accusation is necessary: against me, her father, or anyone else.

She's gone back to being an enigma. Money probably isn't the whole story. I've recently been having other thoughts about the money motive. Long term, she will lose financially. This is because surely there is no way that she will get any of her father's inheritance. John's an ordinary middle-class man, so it isn't as if she would inherit the Chrysler Corporation, but he does own a house. Now she will get no part of it. Of course, not everyone thinks that far into the future. She may even be so few in the pod that she has no idea of the harm she's done, and be deluded enough to think she's still in line for a handout when her father dies.

I also see her again today. As I'm walking back to the car after going to ACC, there is her car right in front of me. She drives past slowly and turns into a private car park adjoining Eagle's Nest Auction House. A blackboard outside advertises an auction of unclaimed goods from police and customs tomorrow at 11 am. I walk into the premises and am hit by a musty smell of old armchairs and bedside cabinets. Only a handful of people are inside, and I don't see her at first, but I immediately see Heinrich walking around holding a clipboard and talking to some elderly browsers sniffing around goods for tomorrow's auction. "Look at these bikes," he says. "Working perfectly, and no one's bothered to claim them." So he works here as well as the other place where I saw him...or has he left the other job and changed to this one? Because the place is almost empty, he and I make eye contact and I think for a moment he's going to approach me, but he wanders into the office, and I can see her also in there through the glass – looking down at something on the desk. What's their role here? Tomorrow I'll turn up at the auction and see what they're up to.

July 11

I go to the auction, and although I'm on time, it's already under way. Heinrich is the auctioneer, up at the lectern efficiently getting through the lot numbers and engaging the buyers with occasional banter. The auction is well attended, with eighty or so people. Verity is there too, behind the glass slide. She and another woman seem to be looking after the clerical side of things, arranging payment from winning bidders and sorting out goods collection. To bid, you have to register at the counter in front of the slide and take a tag with a number. For a moment I'm tempted to register and make a successful bid, so that she could see my name written down. Seeing her reaction may help reveal whether she is deluded or just a liar. If it's the former, she may do a double take and then go sheer white at the horror; if it's the latter, and has she just forgotten the names of the disposable men she's put in the frame, she would just take my bidding tag and my payment, smile, and hand over my waffle maker.

But no, I mustn't be a smart-arse. So after ten minutes I slip away, wondering if he works there and she's helping him out, or the other way round. Or maybe they've even bought the place with seed money our taxes have given her through ACC. Taking over a business is quite a challenge, and I admire people who have the entrepreneurial spirit which I lack. I wish them every failure in their new enterprise.

July 14

I get a very detailed reply from Fridolin, my judge's assistant friend in Switzerland, with some information about how a case like mine would be handled there. The basic approach seems similar, with police gathering initial evidence and then a public prosecutor deciding whether to proceed. If first suspicions are not substantiated, the case is abandoned. If a suspect believes everything is taking too long, he can object to the "unjustified delay", though it is usually easy for a prosecutor to come up with a rationalisation – or excuse. Article 303 of the criminal code allows fines or imprisonment for anyone who brings a false allegation against a person the accuser knows to be innocent. No great differences there with our system, so the real question is how and how often Swiss authorities actually bring prosecutions under such a law, especially in cases like mine. Fridolin tells me that Swiss law would enable me to launch a counter-suit against Verity under article 303, but this wouldn't do me much good because the "main" suit against me would have to be pursued first.

The thought has sometimes crossed my mind of going to the police (not Eva, of course) and lodging my own complaint, which would go something like this: "A woman I have never met has accused me of rape. She has made a sworn statement that it happened. I didn't do it, and can prove it beyond reasonable doubt. Now, what are you going to do about this? Are you going to interrogate her? If not, why not?" It can't be a workable idea, or Dwight would have suggested it. And of course, it suffers from those great legal handicaps of being sensible, intuitive and just.

The Swiss have a unique form of democracy, in which they make many decisions by referendum. In 2008 a shaky majority (52%) voted in a law to eliminate any statute of time limitation on sexual accusations when children are involved. However, rape claims by adults need to be filed within fifteen years. Curse not being Swiss.

This was far too long for Jörg Kachelmann, an unorthodox Swiss-based German TV weather presenter and journalist who became quite famous there. On one occasion he interpreted the weather map while holding a cat which had wandered onto the set, an event that scored over a million Youtube hits. His life changed when his long-time girlfriend accused him of rape, and he was arrested out of the blue at Frankfurt airport in March 2010, on his return from covering the Vancouver Olympics. Despite glaring inconsistencies in the complainant's story, and even her admission that she had faked some evidence, Kachelmann languished in jail for four months and the prosecution continued to press the case. He endured an eight-month trial and was eventually acquitted – far too late to save his career. In a later TV interview, he lamented the fact that women can so readily portray themselves as victims. He also wrote a book about his experience, and when novelist John Grisham heard about the case he gave some thought to turning it into a novel. Kachelmann's case became a gold mine for tabloids in Switzerland and Germany, where people were divided about his guilt.

July 15

I've been reading the New Zealand report of the 2007 Commission of Inquiry into Police Conduct. In the section on appropriate handling of sexual abuse complaints, police policy makes it clear that complainants are to be treated with sympathy and kindness. Above all, under the Victims' Rights Act 2002, accusers are entitled to regular updates on the progress of an investigation:

> Police members are informed that consultation with the victim is a

> priority throughout the investigation process and that decisions must be made in consultation with the victim and the adult sexual assault investigations coordinator.

It's a pity that a still innocent accused man is left to fret in the dark for months without hearing a word from the "investigators".

The Commission report adds that

> All sexual assault complaints will be investigated in a timely, fair and sensitive manner and by specially trained investigators and interviewers, unless there is a valid reason to not do so *(sic)*.

I also learn today that I will need a new lawyer. The Draketown Post has an article about Dwight having been appointed as a district court judge, to be based in Houwhanga, of all places. He takes up his new position in just three weeks.

July 17

I get a letter from Dwight. He seems to be doing some tidying up of cases before he leaves for his new position. He thanks me for my custom and gives me contact details for Monty, whom he suggests I should get to take over my case. He also tells me that he has phoned Eva to ask if there is any news, and she confirms that the police are continuing to leave every stone unturned in their unremitting pursuit of the truth. Dwight reports that she has elevated the file to "extremely complex" – stronger adverbs no doubt justify more delay – with "multiple offenders and multiple scenes around New Zealand" and it is still being worked on by another detective. I don't envy him (or her), because the more pesky facts get in the way, the harder it is to stick to your confirmation bias.

The Rape Survivor's Legal Guide is produced by the Wellington Community Law Centre, with input from the Ministry of Justice. The section entitled The Police Investigation informs the alleged victim that the investigation can be intensive and time-consuming, especially since the physical evidence needs to be collected and analysed. This may include "items of your belongings, such as clothing, or items from your house or car." Of course, this assumes that the alleged incident has only just happened. The other aspect of the investigation is the interview with the suspect. That's it; there is no third aspect of an investigation. What I can't figure out about our case is that, because it's historic, there is no analysis of immediate DNA evidence from the night before to be rushed off to the lab. All that's left is interrogating suspects. One whole dimension of investigation is missing in an historic case like this one. So why are the police doing nothing with the only dimension that remains: interviewing?

The guide also makes the point that all crimes are considered to be crimes against the state, rather than against the individual victim. This is an interesting distinction, which I've never really thought about. It says, "While the state does not need your consent to prosecute, it is likely to need your cooperation." However, even if the alleged victim decides to withdraw her complaint, the police may still proceed if they think they have enough evidence and are convinced it serves the broader public interest. This makes sense, because they may suspect that other people need to be protected from a dangerous perpetrator. Yet surely this should also apply to false rape complainants. Of course, if the police were to suggest they want to prosecute her, there is no chance I would hold them back. But even if I did, it would surely serve broader public interest for them to go for her without my consent.

It's odd how the numbers game plays in historic abuse cases. In the UK, police have been on a crusade for some years now to prosecute alleged offenders in historic rape and sexual abuse, especially in institutions. In a process labelled "trawling", they interview potential complainants in the hope of uncovering an historic crime, which they can then "solve" and boost their crime clearance rates. In the worst examples, this is rather like a fire department starting fires and then getting praised for extinguishing them. One complaint of historic abuse with no corroboration may not be enough to get a conviction, so other potential complainants may leap on board, often with the lure of huge compensation. Quantity evidence therefore comes to stand in for quality evidence. The jury members, caught up in the sexual abuse hysteria that has convinced them that our children must be protected from these perverts who lurk under every rock, get a whiff of something resembling smoke and usually convict. Their sense of civic responsibility is too high to risk leaving a paedophile free to roam the streets.

So what we have here is the police searching for a crime that most likely does not exist, and offering the lure of a crisp wad of cash to as many people as they can track down, until they have enough to make it look like a case. Given the opportunity, I would like to ask this question to the police, the prosecutors, the juries, the judges, the journalists and those few members of the public who still keep up with the news: Have you ever thought that a system like this may be open to miscarriages of justice? Even for a moment?

Numbers are very different in our case, and its particular form of complexity, with "multiple offenders", may be a reassuring sign. Instead of (usually) one alleged pervert and several complainants, ours has multiple alleged perverts and just one complainant. All pseudo-evidence must come from her alone. An epic with a cast of thousands must surely make it hard for Verity to write plot lines which are consistent and coherent, unless the police are so convinced she is telling the truth that they guide her with the screenplay. On the other hand, I'm worried that the more time and money the police commit on what they call investigation, the less inclined they may be to throw their arms in the air and say, "This liar has been stringing us along."

Where is the doubt? With all these paedophiles, has Verity ever questioned whether she's got the details right? I assume that her mother's also in on this. Was there ever a time when Charlotte sat down with Verity and said, "Now dear, are you sure all these names are correct? Let's go through your spreadsheet. This man on page three – the one between Magic Johnson and Val Kilmer – are you sure he raped you? Because you know, if you get one of them wrong, some bad things may happen to him, and… well, I must say that in some ways it wouldn't be fair. He may not like it."

July 20

I phone Dwight, and speak to him for the first time since the police interview on February 10. I congratulate him on his new appointment. He tells me that he still thinks it's unlikely the nonsense will come to court. I respond that I find that encouraging, but I don't feel confident that the system will necessarily clear me just because I happen to be innocent. He says that he knows how the system works and admits I'm right: I have every reason to be hopeful but not complacent. Paedophilia could bring a ten-year sentence. Of course, I probably won't be prosecuted, as Dwight has told me. But the stakes are huge.

July 23

I wake up from my first dream about this allegation. At least, it seems to have a connection, but interpreting dreams is as unscientific as recovering memories of sexual abuse. I'm walking through a flat open field of grass, and in front of me is a policeman at a desk. It's a bit like one of those old Monty Python links, where John Cleese is sitting at a desk in the middle of nowhere and says, "And now for something completely different…." When I get up to the desk, I start railing and cursing at the policeman, though I can't decipher any of my own words, and I can't make out his face, only a uniform. I perceive him as male, so it isn't Eva. I start picking things up off his desk and flinging them at him. I'm not a violent man, so nothing heavy, just pencils and erasers and other sundry stationery. He just dodges it all and laughs.

There may be something useful here, and when I wake up it gives me an idea. Before the big step of going to the Police Conduct Authority in Wellington, maybe it would make sense to make the smaller step of complaining at the Draketown Police Station. Not to Eva, of course, but maybe the local police commander.

Charles mentions an angle neither of us has thought of before: visual identification. How has Verity identified me in a way that enabled the police to confirm I am the Peter Joyce she thinks I am? There are other Peter Joyces around. My grandfather once bought a vacuum cleaner from one who came to his door. Years later, by an amazing quirk, another one was the funeral director when the same grandfather died. If this nonsense comes to court, is it really like in the movies, where the trembling victim points and stammers out, "It was that man over there – the brute in the blue serge suit and string tie"? But if I'm in the dock between two court officers, can she just say "That's him there – the guy on trial"? That sounds a bit easy. But Charles assures me that visual identification of an accused person is an essential point of law, and says I should mention this to my new lawyer. Now that I know where Verity appears to work, I'd better be careful to keep away from Eagle's Nest, in case she gets to know my face. If we need a waffle maker, we'll just have to buy a new one.

July 24

I am in town and on the spur of the moment head into Monty's office. I still haven't decided on a replacement lawyer, and he's one of the main candidates, since he knows the case already. He's very welcoming and asks me to sit down and have a talk. I say that this is "off the record", which is my polite way of saying I'm not expecting to pay six dollars a minute for chatting. He smiles and gives a dismissive wave, which is ambiguous at best. I'm amazed that he says he has three cases of sexual abuse coming up in the next few months, and wants to portray himself as someone I would do well to take on. So there's good business for lawyers in this whole sad area, and I find his soft sell dispiriting. I'm not buying an insurance policy or a car. I say, "Well, I'm still hoping that nothing will come of this." I repeat my outrage at being in this situation, but he says nothing that suggests he shares it. He could at least pretend.

The subject of a false complainant's motivation comes up. He says the ones who are just after money are usually not so successful in court – so there must be some like that. It's the True Believers who are the real danger, because their heart-rending accounts can sway some juries. Their invented memories are as dear to them as their own children. Then I ask him if he knows anything about researchers into false memory, such as Elizabeth Loftus. No, never heard of her. I find this odd. If he deals with this sort of case, why hasn't he been hungering to find out the psychology behind it all? If he isn't convinced that "recovered memory" is really false memory, how can he be sure his clients are innocent? However, I shouldn't be too hard on him. He has a job to do, and I have no reason to assume he doesn't do it well.

Some may say that no lawyers who handle sexual cases would be interested in challenging the social and legal milieu that keeps producing so many outrageous prosecutions. After all, they make so much money from them. I'm just not sure about this; it may be too cynical. Doesn't a dentist want her patients to have good oral hygiene, even if it loses her work?

July 26

In the shower this morning I have a brainwave. I've just thought of the best character witness I could possibly imagine. In 2006 I gave one-on-one English tuition to a sixteen-year-old high school girl called Julia. The lessons were here at home, and as Angela was working, it was sometimes just Julia and I in the house (my god – what was I thinking?): such a perfect opportunity for the lecher I am not. Why didn't I think of this before? This is the most rewarding revelation I've had. I'm pretty sure I can track her down. Tennis is rained off, so Les and I play snooker. I'm too hyped up to play those delicate shots it takes to win, but who cares?

Now, what's the best way of using her testimony to my advantage? Obviously she would be invaluable in court, in case the geographical defence isn't enough to save me. But maybe it would be more effective to ask her to go to the police now. She could testify to my trustworthy character and tell them that, if need be, she will speak for me in the courtroom. That may make Eva or her puppeteer say, "Hmm, this young woman may tip the balance. If she testifies in court, we won't be able to get this guy. Prosecution is off." Of course, I wouldn't play the Julia card pre-emptively unless my new tactician recommends it, so there's no need even to trace her just now.

August 1

Six months today since this nonsense first hit us. As nothing has happened, the only thing that needs to be monitored is how we are coping. Angela remains a rock. This doesn't mean she isn't worried about it, just pragmatic enough to know that no anxiety or analysis or sleuthing is likely to bring any real advantage. Even I am learning to live with it in some respects. I'm sleeping a little longer, and when the Verity problem does keep me awake it's usually because I'm furious. I've learnt that anger sleeplessness is better than worry sleeplessness.

Last night we were watching a TV show with a court scene, and the judge warned a witness who had made an angry outburst that he could be held for contempt of court.

I have always found courts daunting places, with their atmosphere of fusty authority. Many years ago I was called for jury service. I saw this as a solemn duty and I was disappointed that the whole thing ended in an anti-climax: I wasn't called and just sidled back to work. I really wanted to show I was a responsible citizen with a useful role to play in one of the great processes of our democratic system.

When I visited court back in May, I learnt enough about it to realise that defending myself wouldn't be smart. But I also learnt that if I do get taken to court over this, I'll have no nerves when I'm questioned. The reason is that all my respect for the institution of the court and the system that lies behind it has evaporated. Of course, I'm far too restrained to deliver any sort of outburst. Mine would not be contempt of court, but rather contempt for the court. What's the opposite of contempt? Respect, I suppose. How could I respect any system which has unfairly placed me in such a position, which has so little regard for the simple and obvious truth? It deserves only contempt. I'll be a reluctant performer forced to play in a third-rate drama with an implausible plot. If the prosecution lawyer gets stroppy with me, I'll be assertive enough to look him in the eye as the ham actor he is.

August 2

Angela rings Gloria tonight, for the first time in four weeks. Nothing. Nothing! Unbelievable and yet expected. Is Eva asleep at the wheel? With some editing suggestions from Jackie, I've composed my letter of complaint to the IPCA. I am tempted just to send it in, but I suppose I'd better choose another lawyer and run it past him.

Here is a tiny sign of progress in the statistics war. Washington Examiner columnist Ashe Schow reports that New York Senator Kirsten Gillibrand, whom I mentioned back in March as a ceaseless campaigner on behalf of those countless young women raped on campuses, has discreetly taken the one-in-five figure from her website. Schow writes that the figure seems to have been removed back in December, a week after the Bureau of Justice Statistics revealed that the actual number of female students experiencing sexual assault while in college is closer to one in forty-five. Schow reports that Gillibrand's spokesman declined to say why the factoid had been removed, but "condemned those who disputed the statistic." So why not leave it there? Shouldn't we bravely stick by the friends and the facts we know we can trust?

August 3

A bad day, and all the worse because I have no explanation for it. It's Verity, of course, but more than that I can't say. Is it the six-month "anniversary", or perhaps the continued lack of news from John and Gloria? I sit at home doing nothing, feeling hollow and powerless. It's as if I'm just floating in my armchair. I count the minutes until Angela gets home, because I need to talk to her, to say…what? Nothing new, but it's just her comfort that I need, just the fact of her beside me. This is the worst I've felt for months. I'm angry with myself that I can't say why. I've always been a stable person, a person in control. I don't do inexplicable mood swings.

When Angela gets home I break down for a while, alternating between tears and fury, but no kitchen utensil suffers this time. Today's Monday, so it's a VFD, but she sees this is a special case. She brings me back to normality, and together we hit on a great new comforting rationalisation. Before this nonsense hit us, our lives had been close to perfect. Most people have to bear a cross: a chronic and debilitating sickness perhaps, or a miserable marriage, or insurmountable debts. We had nothing like that. Some sort of suffering is part of being human, and Verity's long and lethal reach is what we have to endure. We were naive to think our complacent and isolated lives would cosset us for ever. Why be satisfied with mere happiness when you can be human instead? Of course, this is a very odd way of suffering: false rape complaints aren't uncommon, but it must be a rare thing for someone to be targeted by a stranger in this way. It's wilful and malicious, and it would be so easy to fix. Verity could just go to the police tomorrow, say she was upset and confused, that it was a little lie that just got out of hand. She could apologise and it would all be over.

But any rationalisation is a tool worth trying, and this one works for now. By the evening we're laughing at *Seinfeld* reruns, and by bedtime all our emotion is spent. Verity becomes curiously human. This would be a good time to talk to her. If the Eagle's Nest Auction House were open at night, I could just walk right up to her, introduce myself, and ask flatly, "Why are you doing this? Just tell me why."

August 4

I hear the BBC4 podcast *Ritual Sexual Abuse: Anatomy of a Panic*, presented by David Aaronovitch, columnist for The Times. Aaronovitch says

> I'm not disputing the idea that the society I grew up in was one that was often in denial about the existence of child sexual abuse. Some of our most trusted institutions dismissed the complaints of victims, and colluded in protecting their abusers. But how did we go from a state of denial to one of credulity?

The documentary examines the social climate that led to witch hunts in cases of alleged paedophile rings not just abusing children but torturing and even sacrificing them in depraved satanic ceremonies. I've never considered it likely that Verity has made any accusations as outlandish as this, so the connection with "our" case at first looks tenuous. However, producer Hannah Barnes says that the greatest surprise thrown up by her research is that what she assumed was a relic of the eighties and nineties is in fact alive and flourishing. Perhaps Verity really has alleged weird rituals with sacrifices, and Eva made no mention of them in my interview because she thought of them as "discrepancies" which might undermine the fundamental truth of her accusations.

Aaronovitch interviews Sue Hampson, a former counsellor for victims of sexual abuse. Hampson these days trains abuse counsellors and is co-director of Safe to Say, a Scottish organisation that treats sexual abuse "survivors". A career veteran, then. Aaronovitch asks about her attitude to what he politely calls "implausible" claims by clients. She is taken aback and asks him to clarify *implausible*. Clearly she is unused to facing hard questions. He mentions "childhood sacrifice, sacrifice of animals, altars... that sort of thing." She bridles at his skepticism, and says

> It wasn't my job to not believe (sic) people who was (sic) clearly scarred, physically and mentally, by what they'd gone through, so for me it's not implausible at all, no...It was my job to work with them, and support them...I'm very curious about why wouldn't (sic) people believe somebody telling you something which is clearly horrendous. It feels to me very anti-children, very anti-recovery, and on the side of abusers.

So our conviction that an event would, if it occurred, be "horrendous" is all the evidence we need that it occurred. Aaronovitch treats her kindly, but Hampson clearly takes the nurturing role of a counsellor to bizarre and irrational extremes. She implies that the client is entitled to her truth and must always be believed. It would be bad enough if she always answered yes to the question "Is this client telling the truth?" But it is immeasurably worse than this: Hampson would never even ask the question, and is puzzled that anyone would. As for false allegations, she says, "My belief is that it doesn't happen that much at all."

Granted, a counsellor is not an investigator, and she must mainly deal with a client's mental well-being. But facts are facts, and Hampson's unquestioning belief is clearly more than just an *ad hoc* professional pretence to help the client get over some psychological hurdle. It makes me wonder if counsellors like Hampson would consider anything implausible – ever. Does she believe there is any such thing as an hallucination? An open mind is usually a virtue but, as the old saying goes, you should never open your mind so far that your brain falls out.

All this makes it seem even more likely that a counsellor has played a sinister role in "our" case. When a counsellor shows this sort of credulity, it means that what the client can be encouraged to imagine in therapy becomes unquestioned reality. If a client comes to a counsellor like Hampson convinced that she has been abused in some bizarre and ritualised manner, Hampson will always indulge the poor woman's fantasy. Yet the danger goes further: such an explanation can be implanted in the mind of a client who never considered it. If a counsellor is sure that such far-fetched networks of satanic abusers exist, despite the absence of bodies, bones and blood, she can surely convince her client to think the same way. This can have terrible consequences for anyone caught in the web of delusion, because the police seem to be gullible enough to believe all "survivors". If Verity's counsellor had shared Hampson's attitude and had been contacted by the police, she would have said, "Believe her. It must be true." The police, seeing the counsellor as an expert, would decide, "Okay, let's get these perverts." Clearly this is disastrous for me, but ultimately I doubt that such total credulity really helps the client either. Sooner or later all of us – including vulnerable people undergoing counselling – benefit from confronting the truth.

August 10

I go to Draketown MP Niccolo Ferrari's office to arrange a meeting with him. His secretary-assistant asks what I want to see him about. Other people are milling around, and I tell her it's a slightly delicate matter. Could we go to a quiet room somewhere? So I outline the story to her, avoiding names of course. She is aghast. She shakes her head at the state of world that anyone should bring such a false charge. She never betrays any suggestion that she thinks I may be guilty, so she knows how the game goes. I like this woman immediately for her sense of outrage. She seethes with fabulous anger. I arrange to drop off the text of my police interview and a copy of my draft letter to the IPCA. She will get back to me some time in the next couple of weeks to arrange a meeting with Niccolo, to give him time to read the literature. I leave feeling buoyant.

August 12

With my IPCA complaint letter I bike in to the office of David, hopefully my replacement lawyer – or at least the one to check the letter out. He's the one who phoned me back on June 8. He says that he's not taking on much work these days, and won't even give the letter a once-over. Fair enough. But he does chat with me for a few minutes. He asks what detective is working on my case. When I tell him it's Eva he takes in a gulp of air and says she can be very determined. He implies she buys into the smoke and fire assumption. He even adds that there is a tacit gender war in historic sex cases, and men would be more likely to get justice if only male detectives were assigned to them. Try saying that to women's groups.

One thing he says is most interesting. This case, like so many others, is really about police inefficiency, or imbalance, or tunnel vision....call it what you like, but one way or another it has been mishandled. The police will do anything to preserve their image. If they make a blunder, there are two ways that can be exposed. One is if the case goes through official channels and fails in court, with the unfairly accused person playing a purely passive role throughout. The other is if a determined individual with enough time and enough anger (my words) takes them to task and draws attention to what they've done wrong. I take this as support for what I've been doing and will do in the near future in my crusade mode: the official complaint, seeing my MP, and eventually going public if necessary. He seems to be implying that the police are trapped by procedure, and can be blindsided by anyone who doesn't just follow the dots. I decide I won't get a lawyer to check out the letter. Instead, I'll just send it.

But not just yet. Back on July 23 I had that dream about confronting a policeman at a desk, and I decide to go with my subconscious. On the spur of the moment I head for the Draketown Police Station to complain to someone senior about my so-called case. Not many suitable officers are available, and for maybe ten minutes I mill around in the front office. On the wall is a poster headed "Service Excellence – making every contact count", with cute photos of smiling police officers dealing with the public. Each has its own subheading with an anonymous quote under it. Under "Positive" is "I was treated fairly." What a joke. The heading "Excellence" has "It's an example of good value for tax dollars spent." Let's look at what I've received here. My tax dollars have contributed to paying the salary of a detective who has not yet investigated the transparent lies of a vindictive woman I've obviously never met and who would happily ruin my life. In some respects the value looks doubtful to me.

Finally the receptionist tracks down a sergeant who will talk to me. I imagined someone grizzled and morose, but he's fresh-faced and quite cheerful. He introduces himself as Mike. He looks boyish enough to be my own son. He listens – really listens – to the whole tale of woe. I tell him I'm sending in a formal complaint to the IPCA, and wave the pages to show that it isn't empty talk. I even quote from parts of it during our discussion. I think I come across as angry and determined, but measured. He seems to be on my side – as much as he can be – and says the letter is a reasonable action in the circumstances.

Whenever he plays the devil's advocate in favour of police policy ("Too often in the past we dismissed a woman's complaint") I have a ready reply which I throw back ("Yes, but valid and ethical law is never about retribution; it must consider individual cases and have nothing to do with trends and groups and swinging pendulums"). I'm astounded how little he knows about how the law works. Changes to the Evidence Act? Never heard of them. Statute of limitations? Silence. To be fair, maybe these issues seldom apply in his special field, which he tells me is domestic violence. He asks if he can have a copy of the complaint letter, and would I perhaps like to file it through this station? I say no, of course. I tell him the "investigation" has passed the first of the deadlines I've set myself, hence the formal complaint. When it passes my second deadline, I will go public. He asks when my second deadline is, but I won't say. He seems to prefer chatting to chasing villains, and I'm the one who has to break away, so after forty-five minutes I thank him and say he'd better go and attend to other things. Talking to disgruntled suspects all afternoon isn't good value for our tax dollars either.

Mike made notes, and said he has to put in a report on our meeting. Good. I mentioned Eva by name throughout, so she will soon know that a formal complaint has been made against her. I'm happy that she may be running just a little bit scared after revelling in unrestricted power for six months – that is, unless all police officers know they'll never be held to account by the public. As I leave, I look up at the windows of the blue citadel above. After such an agreeable conversation with the good cop, it's odd to think that somewhere up there, in one of those offices, bad cop Eva or her puppeteer may be plotting my demise right now. But probably not. More likely the pages of my file are just yellowing in an in-tray.

How much more satisfying this meeting has been than my last time in the very same building – the police interview six months ago. Back then I felt hamstrung by procedures and tactics I didn't understand. Today I may have seized some measure of power from misdirected people who can't be trusted with it. More than that, I feel like a different person. It's been a good day. Even in adversity, life can be sweet.

August 14

I send off my letter of complaint to the IPCA. It's a few days short of my deadline, but I'm keen to get things moving, so my excuse is that it will take some time to get to Wellington.

August 16

Gloria rings Angela. No news. Back in February Eva called the case "very complex" and seemed to think two months might do it. In July it was "extremely complex". Maybe now it's been elevated to the highest level of inaction: "extraordinarily complex".

But in a sense there is some news, or at least a new angle on something we'd overlooked. Verity arrived in Houwhanga to attend Westchester High School in July 1991. However, it turns out she didn't start attending school until the start of the third term in September. This means that her claim has changed from far-fetched to impossible. Central to her story is her insistence that I picked her up from school, yet my pay records confirm that while she attended Westchester I missed not a single day's work here in Draketown.

If the police finally work out that Verity has been lying, this alleged complexity of the case should persuade them to charge her, at the very least for wasting so much police time. They cannot on the one hand say that this has been a very difficult case which has had them running around "investigating", and on the other hand say that she hasn't caused them enough trouble to warrant prosecution.

We see most of the Danish film *The Hunt*, about Lucas, a kindergarten teacher (what was he thinking?) in a small town who gets accused of sexually abusing Klara, one of his charges and the daughter of his close friend. It's very moving and disturbing, the way he is ostracised to the extent that almost everyone turns on him. This in liberal and rational Denmark. It makes me grateful to have all these people around who believe me. Some things are just like in my case. At one point Lucas says, "The police are involved, but they tell me squat." Does Eva work for Interpol? Of course, in other ways our cases are quite different, because he doesn't have my geographical defence and the alleged offences have been committed recently on a very young "victim". Klara can't be blamed because she's a little girl who can't always separate reality and fantasy. Verity's pushing forty now – old enough for her reasons to be called excuses.

August 18

Sixty-three today. I treat myself to a day totally free of all issues to do with Verity, apart from writing this short entry. Hopefully my complaint will be arriving at the IPCA today, and it gives me pleasure thinking of some investigator reading it, rubbing his chops in disbelief and then saying, "My god, this is outrageous! Let's get a team down to the Draketown station this afternoon." It won't happen anything like that – more likely I'll just have files lying in two trays rather than one – but thinking of the possibility brings birthday cheer.

August 19

I get an email from the IPCA acknowledging that they've received my complaint. It has been allocated the case number 15-0330 KFI, which looks encouraging, and the body of the reply says, "The Authority is making enquiries into the matter, following which a decision will be made on the appropriate way to deal with your complaint." It's little more than a form letter, but I'm impressed that this first contact has come so promptly, and I can only hope that they work faster than the police. I just wonder if they define *enquiries* the same way I do. If they use the same dictionary the police use for *investigation*, I'm in for a long and exasperating wait.

The police themselves certainly struggle with the word *enquiries.* I download a brochure entitled *Information for Victims of Sexual Assault* from the New Zealand Police website. It offers accusers guidance about the procedure after a sexual complaint has been made. Everything is as I would imagine, but this catches my eye: *Suspects are usually spoken to after key enquiries are completed.* Let's follow the logic here. I am obviously a suspect, and I have been spoken to. Therefore, according to this procedure, key enquiries about my possible involvement should have been completed. Yet if they have been completed, what form did they take, and why have the relevant facts of place and time not exonerated me? It appears that when the police use the expression *complete key enquiries,* what they really mean is *speak to the accuser and treat her word as gospel.* Isn't it enough that we falsely accused have to learn about the law and psychology? Must we become bilingual as well?

August 27

I hear from the office of Draketown M.P. Niccolo Ferrari, confirming that I have an appointment to meet him on Saturday morning.

August 28

After so long in limbo, two things happen tonight. Mary comes round for our monthly movie session, and asks us if we've seen the article in a free local newspaper about Eagle's Nest Auction House, with a photo of a woman who may be her. She didn't see it herself, but a woman she knows, who's also in the V-loop, read it and wondered if that was the she-devil. We have it in an unread pile of junk mail, and I dig it out. There she is, grinning toothily behind a collection of salt and pepper shakers which is going to feature in tomorrow's auction. It's interesting that she's described as co-owner of the business. This article is the best news in a long time, because she's made the mistake of putting herself out there for everyone to see. Although I've been discreet enough not to use her real name, many on the Draketown grapevine already know she works at Eagle's Nest and will figure out it's her. So now they'll have a name and a face. Poor woman - that may really cost her. Of course, she knows even less about tactics than I do. This battle is of no consequence to her, and she's too naïve to know how high the stakes are for me...and could be for her.

Just as the first movie finishes, the phone rings. When I see Gloria's name on the handset I know it has to be something important, because this is Friday night, and the wives' calls are every second Sunday. It's happened: they've got a call from Eva. She will fly up to Houwhanga and interview John on September 14. Still almost three weeks away, but at least cogs are starting to turn. Gloria suggests that Eva has been put under pressure because the IPCA complaint has been received at the Draketown police station, and she's probably right. It's interesting that Eva is flying up there. What happened to the foot-dragging North Island detective? I get the impression that was just an Eva lie to cover up for her own procrastination.

Adrenaline keeps me firing until about two. I do an online search and find the article and photo. I'm happy about both of today's developments, but I'm also nervous about John's interview. This will bring things to a head. I assume that after Eva talks to John, a decision may be made. Which way will it go? Will the police prosecute, or will they see sense? Some old questions come up again. If they go for prosecution, will they thump on the door one day, muscle their way in and take my computers? Will it be one trial or an indefinite number in different cities, one for each pervert, perhaps using video links and even an army of translators? I assume one trial makes sense, because otherwise poor Verity will have to endure the stress and indignity of reliving her ordeal several times over. Does that mean it will be in Draketown, because that's where she lives and where the lie was first filed? Probably. So we can host some defendants, but our house isn't huge. This trial could be quite a boon for the Draketown accommodation industry.

August 29

Predictably, the first email response I get to Verity's photo is from Jackie, who boasts that she looks exactly the way she'd pictured her. A friend in Christchurch says that Verity looks so different from the way she'd imagined her that she has reversed her assessment from "malicious and spiteful bitch" to "helpless fruitcake". Jackie also says, "You need a totally trustworthy spy who haunts the auction house and gets pally." Yes, brilliant – a woman who could get accepted into the control room behind the glass partition, someone with enough loyalty never to be enticed into becoming a double agent, not even by gifts of antique cruet sets.

I get an email from Fridolin in Switzerland. It contains a link to a research article on rape statistics from Bavaria and he promises me that the findings are most revealing. My German's not bad, but it's not good enough. After struggling for a couple of hours I take up Fridolin's kind offer to translate the main points. He'll get back to me.

Angela comes with me to see Niccolo Ferrari this morning. He's happy to talk, and gives us a full forty-five minutes. As I expected, he stresses that he cannot intervene in any way, but he is at least interested in the wider issue of police efficiency. I would have liked some of the glorious outrage his secretary showed, but of course that would be asking too much. Like Dwight, he says the legal system is all about balance, and he's confident that it gets that balance right almost all the time. He's familiar with at least the broad principles behind sexual allegations, and is realistic enough to know that some of them are false. He plays devil's advocate for the police: they have to counter historic perceptions that sexual allegations were not properly followed up. He concedes that police investigations do take time, and we have to live with that, however unsettling it can be. In other words, he says what we expect a politician to say. He adds that being outwardly respectable isn't and shouldn't be any defence, and of course we know that. In some respects he underestimates how much my "case" differs from most others: the simple geographical facts, and the ease with which police could exonerate me then turn things around and prosecute Verity. He also makes light of my suggestion that even if she's seen to be a liar, the police should charge her. He reminds me that one of the great merits of our legal system is that we are free to take out a private prosecution. This is rather glib. Police will prosecute an alleged rapist if they have a case they think they can win. Why should they not prosecute an alleged false rape complainant if they also have a case they think they can win?

He casts some doubt on the professionalism of counsellors in sexual abuse cases, but he doesn't seem to know much about "recovered" memory, or about the way false statistics have shaped policy. He tells us about one encouraging legal requirement, which I vaguely knew about: even if the police do decide to prosecute me, the case must get presented to a judge for a preliminary ruling. This judge has the power to say, "No, this is pure bunkum. There's not enough convincing evidence to prosecute here, so it can go no further." That must be good news. If ever a file was fit for screwing up and tossing into the bin, this is the one. He ends by saying that I should contact him again when there is any development, and he is particularly interested in the way the IPCA handles the matter. It's an organisation he helped set up as a citizen's check against police power, and he's keen to see whether it functions the way it should. His last words are that we should take comfort that I have only been accused, not charged. He appears genuinely interested in the case, but we emerge not much wiser…and I wasn't impressed that while we were talking he seemed to be skim-reading the notes

I'd already given his secretary. Multi-tasking cannot reveal how my case differs from the normal he said/she said.

September 1

Back in July the celebrity being grilled in the news was Bill Cosby, for his alleged abuse. This week it's the turn of Pretenders singer Chrissie Hynde, who's in trouble for her reaction to being abused decades ago. In her recent autobiography, *Reckless*, she mentions that when she was twenty-one and out of her tree on alcohol or drugs she was sexually abused by a group of motorcycle gang members who said they would take her home, but instead took her somewhere else and performed unmentioned indecencies on her against her will. If she still has any anger, it is only with herself for her carelessness. She says

> This was all my doing and I take full responsibility You can't paint yourself into a corner and then say whose brush is this? You have to take responsibility. I mean, I was naïve.

She adds that women who dress provocatively in public are to blame for their own attacks. She says, "I don't think I'm saying anything controversial, am I?" Chrissie, where have you been?

Such victim-blaming naturally couldn't escape fury from women's organisations. Some former fans almost seemed ready to burn all her albums in disgust, as Christians did in 1966 when John Lennon joked that the fab four had become more popular than Christ. And her critics are right: no victim of any crime should take the blame. However, active blame and passive responsibility are not mutually exclusive. We live in an imperfect world, and it is fitting to discourage inappropriate actions that may tempt others to take advantage of you. You aren't the primary wrongdoer if you leave your house unlocked and get burgled, but no one should criticise me for telling you it wasn't smart to neglect your security. At least, not until humanity achieves nirvana, crime becomes obsolete, and all the police and lawyers are forced to get other jobs. Until then, you are a naïve young woman if you're in a club wearing next to nothing, knock back half a dozen vodkas and drape your arms around hormone-fuelled young men who are also boozed. The chances that one will rape you are still slim, but they are greater than they would be the next morning, when you're hung over and traipsing through a crowded mall in your baggy tracksuit pants and sports top. Live with it, and don't rail against people who urge you to take some responsibility for your own safety. Above all, don't leave your house unlocked and don't tease out-of-control young males just because you want to assert your right to do so.

One aspect of Hynde's comments has drawn little response. Maybe she goes too far in taking full responsibility, but what interests me most of all is her apparent resilience. She obviously hasn't forgotten the indecencies done to her (no sign of a repressed memory here, then), but she seems to have shaken off their effects. "Survivors" should respect her as a role model. She has been hardy enough not to have let this incident define her as a permanent victim, or to become bitter about men or about life in general. She is in fact the strongest kind of sexual abuse survivor: the kind who dismisses it as just one of those volleys that life fires at all of us from time to time.

Yet some readers who have been posting on sites reporting Hynde's comments are determined to deprive her of that resilience, of her prerogative to interpret the events of her own life in any way she chooses. They insist that the only reason she is reacting so dismissively is that subconsciously she is still traumatised, and this is her only way of coping. How dare she betray the sisterhood by denying she is a victim, and how dare she assume that the opinion she thinks she holds about the sexual abuse she suffered is her actual opinion!

I commend Hynde's determination to keep the kind of perspective that is rare in any talk of sexual crime. I have little doubt the most depraved sexual crimes do permanently affect the quality of victims' lives, but the lure of financial compensation surely inflates the real number. I am sure that all sorts of crimes can do the same, but no one makes the claim because they expect not to be treated seriously. When I was a teenager some low-life smashed me in the face when I was waiting for a hamburger. It was nasty and painful but the sergeant on duty at Christchurch Central police station saw no blood and in effect refused to follow it up, despite the fact that my witness and I both got the registration number of the car the attacker got away in. If I had claimed that the shock of this attack could permanently affect me, the sergeant would likely have abandoned all pretence of sympathy and burst out laughing. Perhaps his modern equivalent would do the same, but heaven help him if he reacted this way with a woman who reported she had been groped.

The BBC has got in trouble for hosting a discussion on *Sunday Morning Live* entitled "Is there too much panic around rape?" Back on March 17 I outlined the way the notion of rape has been broadened so much that it's quite possible to say that many instances of what we now call rape are not really so damaging. If we accept this is true, the title the BBC chose for the discussion is perfectly reasonable. Yet viewers reacted with predictable fury at the callousness of the BBC, with one (male) tweeting "This whole debate is revolting. Rape is the worst of crimes. Exactly how much panic is too much?" Rape, the way it is now defined, is not necessarily the worst of crimes.

September 5

I'm especially interested in cases when the "victim" herself didn't appear to consider the encounter to be rape until a more savvy and socially aware friend brought her up to speed with the latest thinking and convinced her to be devastated. Emma Sulkowicz, who graduated from Columbia University in May this year carrying a mattress, is one example. The mattress was the one Sulkowicz was allegedly raped on, and she had carried it around campus for months in protest at what she saw as the university's reluctance to treat her rape accusation against another student seriously enough. She was a visual arts major, and carting the mattress around was her art project – a performance. She said the work of "endurance performance art" would end only when her attacker left or was expelled from campus. The fact that she and her mattress attended the graduation ceremony suggests that she passed, but I cannot find out what grade she was awarded. Women's campaigner Camille Paglia wrote off Sulkowicz's effort as "mattress feminism" and said a *D* would have been about right.

The young man she accused was named and shamed in a manner that recalls the era of lynch mobs, despite the fact that he had been cleared of any wrongdoing even according to the victim-friendly "preponderance of evidence" requirements applied by the university. The crucial question of whether she was actually raped got lost in all the hype surrounding the spectacularly original way she expressed her outrage. First reports presented her accusation as if it was gospel, and she was lauded as a courageous representative of all those silent victims. It was only later that it became known – at least to those few who cared to find out – that Sulkowicz's story didn't stand up to scrutiny except to those who believe in rape myths as articles of faith. She reported the rape as an especially brutal attack, but had sent friendly messages to her "attacker" on Facebook after the encounter and a female friend told her the day after that what had happened was rape.

Her alleged rapist was really a victim of outrageous gender-based discrimination, legitimised by a widespread "believe the victim" mentality and supported by influential people working for Columbia University. An art professor encouraged Sulkowicz with the mattress concept, and Columbia provided transportation to help her carry the mattress. The university also featured her project on its website and helped pay the cleanup fee for a "Carry that Weight" rally.

The particular rape myth that is applied here is the notion that in rape accounts there can never be lies or even untruths, only forgivable discrepancies. So what if an alleged victim exchanged flirtatious messages with the monster after the event? It was her way of coping. This outlook reaches its zenith in the tweet *#TheresNoPerfectVictim*. Here are some examples of its use, as reported in an article by Claire Biggs on MTV.com:

> We have to be traumatized enough to be believable, but if we're too traumatized we're 'crazy' and unreliable. #TheresNoPerfectVictim

> Changing your story or misremembering details is a CLASSIC sign of trauma, not an attempt to fool people. #TheresNoPerfectVictim

> We cannot dictate how others should react to trauma. We can always choose to have compassion. #TheresNoPerfectVictim

This form of hashtag logic could take the form #ThereAreNoComplainantsOnlyVictims. Begin with the certainty that anyone making a sexual allegation is telling the truth, and work backwards from there. Find a way to explain what doesn't seem to fit. Discard anything you may once have valued about the presumption of innocence. Do anything it takes, but *believe*.

Huffpost College gives another example of friend-defined rape from the sexual autobiography of Lena Dunham, creator of the TV series *Girls*. Huffpost says that Dunham recalls an "ill-fated evening of lovemaking" with an infamous on-campus Republican. Describing the lead-up to the incident, she writes:

> All I knew when I stumbled home from a party behind him was that he was sullen, thuggish, and a poor loser at poker. How that led to intercourse was a study in the way revulsion can quickly become desire when mixed with the right muscle relaxants.

The following day her roommate, after hearing about the encounter, said, "You were raped." Dunham was a slow convert. Her first response was to burst out laughing. Years later her *Girls* co-writers heard the account and agreed that she was raped, but she still didn't see it that way. It took her years to understand what happened and to approach the experience "in a way that felt truthful to her" (Huffpost's words).

Truthful to her? We don't need to know any grubby details of what happened (though she does offer them). It may have been just an unpleasant sexual encounter, or it may have been what all of us would call rape. The point is that it's surely hard to consider Sulkowicz or Dunham sexual victims when it took other people to convince them. I don't like any expression referring to personal truth, but if I had to choose whether Lena Dunham or Chrissie Hynde had found an interpretation which was "truthful to her", I'd go for Hynde. Sulkowicz and Dunham were swayed by interpretations that were truthful to friends with fashionable agendas.

Yes, fashionable. I confess I am out of touch with what can get you a place at the table of trendy females – if indeed I ever knew. But I get the impression that being a sexual assault victim has developed a certain cachet among some young women. This is the angle taken by Steven Crowder in a hilarious and hard-hitting video ridiculing Dunham on *louderwithcrowder.com.*

September 7

We've all seen cop shows in which a gnarled detective has a hunch about a crime. His boss and his green deputy insist that the evidence points in the opposite direction, but he sticks with his instinct and events finally prove him correct. The real world seems to have detectives like that. The difference is that they're usually wrong, especially when it comes to unfounded historic sex accusations.

For some weeks now there has been news of an investigation into supposed paedophilia by former British Prime Minister Edward Heath, who died in 2005. Today's online edition of the UK Daily Mail newspaper has a column by Dominic Lawson, who exposes this operation as misguided and pointless – unless sullying the reputation of deceased politicians has purpose of its own. Lawson writes that a man using the pseudonym Nick claims that back in the 1970s Heath – along with sundry politicians, generals and secret service chiefs – raped, tortured and even murdered children.

Detective Superintendent Kenny McDonald had called Nick's claims "credible and true." Lawson reveals that McDonald's judgment appeared not to have been based on any actual investigation of even the most fundamental kind. It was just a feeling, a whiff of smoke. Police did not interview any of Heath's drivers or special branch protection officers or anyone who lived in neighbouring apartments. Lord Robinson, Heath's "closest civil service advisor", revealed in a recent radio interview that he has not been questioned. This is despite the fact that the two remained good friends after Heath retired, and he is chairman of the trust that owns the ex-Prime Minister's house.

Probably because of the lack of any convincing evidence or witnesses, last month the police resorted to having broadcasters film one of their officers outside Heath's house. The officer appealed to any of Heath's victims to come forward. Recently other detectives have looked at the case and not found "a shred of evidence". Sense at last from the police in London. Now, can they come to the antipodes and talk to Eva about what appears to be her own baseless hunch?

September 9

This afternoon I get a call from a friend in the V-loop who knows someone called Eric, who is in a similar predicament to me and is also writing a book. My friend tells the other guy about me, and gives me his mobile number. We keep missing each other's calls, but we're likely to make proper contact this weekend. He seems keen to talk. So he's a rival in a sense, but never mind: so many guys seem to be victims of false rape complaints that it could become a whole new genre of books or even films. If martial arts can do it, we can.

The other side already has its genre. When I do a search for "sexual abuse" on Amazon, I get hundreds of pages of titles like *Hush, Endless Tears, Dear Daddy, Daddy's Wicked Parties, From Pain to Power, Rag Doll* and *Life Uncaged*. Almost all appear to be stories told by "survivors". No doubt some are genuine, but it's impossible to do a count. Let me put it this way: if Verity wrote a book, it would be there. Once she made some minor embellishments to the facts, it would no doubt be a compelling story. How many of these books are the same?

September 11

Two days ago I wrote that Eric and I are in a similar predicament. He and I finally make contact. I learn that he is six years down the track, and he has suffered much more than we have. We compare our cases on the phone for about an hour, and in that time I say and hear the word "outrageous" more often than in all my life so far. Everything I have learnt about the injustice of the system and the vindictiveness of the police gets multiplied by about ten. I would rather not give more detail unless he gives me permission when he comes to meet me on September 20.

September 12

Two weeks ago I wrote that Fridolin would translate the most important points from the German article about rape statistics in Bavaria, and I get his message today. The figures should have the two-percenters sweating, but it won't because they will just ignore them. The data come from a very thorough investigation in 2000 by Erich Elsner and Wiebke Steffen. In that year women made 1754 accusations of rape in the state, which has a population of about twelve million. A third of these accusations were judged to be probably not true. No prosecution of an alleged rapist was pursued in half of the total. Reasons for abandoning prosecution were divided into four groups (figures rounded to nearest whole number): lack of evidence 38%; contradictory statements by the women 25%; no punishable action 14%; no offender found 22%. Of the 1754 complainants, 7.4% were investigated for making a false complaint, and of that 7.4%, *every single one* admitted she had lied. Police prosecuted three-quarters of the false complainants; the other quarter were let off because of mental instability. The study also found that female police officers were more skeptical about rape accusations than male officers. This surprising discovery certainly goes against what lawyer David suggested when I spoke to him back on August 12.

These figures tell us plenty. They suggest that there is no conspiracy to disbelieve women who make a complaint. Although a third of all allegations were believed not to be true, fewer than a tenth of complainants were investigated for making a false accusation. This means that it was very unlikely that a woman making a complaint the police suspected was false would face any consequences. In fact, fewer than half of the women found to have given contradictory accounts were investigated. I am not suggesting that they always should be, because I accept that some who get details wrong may in fact have been raped; I just want to point out that these figures show no systematic policy to deprive women of justice.

Most interesting is that 7.4% of the 1754 total admitted they had lied. This means that the *absolute minimum* of false rape complaints in this study is 7.4%. The true percentage of false rape complaints could never be determined, but it must have comprised two numbers: the known 7.4% plus an unknown additional number: those who lied but could hide under enough doubt to escape blame. A woman who is part of that 7.4% of confessed liars still had a one-in-four chance of escaping prosecution because of her mental state.

Of course, this report has its limitations – or at least, my knowledge of it has. The figures are dated, and they are from Germany, which may be culturally different. I admit I don't know about the study procedures, but it was commissioned by the Bavarian State Ministry of the Interior and carried out by the Criminological Research Group of the Bavarian police. This source is clearly more reputable than the source of the two percent factoid, which is also foreign and even more dated – when it isn't just plucked out of the air.

I search for this report online, and I find that it hasn't attracted sufficient interest to be translated into English. It is available from the website of the Bavarian police, and from Amazon Germany, where it probably hasn't sold enough copies to buy the authors a shared lager at the beer festival, let alone a new BMW 7-series. No one has even reviewed it yet. Why do I have the impression that if its findings were very different they would be all over the blogosphere?

I email the data without elaboration to the comments section of Auckland Rape Education *(rpe.co.nz)*, a site that helps victims of sexual abuse. I want to see whether anyone there accepts them, challenges them or responds to them in any way. They don't, of course.

Today Angela tells me that she's changed her mind about anonymity: she's now happy for me not to hide behind a tree. This was quite spontaneous, with no prodding or cajoling from me. Excellent! Not only does this mean that justice is more likely to be served, but it also means the first sentence of this diary isn't contradicted by my later retraction. She wants to be anonymous herself, and she chooses the name Angela. Maybe I didn't need to write that.

September 14

Today is defined by one event: John's interview with Eva. Angela rings at 7:30 and speaks to him, because Gloria has to attend a meeting at the school where she teaches.

The report over the phone is a whirl of places and days and names, but I can hopefully have any unclear details clarified later. The interview was done by audio, which I suppose is a compromise between being filmed and having written notes. I would rather have the notes, so that I could get my hands on them, but the agreement appears to be based on the expectation of a very long interview, which it was: around three hours. Hand-written notes would have extended it much further, and Eva probably had to rush back to Draketown to attend to other cases she was busy ignoring.

Before it started John's lawyer told John and Gloria that he could have been simply charged, with the interview coming afterwards. That put both of them on edge. Gloria wanted to be at John's side in the interview, but the lawyer told her she had to wait in the outer office.

Our accuser seems further out of her tree than any of us ever imagined. Eva had reams of paper, with Verity's twenty-eight separate accusations against him neatly stacked with coloured tags. John was questioned about these alleged incidents one at a time. Most were from her infancy or shortly after, and centred on recognisable childhood environments superimposed with a sinister sexual overlay, such as a swimming pool where her father's deviant friends were lurking in the changing rooms. All involved John in company with other men, who were unnamed except for Lance Boyle and myself. Lance has been hunted down and interviewed, apparently, but apparently none of the others could be identified through the murk. Eva made only brief mention of the Skeptics Association. Some allegations were from when

John was in the mountain ski patrol. With each one, John's response was that all the claims were outlandish, because whoever these unknown men were, the alleged places and times just didn't match. Surprise surprise. I seldom featured, because I'm really just a bit player unlucky enough to have a name Verity remembered. Eva asked if I owned a house in Houwhanga, which is an odd change from what she asked me. John felt stressed throughout, and Eva offered breaks, but John carried on without them. After a harrowing three hours and with still only ten of the incidents covered, the interview ended.

Nuttiness and stupidity don't always go together, but in her case they surely do. After my interview back in February I wrote that her lie was "inexpertly crafted", and I see now what an understatement that was. Her brain contains a mishmash of cars and water slides and houses and rapists and towns and bouncy castles and streets and times and changing rooms and ski wax and dates, any of which she just spits out in an inconsistent and random way to the only people who will listen to her: anyone wearing blue. Yet surely this interview marks the end for her. Even the police must get it now. Eva assured John that the police will tell him by this Friday whether or not he will be prosecuted. This Friday! And if he's scripted out by then, surely that applies to Lance and me. Will the police have to tell us we're vindicated, or if they don't like any of us (if we made a complaint to the IPCA, for example) can they leave us dangling?

I'm not sure whether this featured in the interview or whether it was a part of John's reflection afterwards, but Angela says John is now totally convinced that a counsellor has played a sinister role in all this, because the times of Verity's most intense allegations coincide with those times he knew she was taking counselling. That's what I've come round to believing too – and it was my initial impression, formed just seconds after the allegation first hit me seven months ago. What seems to confirm it now is the inconsistency and plain incompetence of her accusations.

After this, I've shifted towards feeling just a little sorry for her again: she is clearly disturbed. But if Eva contacts me on Friday and tells me I'm in the clear, I'll still furiously pedal in to the police station and demand that Verity be prosecuted. The consequences of her accusations have just been too damaging. If a man had caused as much trouble as this, no mental condition would keep him out of court, so why should it be different for her? She has broken a law for which she can be sentenced to years in jail. Let her be named and tried. If she is convicted, let a sympathetic judge give her a moderate sentence because of her mental frailty.

John's interview gives us another angle on Eva's delay in handling this case. Although there were probably scores of alleged perpetrators, Verity could name only three. The others were unidentified friends John had recruited. This seems to mean that it took seven and a half months to interview three suspects, unless unnamed members of the ski patrol were questioned. Something else about the interview gets me thinking. It ended after three hours, but with only ten of the twenty-eight charges against John discussed. It wasn't adjourned till the next day so that the other eighteen could be covered; it just ended. This means that, in Eva's eyes, fewer than half the cases were enough to establish a pattern that exonerated John and, by implication, other suspects. It makes me wonder why the "investigation" itself had to cover all the alleged incidents. If ten allegations were enough to shoot Verity out of the sky in the interview, why not in the "investigation"? It seems to suggest that the interview was the first time Eva had been presented with facts. We also know she probably hadn't interviewed people, so…what is a police investigation again?

September 15

It's all happening this week. Today I get an email from the IPCA, saying that Detective Braun "has advised the Authority that the investigation has progressed to a stage where she expects to be able to discuss matters with you by the end of September." The Authority seems overjoyed with this noble promise, and has decided that it has performed its role admirably, so it tells me that file 15-0330 is closed.

That's encouraging, of course: some sort of resolution will come soon, and it appears after the interview with John that it will be one to celebrate. Surely. Won't it?

In one sense my complaint has received no response, however. I wasn't just furious about the delay. The original complaint contained three specific points, the third of which was this: "The attitude of Detective Eva Braun at Draketown Police Station has been unprofessional," and it went on to give details of her response to my phone call on April 7. No mention was made in the IPCA letter about whether she was questioned about this, and I'll bet a dollar to a dime that she wasn't.

Yet why not? With any other company or organisation, if a member of the public makes an official complaint through the established channels about the attitude of an employee who deals with the public, action is taken. Maybe the boss hears the complaint and sides with the employee if she is found to have acted reasonably, but the person who complains will at least take comfort in the fact that she was asked for an explanation. The IPCA says nothing about this specific complaint, and I'm keen to know why not. It's not as if the police can claim they don't care about public perceptions. Back on August 12 I recorded that when I was at Draketown police station waiting for someone to see me, I read all those cutesy posters they had in the foyer with smiling officers dealing with the public. Police attitude seems to matter only when it's pasted on a wall.

September 18

At about 8:45 this morning I am writing lesson notes on my whiteboard when my mobile phone rings. It's Eva, after all these months. I'm ready for this, and have even planned my response, at least in part. I'm determined to resist any instinct to thank her as the bearer of good news. The conversation is less than a minute. She says that my file has been closed, and no further action will be taken. Her voice has that same chilling detachment I can remember. I tell her that the police have finally concluded what any ten-year-old would have concluded after ten minutes. I ask if Verity will be charged. Her reply is so immediate that maybe she expected the question: "No." I ask why not. I say that she has broken the law, after all. She snaps that I have no reason to think so, that I know nothing about the law, and that there is no point talking about this. "Goodbye," I say. Damn! I should have just hung up rather than waste a single polite word.

So this is it. This is it! The rest of the morning passes in a whirr, and my lesson on countable and uncountable nouns is a write-off. I get home in the early afternoon. Angela's already there and I give her the news. We hug and dance around the room. It's over.

Early in the late afternoon I ring Houwhanga, and John answers. It doesn't matter that we're talking directly now. He was also cleared, a few minutes before I was. We share thoughts on our clearance, on all aspects of this terrible business.

Eva's terse "No" in answer to my question about charging Verity shows that the outrage continues. It's revealing to compare two parallel situations. I, an innocent man, ask for the police to take legal action against a woman who has committed a crime that has brought misery upon who knows how many people over a period of months. Eva's response to this request takes less than a second but manages to spit in the faces of all of the innocent people this outrage has touched. By now Verity will have got the news that, long after she filed for her malicious (and free) legal action against us, the police have declined her request. Even though they must finally know she hasn't been telling the truth, she is the one who will probably get the news with a face-to-face explanation ("We're just not confident we can get a conviction") and with sympathy ("It doesn't mean we don't believe you"). As she's a victim rather than one of those evil perpetrators, maybe the police manual even requires them to provide a trained support person to console the little liar. More important, her preposterous accusations have been entertained by the police for…how long? Maybe more than a year. Yet a request for action on the only crime that clearly has been committed gets rejected in one terse second. I do the arithmetic: Verity's request has received 31,536,000 times more consideration than mine.

What will Verity's reaction be to the news that no charges will be laid against us? I would give anything to be there and see it. Will she break into a furious tirade against the injustice of the system, beating her fists on the wall? Will she sit with sad puppy eyes and weep silently on the shoulder of her paid support person? Or will she say, "Sorry, what are you talking about? Who are you people?...Oh, that rape thing? Did you actually follow that up in the finish?"

September 19

We call John and Gloria in the evening and speak about the case for about an hour and a half. There's little new, but John confirms Verity's consistent dependence on counsellors, going right back to when she was about sixteen, when the first historic sexual abuse imaginings began, centring on her very early childhood. John confirms that her counsellor at the time told her she must have been abused. He also reveals that Verity's most recent accusation was from just eight years ago, when John was visiting Draketown and stayed in a hostel. She claimed he arranged to meet her there, but when she arrived he had a line of friends queuing up to rape her. This in the middle of the city when she was thirty years old. Why didn't she scream?

We learn the fate of the two letters John sent, one to Jennifer and the other Charlotte. Both mother and younger daughter turned these in to the police, because Eva had them at the interview. After our conversation, John and Gloria email us the letter to Charlotte and a scanned copy of the last communication John ever received from Verity: a hand-written letter she sent to him about five years ago. The counsellor remains prominent. Here are the actual words (reported with John's permission):

> Dear Dad
>
> I'm going thu some stuff from my childhood right now and would like to not see you for a bit I'll contact you when I feel better. Pls don't ask Mum about it. It's my busniss. Pls don't respond. I want to calm down before I talk to you about it.
>
> It's ok. I'll be alright. Lot of anger at divorce and I'd rather it stayed between me and my councillor. It's all a bit new age isn't it?
>
> Thanks, Verity

Yes, I suspect it is *very* new age – a term which famous skeptic James Randi pronounces so that it rhymes with *sewage*.

John's letter to Charlotte was very articulate and reasonable. It showed concern for

Verity as his daughter, but warned that this behaviour could not continue, that Verity was in danger of "serious litigation." He said, "While I understand Verity's situation and can make allowances, others will not be so generous."

Verity's five-year-old note to John was most interesting. The "rape myths" argument consistently reminds us not to be duped by the passage of time. It insists that genuine rape victims have every reason not to report the crime immediately: they may be suffering trauma; they may not have perceived the event as rape; they may feel unwarranted guilt themselves; they may have some emotional ties to the rapist. All possible, of course. However, the fact that almost two decades after her parents' divorce Verity admits to continuing anger shows that motives for the spiteful can also last for a long time. So can mental illness, not to mention state-funded quack counselling.

Today Eric comes round to meet us and have a chat. He's the guy I made email contact with back on September 9. He tells us about the horrifying things that have happened to him after his stepdaughter accused him of molesting her in a situation where it simply couldn't have happened. He was convicted after the police clearly refused evidence and witnesses that could have exonerated him. The six-year legal ordeal has left him penniless. How do I know he's innocent? Because of facts I cannot reveal.

So we've been cleared. On the face of it, that makes us winners, but John told me he doesn't feel like one, and neither do I. The process itself has been a terrible punishment, and three questions are still to be answered. What happens to Verity? If she's to be prosecuted, ideally the police will do it, but Eva's terse monosyllable almost certainly rules that out. In fact, however often the police say they do prosecute false accusers, my hunch is that they have not even considered it in this case. Also, where are our formal clearance letters? A phone call just doesn't cut it with an accusation as devastating as this one. Are we to be content that the police grip on us has changed from temporary full nelson to permanent half nelson? What can be done to get the story told, to draw public attention to police mishandling of the case and the wider issues of false accusations, "recovered" memory and changes to the law that have taken away the presumption of innocence?

I'm convinced it is wrong that after Verity has forced us to participate in this lethal contest, when the run of play swings against her she can just whimper that she doesn't like the game any more and demand to go home. How fair are the rules if the possible results for us are a loss and a draw, but for her they are a win and a draw?

One thing is certain – Angela and I are no longer victims. Yes, there is still a chance that the police will take my file out of the cabinet and come and get me one day, but the chances of this are slim enough that we can get on with our lives. Yet a sense of outrage remains, from what did happen to us and what can happen to others.

September 21

First Monday after clearance, and the remaining covers start to come off. People around me have to receive the news directly, because I don't want friends learning about it for the first time from the newspaper. At work, when my colleagues casually ask me about my weekend, I say it was wonderful just enjoying a couple of days of without having this rape charge hanging over me. Eyes bulge and jaws drop. They look at me fixedly and say, "You're kidding, right?" and I give them a quick rundown. At morning break time, I'm walking down Gravelines Street and I run into my old friend Dick. I casually mention it to him as well. I may have let Verity's place of work slip out during the conversation, but it's important that I try not to let that happen again.

September 22

After work I go to the police station to try to get an interview with Malcolm, the top Draketown policeman, but it's like getting to see the Pope ("He makes his own appointments," I'm firmly told), so I give that up. However, I talk on the phone early this evening with Richard, Eva's superior. He seems to know a lot about the case. I begin by asking if I can have a letter confirming that the case is over and no action can be taken against me. Yes, I know it's unlikely the police will prosecute us now. If they could build a case which they think could win over a jury, they would have charged us; if they don't have such a case now, what can change that in the future – a twenty-ninth accusation against John? A second yellow car I never owned?

But so many other people have said I should insist on a definite clearance letter, including Angela and Eric, that they've convinced me it's vital. How can something as devastating as this rape accusation, with no statute of limitations, be considered over after a phone call from a woman who said she was Eva? Richard admits that clearance letters are given if the police are convinced no crime has been committed, so I insist that one is issued to me. He replies that the police will not take any such action unless they are certain that the accuser is not telling the truth. How certain? At one point he says "absolutely certain" and at another he says "beyond reasonable doubt". I protest that Verity's lies are about as transparent as the police will ever find in such a case. Yet he says that the police still believe that Verity may be telling the truth, so I'll get no letter. My god – still a whiff of smoke.

Richard says Eva's investigation has been thorough, especially since it was a "very complex case". Oh really? I ask whether he has given any thought to the *where* and the *when* of the accusation, and point out that I have my pay records to confirm where I was on all but one day. He doesn't sound interested. How odd. He just says Eva may be disappointed that all her work has come to nothing. My heart bleeds. Shouldn't the police celebrate the news that an adult woman's problems were not in fact caused by horrific abuse decades ago? Shouldn't exonerating innocent men bring its own kind of satisfaction?

He tells me that the police had to conduct more interviews than he can reveal. Now that's interesting. They would have spoken to Charlotte and Jennifer, of course, who would no doubt have told them that Verity's stories were too convincing to be fake. Angela suggests they may also have spoken to counsellors who had "guided" Verity, but the police couldn't say who they were because the counsellors would have been hamstrung by confidentiality requirements. Maybe Verity went to the police and they sneaked a visit to the "experts" to see if they thought she was telling the truth. And of course, there is the ski patrol. We'll never know.

He adds that the police investigation had balance. Let's test this. Police balance in this case, at its very least, would run as follows. Either the woman or the men are telling the truth, but the police can't be one hundred percent sure who. They've finally sided with the men enough to tell us that they're not taking any action against us, but they won't commit themselves so completely to our innocence that they'll write formal letters to exonerate us. They're also not sure Verity hasn't committed a crime by making false sworn statements. Therefore they must keep open the possibility of prosecuting her. Furthermore, in fairness to her, they have to let her know this may happen. Now, has she been given such a warning about possible legal action? You can bet your life she hasn't.

For the police, the guiding question throughout this travesty of an investigation has been "How can we get these guys into court?" Now that we've been cleared, it's turned to "How can we keep this woman out of court?" and their simple answer is not even to consider charging her.

He defends what he calls balance by insisting there have been plenty of cases in which false complainants were charged for wasting police time (though he makes no suggestion of more serious charges or what their sentences were). I respond that if that happens in other cases, why can't it now? I can hardly imagine an accusation more demonstrably false than this one. It's hard to believe that they can still think she may be telling the truth, despite what he said. Perhaps they feel sorry for her because she does have issues, after all. Yet if she's sane enough to be believed for month after month of "investigation", she's sane enough to face some consequences. Angela thinks one of the reasons the police are reluctant to prosecute is that they're embarrassed that her True Believer credibility had them fooled for so long. Now they just want the whole story to fade away.

Our conversation runs to about fifteen minutes, and most of the time is taken up by my railing against police inefficiency and bias. To the guy's credit, he doesn't hang up on me. There's a trace of humanity here I never detected in Eva. When I spit with anger about Eva's attitude back in April, and about her monosyllabic rejection of my very reasonable request to charge Verity, he even concedes I have a point: that wasn't the right way for her to respond. When I declaim against the current system that has abandoned the presumption of innocence in sexual accusations, his silence seems to give support. I can deal with this guy. I wonder if I should take in a copy of my pay records and wave them so close to his nose that he can no longer treat them as insignificant. Was he even aware of this factual evidence before I mentioned it? Of course, Dwight would say this is a tactical mistake, but it's unlikely the police will charge us now, so what's there to lose? Dwight's no longer around anyway. If Richard simply doesn't know I can prove I was in Draketown when the rape supposedly happened, seeing my pay records may get him and the police worried, especially if I drop a hint that I'm either contacting the media or looking at a private prosecution. It won't look good if this incompetence gets leaked.

After I hang up, I start wondering about those cases where Richard said women were prosecuted for making complaints that turned out to be false. I don't know any details, but I'd be surprised if any were as worthy of prosecution as this one. Most likely some young binge drinker had had one tequila too many and got horizontal with a guy who wasn't her boyfriend. To cover herself she invented a rape story, and buried herself too deeply in the lie to clamber out. Fresh forensic evidence soon showed she was lying, and the police abandoned her case. This sort of thing happens. No premeditation, and probably no identifiable perpetrator, so the only people who really suffer are the police. I almost feel sorry for these young women. Verity's crime is far more serious on every level. It has been sustained, deliberate and deadly. It has reached into the lives of named men and put them in fear of their lives. Richard said false accusers have been charged. Then I repeat, why not Verity? Why has the request for prosecution been dismissed apparently without even a moment's consideration?

September 25

Gloria rings tonight. She and Angela chat, and I hear a lot of laughter. I love this new phone atmosphere, free of the worry of jail and financial ruin, when I'm not hovering around waiting for the call to end so that I can ask, "What did she say? What's the latest?" Sure enough, Angela tells me afterwards that they talk about plenty of other stuff. On the subject of Verity, Gloria says that she still thinks she got an ACC payout, and that may have allowed her to put up some money for the partnership in the auction room. I'm not sure about this. John insists that his daughter is a menace to society, and agrees with us that she has to face some consequences. He's rung his lawyer and asked if he can storm into the police station and report a crime. Why not complain that Verity's accusation broke the law because it was a lie and it has turned him into a victim? The lawyer just shrugged it off and told him it won't work, and he should just put all this behind him and get on with his life. Does she moonlight as a counsellor too? Gloria asks how Verity can be forced to face some sort of justice. Angela points out that a private prosecution is still possible, despite what John's lawyer said.

However, if it comes down to "he said/she said" and she gets all sincere and weepy, a jury probably won't convict her. If we go for her, the best way is to pool our resources and get her on the lie that can be refuted factually: not John's case but my case. We have to do something for the broader public good. If no victim ever takes his dishonest accuser to task, but just eases into safe anonymity, these travesties continue and most people keep believing that accusers never lie. The very vicious circle is perpetuated, and innocent victims of True Believers and spiteful stepdaughters keep going to jail. Herb has said that someone has to publicise a test case. Someone has to stop the police giving more innocent men black tickets in this awful lottery. If I don't at least draw the public's attention to this, how can I ever look him in the eye again? I've decided to attach the label "the Herb hypothesis" to this determination to pursue the wider issue of men's rights. Of course, it isn't really a hypothesis, but the name alliterates nicely. The Herb hypothesis is what keeps me going long after my fear subsides.

September 28

The first open skirmish with enemy forces happens today, and it's unplanned. I am walking through the city at lunchtime, and there's bald and beefy Heinrich strutting straight towards me, briefcase in hand. I approach him and say, "Aren't you the auctioneer guy?" His face twists into a joyful rictus and he says he is. Maybe he thinks I've got some business for him. I add, "…from the place where there's a woman who accused someone I know of rape." I don't say I'm the victim, of course. I've never seen anyone's demeanour change so totally so fast. He reddens with barely controlled fury, and says through clenched teeth, "She happens to be my partner." He walks on, but pauses and turns around. He hisses, "…and I'd be very careful what I said if I were you. Very careful." Whew. My heart's pulsing afterwards. When I calm down and reflect on this little exchange, I get a glow of satisfaction. It confirms that he knows about Verity's accusations, and the way he sprang to her defence tells me he believes her. So he isn't a victim; he's firmly in the enemy camp. His reaction was more fury than surprise, which suggests that he already knows that people know. He hurled a threat at me, but it's an empty one. What are his options? Is he going to get some heavies onto me? If he's going to call the cops, what would the charge be? After all, I made a statement of plain fact: a woman at his auction house has made a rape accusation. Maybe my next sentence, before he rudely interrupted, would have been, "Good for her! It's about time a victim managed to pin a charge on that Joyce pervert." The threat just shows he's feeling the heat. He may be worried that if news of this gets to too many people it may affect business, and this may cause friction between him and Verity.

I did something. How things have changed since May 20, when I saw Heinrich in his café and was tempted to approach him but was too scared. What happened today was only a fleeting exchange of words, but thinking back on it makes me smile. After months cowering under a sustained attack, I feel like I've established a small but secure beachhead on enemy territory.

It's a cloudless spring day. Back home I sit under the sun umbrella in our courtyard with a beer. I've been labouring hard under this accusation for months, and I feel like I deserve a little shot of joy. A few twittering sparrows flutter around the birdbath. I'm so happy I almost get spiritual. When was life ever so sweet?

September 30

I have my third meeting with Lionel at The Men's Room. With all the anguish of Verity's threat behind me, we're upbeat. It's like a campaign meeting for the final push. Lionel seems excited at the possibility of getting the story into the media in some way – ideally on television, because he thinks it could be national news if it's pitched right. Then maybe some attention can be drawn to those issues we're both concerned about: abandonment of the presumption of innocence, changes to the Evidence Act and the persecution of innocent people – usually men. Neither of us is so naïve as to think these things can change overnight, of course, but someone has to start.

Walking down Gravelines Street again, I run into my friend Jeff. I slot the Verity story into the conversation – as you do when you're accused of rape. I may have mentioned her actual name, but I don't think so. I hope not, because Draketown can be such a small place.

October 2

Now that we've all finally emerged from the fear, I decide to track down Lance Boyle, the third named man. I go to the library and start to look through all the electoral rolls in the North Island, hoping I don't have to start on the South as well. But I get him on my third attempt. There he is living in a central North Island village miles from anywhere. I'll write him a letter inviting him to share his experience with ours. He may want to put all this despair behind him, but it's worth a try.

October 5

I read *No Smoke, No Fire* (uncannily similar to my title). This is the autobiography of Dave Jones, former manager of Southampton football club. He was hit with an historic sex charge dating back to when he worked in an institution for at-risk young people. Some of them ended up in jail years later, and the police interviewed them in a trawling operation, hanging the carrot of compensation in front of them. The police were clearly keen to snare someone prominent to show the public they were serious about sexual abuse clearance rates. Despite the total absence of corroborating evidence, the case eventually went to trial after an intolerable delay, but the judge threw it out almost immediately when the witnesses' stories collapsed. He criticised the police for taking Jones to court. The whole travesty cost Jones around £400,000, and he remains justifiably angry at the police for this preposterous witch-hunt. In particular, he's furious that the woman from the Crown Prosecution Service – the woman who had coached the complainants in how to lie – received no official rebuke. In fact, she was promoted soon afterwards.

One encouraging aspect of his case was how little mud stuck to him. He and his family did have to endure some boorish and offensive comments from a small number of idiots, but overwhelming numbers of people knew he was innocent and that the so-called case against him was just a police beat-up. Even the enemy – supporters of rival clubs – slapped him on the shoulder in solidarity. Maybe all of us falsely accused worry too much about our reputations. Or maybe that's just what I want to think because I'm about to go public.

October 9

I write a letter to Richard, Eva's superior. I thank him for hearing me out when we spoke over the phone on September 22. I tell him that I am still outraged by two things: that the police will not issue a letter exonerating me and that they will not prosecute Verity. Since nothing spoken really counts for anything, I ask him to correct me in writing if my impression on either of those matters is mistaken, or if the police have changed their minds. I don't expect to hear from him, but it allows me to say that I gave them a chance. The main purpose of the letter is really to let the police know that from my point of view the case which they thought they could bury isn't over, and hopefully to have them wonder what I will do next.

October 10

We run into old friends Paul and Alison, and bring them into the V-loop. It turns out Alison knows Heinrich. She describes him as "completely untrustworthy, dishonest, sly and deceptive." She tells me that Heinrich has been declared bankrupt not once but twice. I see I should have recruited her much earlier, because she is immediately interested in the case. She reads all the diary up to this point at one sitting, and sends me a whole series of emails about avenues to pursue and people to talk to. I have set up a new folder in my email directory to store all her messages. She even sets me homework, with reminders ("Have you done this yet?"). If she demands a salary, this could break us.

She has worked in the legal field, and she has some nuggets about the police. The new head of police for the whole Draketown-Schouten region is Hannah, the woman who has specialised in sex abuse cases. In fact, she led the investigation of a couple of teenage guys in Auckland who boasted online of having sex with underage girls. The police took a lot of flak when they decided they didn't have enough evidence to prosecute. Maybe she has to compensate for what the public sees as a slip-up. Alison also tells me that police operations are underfunded, which means that there just isn't time to investigate properly. This in turn means that police must give the appearance of thorough investigation. The easiest way to give this impression is simply to delay. The same even applies to judges. She writes

> A colleague who is now a district court judge told me about a new judge who was criticised for giving decisions straight away and also criticised for not getting them right because they were too rushed. He took the criticisms on board: he still made every decision before he left court each day but signed and dated them with a two-months-later date and then put them in his bottom drawer until that date came round. Result? Huge praise for correct and considered judgments.

So the trick is to appear to give detailed attention to a file which is actually just gathering dust in an in-tray. It reminds me of the episode of *Seinfeld* in which George Costanza is employed as a minor executive. He is supposed to be working on a customer's file but, having not the slightest idea how to do so, he simply sits at his desk doing nothing all day. But he hits upon the secret of appearing busy: whenever anyone enters his office, he acts bad-tempered, as if the complexities of the file are driving him nuts. There's more than one way to seem to be doing things.

Part Four

October 11

I read in the UK paper the Daily Mail that the reports of a sadistic paedophile ring from decades ago involving politicians and celebrities (which I first mentioned on September 7) have been exposed as pure nonsense. In fact, it's been revealed that police knew two years ago that the credibility of the "witnesses" was close to zero, and had decided to take no further action in what they labelled "Operation Midland". The "witness" who got the whole thing off the ground was a convicted fraudster and former Labour councillor who clearly had a political motive. The politicians who had been investigated were Conservatives, and this man said he was "right up for witch-hunts against right-wing Tories." However, Tom Watson, the politician who later became the Labour Party deputy leader, wrote to the director of public prosecutions to complain that the officer in charge, Detective Chief Inspector Paul Settle, had dropped the investigation. Tom Watson has got into hot water for this political interference. The police have also been lambasted for their incompetence and insensitivity. Head of their list of debauched public figures was Lord Brittan. He had terminal cancer when they interviewed him, and they let him die without telling him that the investigation had been dropped and he had been exonerated. Watson issued a tepid apology for calling falsely accused peer Lord Brittan "evil". The Daily Mail adds that Watson

> showed no sympathy for those wrongly accused of VIP child abuse. Nor did he address concerns that witnesses have been coerced into making

> false allegations. Sir Samuel Brittan, the former Home Secretary's brother, said Mr Watson's apology was inadequate.

This sorry saga has no winners. I should be grateful that our case, complex though Eva always claimed it was, at least was too insignificant to be tainted by political interference. However, all such cases are bolstered by the same phenomenon: the public perception that countless undetected paedophile rings are out there in some murky netherworld, and the perverts who participate are not the rough-hewn weirdos who are used to ending up in court but outwardly normal and successful men astute enough to hide behind a veil of respectability. The public wants this to be true, and the police want the public to like what they are pretending to be doing. In this regard, what a Daily Mail reporter discovered on a briefing note by one senior detective working on Operation Midland was fascinating. It said, "People are not going to like what we have found out." Was this early in the investigation, when the police thought they had a case? No, it was after it had become clear there was no case to answer. We must wonder what people the detective was referring to, and why on earth they would not want to learn that no children had been raped, tortured and murdered.

October 13

I run into my old friend Steve in Gravelines Street, and we have a brief chat. I give the short version of the Verity story, naturally avoiding the name. He says he served on a jury for a sexual assault case just a couple of months ago. The defendant was some young guy the jury had no hesitation in acquitting. Steve said he wondered at the time why it had come to court, because the prosecution seemed to have no real case. Go figure.

I make my first public move. I phone the office of TV One's Sunday programme, a well-known current affairs show. The producer hears me out for ten minutes or so. She's very polite and I'm amazed how much she seems to know about this sort of case. She says that they have someone contact them around three times a year with a false sexual abuse story, but they haven't run a show on the subject for a variety of reasons: it may not be appropriate for the early evening time slot, it may not be interesting enough for viewers or they may not even be convinced the guy is innocent. I tell her about Verity's claim and my rock-solid defence, and I also suggest that maybe they should look at wider issues, such as changes to the law that have ensnared many innocent men. She seems interested, takes my contact details and tells me she'll certainly bring it up at their next programming meeting in about three weeks. I give her a guarantee I won't contact any rival news organisations for a month. It sounds at least a little promising.

October 15

Lance Boyle, the elusive third pervert, phones this afternoon. He thanks me for writing to him. Unsurprisingly, he says that it's been quite an ordeal. He was interviewed back in March – not by Eva but by some male detective, so there was someone in the North Island handling that side of the case after all. He was asked if he knew me or had any connection with NZ Skeptics. Not likely, bearing in mind what he says next. He wishes me well in any action I take, but he has forgiven her. She is a liar, but who among us has never lied? He sends his love equally to me and to Verity. Love is apparently all any of us needs. It is the key we must turn. He says he is on a "spiritual trip", and that "in love there is no fear." This is useful information, because I'd always suspected there was a place without any fear, but was never sure where it was. He says we all have had different incarnations, and who knows what we were before or what will be next? Sigh. All this forgiveness is commendable but it doesn't get any unfair laws repealed. No point hounding him to toss any time, money or ideas into the pot then. Never mind.

October 16

John sends me a copy of a letter he's sent to the New Zealand Police Vetting Service. These days he works as a van driver, and to have his passenger vehicle licence renewed he needs to get a clearance from the police that confirms he has no black marks against his name. He applied for this on May 22. He's worried because his licence expires next week, and without the renewal he loses his job. Understandably, his letter has an urgent and exasperated tone. He writes

> I am now aware that I am being investigated for alleged historic crimes of which I have no knowledge – presumably the reason for the delay in the vetting process...That a malicious false accusation can result in the loss of my job, with no conviction or charges laid, is disturbing and makes a mockery of the claim "innocent until proven guilty".

The Transport Agency, not having received clearance from the police, gave him temporary extensions when he pressed them to do something. On October 9 he emailed the Houwhanga police directly, and asked them if a clearance had been received from the police in Draketown. In reply, they said they could release such information "only to an official body" (John's words).

Back on May 31 we learnt that John and Gloria no longer had police clearance to host foreign students, and no reason was given. This news about his licence just underlines the outrage over his treatment. What it means is that the police have secretly been waving a red flag that has prevented him from leading a normal life for months, perhaps years. This is because of an accusation he would have known nothing about until his interview last month – unless we had told him. Even after the police decide not to prosecute him, he has to jump through hoops to get his record cleared.

October 19

I hear that Lloyd, a friend of a friend, has been so outraged by this case that he has done his own research and found out Heinrich's mobile phone number. He recently rang Heinrich and asked what his partner thought she was up to accusing an innocent man of rape. Heinrich boiled over on the spot, questioning Lloyd's masculinity for hiding his identity and calling from a public phone box. The two had a bit of a conversation. Heinrich said these unspeakable things definitely happened to Verity, and this case isn't over. Lloyd assured him that it is, and that she is the only villain, trying to ruin the lives of innocent people. Heinrich fumed at his treatment by all these nameless cowards. Some have come into the auction house and confronted Verity, which is news to me. He even had an encounter with some guy in the street. Yes, I concede I know about that one, and it's comforting that if I'm just "some guy", he doesn't know Verity's Draketown victim by sight. He said he's just trying to run a business, and Eva will be interested to hear about this harassment. It's as if he, Verity and Eva are a team, like the Three Stooges. He threatened to take out some sort of protection order to stop this aggravation (against all the citizens of Draketown, perhaps), and warned Lloyd that there will be hell to pay if it affects his family. Family? So Verity and Edda are his family now. Not only that, but he will stick by Verity whatever claims she makes. Is the man in love? How touching.

These encounters with Heinrich bring me particular joy. Clearly he's a man who's used to being in control, and he hates this new impotence. He can't put names or faces to his tormentors, and he has to lash out at shadows.

Back in February I wrote that I felt like the protagonist in a grim novel, frantically scraping at the walls of the narrative trying to escape back into the real world. My clearance on September 18 has changed everything. In Woody Allen's story *The Kugelmass Episode,* a magician has the power to project the main character into the plot of any novel he likes. He chooses *Madame Bovary,* and he slots right into the story as an extra character. He even ends up having an affair with Emma Bovary herself. It's a tantalising thought, to be having it off with a woman whose beauty is limited only by your imagination. But at sixty-three it all seems too edgy, and too much like hard work. As I sit in our courtyard with a beer, and with those sparrows fluttering around the birdbath again, I know that the story I want to be in more than any other is the one in which a puffing bald man called Heinrich lashes out at ghosts. It's just so....so right.

October 20

News is out that Mils Muliaina, the rugby player arrested very publicly after a match in Wales months ago, has been quickly acquitted of sexual abuse. The trial barely got under way before the prosecution withdrew and the whole charade had to be abandoned. Some woman had accused him of fleetingly grasping her rear end on a crowded dance floor. Perhaps I am unqualified to comment on this, because dance floors – whether crowded or sparsely populated – and I have little to do with each other. But from what I see on TV shows, it's astounding that anyone can ever emerge ungroped, just because inebriated and pulsating dancers need to clutch onto something to avoid falling over. Muliaina's lawyer called the prosecution case "wholly defective", which puts it mildly.

I write a letter to the Draketown Post about the Muliaina case. I call it preposterous, and warn readers not to assume that this sort of thing doesn't happen here. On the contrary, innocent men have been victims of vindictive or deluded false accusers, and the police are too feckless to abandon far-fetched cases. I want to stir the pot a little: to try to get women's groups to break cover so that we can have a public squabble about abuse statistics. I once assumed educated and articulate people who are committed to righting some perceived social wrong have always done enough solid research to get their facts right. I now see how naïve I was, and on the matter of rape statistics I'm confident I can show the campaigners are dead wrong…if the letter gets published, which is unlikely.

October 21

I send a letter to Malcolm, Draketown police area commander, so the boss of Richard, Eva's boss. It's similar to the one I sent to Richard, in which I complained about the delay and the lack of real investigation. I stress that it's outrageous I haven't been sent a letter clearing me, especially when I have my pay records to confirm my innocence. I offer to come in and talk about this case. I also make a point of mentioning that I am sending a copy to Kelvin Davis, Opposition spokesman on police matters. This suggestion has come from Alison. She says that Opposition is better than government, because they are hungrily looking for things to change. I'm not sure about this. It may be true with some issues, but what politician wants to be seen to take up the cudgels on behalf of men who say they didn't rape anyone? I don't expect Malcolm to do anything, least of all to ask me in for an audience (he is the Pope, after all), but I just want to make sure he knows about the case.

I run into my former colleague Naomi in Gravelines Street. We haven't spoken for a couple of years. She smiles at me as we pass each other, so it would be rude not to stop. I'm no chatterbox and I never knew her all that well, so I fall back on those old, socially accepted staples of small talk: work, family, rape accusations and the weather. My discretion is beyond reproach, because I definitely avoid using the names *Verity* and *Eagle's Nest Auction House*. She says that a friend of hers went through a difficult emotional time recently, and ended up going to a counsellor. She underwent what Naomi called "deep hypnosis" and – what a surprise – this unearthed repressed sexual abuse from her early childhood. I ask how her friend reacted to this revelation. "She was conflicted," says Naomi.

October 23

Alison has found out that Heinrich doesn't have a current auctioneer's licence, and has complained to the appropriate authority, the Ministry of Business, Innovation and Employment. She'd love a prosecution or heavy fine, but the emailed reply tells her only that the MBIE "seeks compliance with the legislation" and Eagle's Nest Auction House has now been warned to toe the line.

October 24

Phone conversations with John and Gloria happen every weekend now. Today John tells me that Charlotte used to prepare homeopathic and Bach flower "remedies", and she gave astrological readings to clients – presumably for a fee. Her contempt for anyone skeptical knew no bounds. Charlotte may even have convinced Verity that NZ Skeptics were a sinister bunch who used the organisation as a front for their paedophilia. Who can say? In this story, nothing is too weird to be counted out.

October 26

The theme at the moment in Draketown and Houwhanga is building a bridge to

Jennifer. John and I have both drafted letters to her, and read each other's. They have similar content: both concentrate on the total lack of evidence that might corroborate Verity's claims, and on the shameful police investigation. As their father, he moderates his tone considerably, but there is no daughter I need to win back, so I play the bad cop to his good cop. I include the first ten days of this diary, and tell her that if she wants to read the whole thing, she should contact me and I'll happily send the file to her. Maybe then she'll grasp the truth. This may mean she forwards it to her mother and sister, or even the police, but I don't see that as a problem.

October 27

John sends his letter to Jennifer, hoping that the old Sydney address is still valid. I keep mine under wraps. John has even told me that the time may never be right for me to send it. I can accept that.

If the Draketown Post were going to publish my letter on the Mils Muliaina outrage, they would have done so by now, so that's a dead end.

October 30

I have another chat with Cedric, my ex-policeman friend. He agrees that I am safe, even though I haven't received a letter, because the police press charges whenever they like the odds of winning over a jury, and if they've cleared me it means they can't build a convincing case – now or ever. But he also agrees that getting the letter is a useful goal to press for, and he is baffled that they haven't sent one. He seems to think that writing those two letters to Eva's superiors was a good move, because it allows me to say I gave them every opportunity to clear me formally, but they refused to do so.

I had thought of four reasons the police haven't charged Verity, and the real reason may be any one of these, or a combination – or none of them. Perhaps they still think she may be telling the truth, for god's sake. In fact, Richard even told me as much over the phone. The second is that they want the public – and especially vocal women's groups – to see them as relentless trackers of perverts. Another clear possibility is that they see her as so mentally disturbed that no legal action would be fitting. The fourth reason is related to the third, but isn't quite the same: if she truly believes these things happened, she has done nothing malicious in making these accusations. Given that she is deluded, what else could she be expected to do? Cedric floats two other reasons I hadn't really thought about. The first is that, after the police finally saw she has been somewhat economical with the truth, she may have been pressured to retract her accusations. I presume he is implying that this comes down to "Retract or we charge you": a sort of compromise to her benefit. The other suggestion he makes is that she didn't retract, but the police just considered the public interest angle: more social damage would be done by prosecuting her than by letting her off. After all, she has a daughter to look after.

All of these reasons have some merit, but not enough to let her off the hook. If she were a man, I know they would count for nothing.

October 31

I send my second complaint to the IPCA. This one acknowledges that its response to the first complaint is the likely reason we have now been cleared, and I give credit for that. However, I tell them that my requests for Verity to be charged and for a formal clearance letter to be issued have been completely ignored. The police won't even talk to me.

November 2

The UK newspaper The Independent reports that Thames Valley police have launched a publicity campaign labelled "Consent is Everything", with a three-minute cartoon video comparing sexual consent to asking someone if she wants a cup of tea. "Just imagine that instead of initiating sex, you're making them a cup of tea," says the voice-over. It urges the tea-maker to "be aware that they may not drink it and if they don't drink it – and this is the important bit – don't make them drink it."

It's cute, catchy and folksy, and it even tries to cover misunderstandings that get men into court, for example when it insists that her saying yes to "tea around your house last Saturday" doesn't mean she wants tea today. The Independent leaves us in no doubt that the sex-tea campaign works for Christina Diamandopoulos, co-director of Rape Crisis in Wycombe, Chiltern and South Buckinghamshire. It quotes her as saying that myths around a "grey area" in consent had persisted for too long. She says that "confusion around consent has been the result of historical distortions," and she is proud to be associated with the campaign. CPS boss Alison Saunders is also a fan, going so far as to say it's a rape myth to claim that sexual consent is more complex than a cup of tea.

Are the tea analogy fans all virgins? The parallel is infantile. So many occasions in life when we need to give consent are more complex than opting for a cuppa, but none more than sexual consent. In most sexual situations, ambiguity is inescapable. Undercurrents and nuances of communication and perception in the primal dance of love and intimacy make sexual consent infinitely more complex than a simple offer of tea. There are grey areas even in those few situations where the silly analogy can be used. For example, what if she enthusiastically drinks the tea but the following morning has bitter regrets and insists she didn't really want it? What if she eyes the teapot provocatively and expects you to read the signs, but doesn't ask for tea and doesn't answer when you ask, because words would be a turn-off? David Gurnham, law professor from the University of Southampton, explained on the Youtube discussion *Blurred Lines* just one of the many ways the primitive drives of our sexuality defy the simplicity of an analogy like this. He says that inequality in an intimate relationship is sexy for some people. He explains, "People deliberately transgress this offer-acceptance model of sex, because they find that sexy. They don't want to have a conversation about *Do you consent?* That is not sexy." More than anything else we do, sex reminds us we are animals.

Some campaigners for higher rates of rape convictions have proposed something even less sexy (and actually had it passed into law in California): replacing the "no means no" slogan with the much scarier "yes means yes". This builds on the notion that consent is a simple matter. It insists that mere silence is no green light and emphasises that consent has to be actively and unambiguously given. But when, how often and to what? A sexual encounter, like a symphony, has a series of "movements" of varying speed and intensity. Does a yes to cuddling mean a yes to kissing and to any crescendo that follows? Like a conductor, do lovers have to pause between one movement and the next?

November 4

I have a long chat with Simon, a former teaching colleague. He knows the bare bones of the Verity saga, but I want him to get more detail. He shakes his head with laudable outrage at the randomness of it and the legal imbalance: that any man can get the winning ticket in this black lottery and the false accuser will likely face no consequences. Something he says gets me thinking. When I tell him about the way Heinrich expresses no doubt that Verity has been telling the truth, he appears at least partly to be on Heinrich's side, because supporting your partner "is just what you do" when she is under pressure. I find it hard to see it that way. It is a matter of fact, not faith, and Heinrich is no position to know what happened…or did not happen. I suppose I'm just hard-nosed about such things. I say to Simon that Heinrich is of course free to support Verity as much as he likes, but such loyalty can have its price: he has to take any consequences of being wrong. If she falls, he may fall with her.

The truth is the truth. Deal with it however you can, but don't deny it or hide it just because it's unsettling. I've come to realise that this attitude shows itself in the way I regard the other two villains in this story: Eva and Verity. When some people hear about Eva's non-investigation, they make excuses for her. "It's the adversarial justice system. The police are after a result, not the truth. That's the way the game is played. It isn't her fault. Live with it." What this means is that it's only natural for a detective to downplay or disregard any evidence that doesn't strengthen the case she's trying to build. In a sense, this is similar to support for Heinrich: just as Heinrich is being loyal to his partner, Eva is being loyal to the police. Put another way, do I think the "investigation" would have been any different if another detective had been on the case? I'm not sure, and there's probably no point speculating. I can only take the events as I find them, and my disdain for her "investigation" isn't softened by the thought that she was doing what the police always do. If Eva has just been doing what the police expect of her, it just means I extend my contempt for her to cover all police criminal procedure.

Then there is Verity herself. So many people, including some who have played major parts in this story and are very much on my side, are convinced that someone probably abused her. Even John doesn't rule it out. They are not suggesting the abuser was John, Lance Boyle or I, to be sure, but some unnamed and mysterious predator way back in her early childhood. This is really a "smoke and fire" assumption. They are almost certainly wrong. I see no more reason to assume she was abused than to assume that my neighbour, my postman or even I was abused. People who suggest that are underestimating the ease with which certain counselling "treatments" can do much more than just amplify or exaggerate the effects of real events, but actually implant memories of events which are *totally* false. Anyone who doubts that should see Elizabeth Loftus' TED talk again. It comes down to Ockham's Razor: when one explanation is probable and complete, no further explanation is needed.

November 10

Everything seems to be settling into a new limbo, with no word from the Sunday programme, and nothing from Opposition police spokesman Kelvin Davis. Of course, Draketown police haven't been in contact either, and the IPCA haven't even acknowledged that they have received my second complaint. Then I get an email from journalist Fred Hurst from the Draketown Post, the one I saw briefly back in March. He is keen to do a full story on the case, and it will likely feature in other Fairfax papers and websites around the country. We arrange to meet next Monday. It looks like the wheels are starting to turn again.

November 12

I download and read an e-book essay by Linda Fairstein: *Why Some Women Lie about Rape*, which is a brief account of false cases. The author is a New York writer and very experienced criminal lawyer who has dealt with many sexual abuse cases. Of course, most of her cases were genuine, but she has "had to suss out more false rape accusations than you would think." Annual figures put out by the FBI confirm that unfounded claims over all criminal categories run between 1.5 and 5 percent, but the number of unfounded accusations for forcible rape are "as high as nine percent." This causes Fairstein untold anguish because it threatens the freedom and happiness of innocent men and wastes police time and resources. She says, "The most appalling is that these falsehoods trivialize the experience of every real rape survivor." No it isn't. The most appalling effect is the one we know for sure, and the one she mentioned first: that innocent men go through a kind of hell.

Fairstein runs through the reasons a woman would lie about being raped. She suggests that the most common reason is "to get back at a man for something." Other women are trying to cover up their own indiscretion, are trying to extort money, or are mentally unbalanced. Fairstein uncovers nothing startling here, but her experience in the field does throw up some interesting aspects. For example, she says that real victims tend to offer lots of detail in their first interview, but liars offer a sketchy outline to start with, then "pile on features as they make them up." This gets them into trouble, because it's hard to keep all the fabricated details consistent. Fairstein also says that if a woman ever broke down and cried during her account, she would suggest taking a break. True victims usually agreed to this, but the liars "stopped their sniffling" and carried on.

One case she mentions in detail reveals a reason I'd never thought of for false complainants not being prosecuted: the man she put in the frame may have something to hide. Sally made a very calm and convincing accusation that Jim, her boss, had raped her. Shocked at being accused, Jim was forced to admit that the two had been having an affair, and that Sally began to demand that he divorce his wife. These claims alone were not enough to convince the police that the rape had not occurred, because many rapists protest that the victim is a spurned woman who seeks revenge. However, her goose was cooked when Jim produced receipts for their air travel together, and Fairstein called business associates who had attended meetings with Jim and Sally in their hotel rooms in various states of the US – and of undress. Confronted with this evidence, Sally broke down and confessed her lies. Fairstein wanted to prosecute her, but Jim opposed this; he felt guilty about his adultery and wanted to avoid damaging publicity. Like many women exposed in this way, she got away with a reprimand. Here is another likely reason false rape complaints are more common than most people believe: there's a whole category of them in which the victim himself doesn't seek justice, even in the unlikely event the police wanted to pursue it.

Fairstein says that some falsely accused men have tried to sue the police "for the damage done to their reputations and livelihoods," without much success. However, here's an interesting outcome: one judge in Nebraska ordered a woman to take out radio and newspaper ads apologising to her victim.

November 16

It is four weeks since I wrote to Draketown police area commander Malcolm, and I'd filed him away as yet another lost cause, but today I get a brief email from him, saying that he has passed my concerns on to someone called Arthur, the police sergeant in charge of prosecutions, who will be in touch with me soon. I wonder if this means my second IPCA complaint has reached Draketown police.

Fred Hurst and I meet. He is attentive through the whole ninety minutes, which he says is a preliminary meeting. He has no apparent doubt about my innocence. We discuss all aspects of the case, including how much Verity should be held accountable for her big delusion. He calls her "ill" and seems to imply that she should face no consequences. He says that he'll read the whole diary in order to get as full an idea of the whole story as he can, even though the final article will have to leave a lot out. He agrees that there's a story here, and sees the main issue as police incompetence and delay. He's limited to an absolute maximum length of 1200 words, so the article is unlikely to touch on the wider issues of "recovered" memory and rape statistics. That's a pity, but I'm not surprised.

November 18

It's confirmed that I will meet prosecutions supremo Arthur at the police station next Monday at 1 pm. It's only now that I recall the name: he was the policeman quoted in the newspaper back on February 5, saying that the French tourists who made a false robbery complaint would be prosecuted for wasting police time. It pays to keep up with the news.

November 23

I meet Arthur, a tall, solidly built man, probably in his fifties, with close-cropped hair. He looks like an ex-Marine who's kept up with at least some of his fitness routine. He has my letter to his boss on his desk, and it looks like he's been making notes on it.

He seems gruff at first, like someone who's been called in to work on his day off. It's clear he's only meeting me because he's drawn the short straw.

His tetchiness soon evaporates and we end up talking quite freely for about an hour and a quarter. He opens by saying that the police have to keep a balance between victim and perpetrator, and it can be hard to do sometimes. I butt in to make sure he realises that in this case I have been the victim and Verity the perpetrator, but he shrugs this off as trivial. He says the police are only human, and they can sometimes get that balance wrong. He insists that false accusers are sometimes prosecuted, but has no idea of figures and doesn't say what charges are laid. One comment he makes about this is a dead giveway. He says that after a complainant's allegation has been investigated, the police can hardly just turn the tables on her and start to treat her as a suspect. "Why not?" I ask. I assume that's exactly how it would work. When I tell him that is the very reason some false accusers in other countries have ended up in jail, he seems surprised. In other crimes, if new evidence incriminates a complainant or a witness, doesn't it immediately transform him into a suspect? He's also just claimed that false accusers are sometimes prosecuted. I'm not sure how this can happen *except* in this way.

Of course, Arthur defends Eva as a dedicated and thorough investigator. He stresses the fact that I was in Houwhanga, so I could have done the alleged deed. No chance of the police going after her then. He doesn't know anything about the facts of time, place and workplace, so I have to fill him in. I point out that I can forgive him for not knowing those details, because he wasn't involved in the case, but I can't forgive Eva. By the time we finish talking, he seems to understand why I feel badly treated, and he even apologises informally. He concedes that I should have got a letter exonerating me, that the "investigation" took too long and that he "would not like to be spoken to" the way Eva spoke to me. He says he will have words with her about the way she deals with suspects. He even promises me a formal letter, and he says he will "review the case". I'm not sure what that really means. It doesn't sound promising, but I have to give him the benefit of the doubt. We shake hands at the end of the meeting. As I leave, I have the impression this guy knows I'm innocent, but he's not free to say so. If this meeting did nothing apart from give him an insight into how abandoned an innocent man can feel, it has achieved something useful.

Thinking about the conversation afterwards, I realise that at one point he and I were talking at cross purposes. My letter, which he had in front of him, mentioned that probably hundreds of people in Draketown now know about the case. That's my estimate, but it's probably about right. He fastened on this because he thought I was accusing the police of having loose tongues and deliberately or accidentally destroying my reputation. I thought he was accusing *me* of having a loose tongue and deliberately or accidentally destroying the reputation of the police and of Verity. He insisted that the police guard any suspect's reputation as well as they reasonably can, and I have no reason to doubt it. Clearly, the notion didn't occur to him that I'm not worried that friends in the V-loop may have told other people about the case.

I also realise that I stupidly forgot to say anything about the prosecution of the French tourists for falsely claiming they'd been robbed back in February.

December 5

Nothing. Nothing from Arthur or from Fred Hurst. I'll resist the temptation to give Arthur the hurry-up, for two reasons. First, my April phone call to Eva showed that it's pointless to try to rush the police. Secondly, if he doesn't front up with the promised clearance letter and what he called a review of the case, it just gives me another stick to beat the police with. I'll give Fred Hurst another week.

December 9

I read the e-book *My Lie* (subtitled *A True Story of False Memory*) by Meredith Maran. It's the courageous and honest account of the writer's gradual acceptance that her father must have abused her, followed by her gradual rejection of the same idea. She edges into sentimentality during the final reconciliation with her father, but Maran is a fine writer whose humour keeps this in check.

For years Maran was living on "Planet Incest", shacking up with a woman who was convinced she had been the victim of a satanic cult, and reading and editing feminist books about "survival". It was a religion, and doubting the dogma was close to impossible. It was only when I read this book that I saw how pervasive and defining such a belief became for thousands and thousands of women. Central to acceptance was the notion of personal truth, in which dreams, hunches and "therapy" stood in for corroboration. *Believe* and *know* became synonymous verbs. Yet Maran had niggling doubts; she remained logical enough not to buy into this idea of relative truth as completely as the women around her did. When the evidence against the nonsense became too convincing to ignore, she had the clear-sightedness and the guts to leave the faith.

The limbo of recent weeks has cooled my anger, and there have been times when the Verity allegation seems a half-forgotten nightmare. Was *I* really accused of historic rape of a minor? But Maran's book makes me angry again and I can't sleep – again. It isn't personal, because I'm no longer under immediate threat. I'm angry as a skeptic. Maran has painted false memory as a period piece, a discredited throw-back to the eighties and nineties. Verity, you are wrong. Dead wrong. Verity's counsellor, you are dangerous and misguided. It's the twenty-first century now. Haven't you noticed? If you're both too lazy to keep up with the latest findings, you lose the right to be sure you're right. What you consider valid has been discredited as surely as alchemy and blood-letting. You are free to believe any nonsense you choose, as long as it stays between your left ear and your right ear. You don't have the right to endanger innocent people based on your outdated personal truth. *People* – not just me. Men, almost certainly. Yes, there will be other victims of other women like Verity. This is the Herb hypothesis again: I can't let things rest just because I'm lucky enough to be in the clear.

December 11

I email Fred Hurst at the Draketown Post. It appears that all the time I was waiting to hear from him, he was waiting to hear from me. With that misunderstanding cleared up, Fred and I will meet next week. He says he's almost finished reading *Dry Ice*, and he already has plenty of questions based on it.

December 14

I finally get an email from the IPCA in response to my second complaint. They apologise for the delay, which they say happened because of an administrative error. They tell me they have no power to force the police to issue me a formal clearance letter or to put any pressure on them to prosecute a false complainant. However, they have forwarded my letter to the police "for their consideration and response."

How ridiculous is this? The IPCA have the power to put pressure on the police to let me know whether they are going to charge me or not, but not to convey that decision to me in a formal manner. Without such a letter, what do I have? Just a terse phone call from some woman who did convincing Eva impressions and told me that I won't be prosecuted now but said nothing about a couple of decades later.

December 16

Fred Hurst emails me in the morning to arrange a meeting for this afternoon. I ask if Angela can come with me, but he suggests she stays behind, at least on this occasion. At the end of the meeting I learn the reason for this.

As I expected, he hits me with some tough questions and objections. I can't tell whether he's playing the devil's advocate on all, none or some of these. The quotes and responses which follow are approximations, but they recall the spirit of the conversation. "Sure, this has been an ordeal for you, but you seem to have revelled in it in some respects. It's been an adventure, and the idea of writing about it excited you." I reply that this is partly true, but I was just trying to make the best of a desperate situation. If anyone had offered to take the drama away by withdrawing the charge, I would have accepted in a heartbeat, just as Robinson Crusoe would have abandoned his own diary in exchange for rescue.

"You refuse to see this woman as mentally ill. You despise her; you call her a bitch." I have every reason to despise her, and I don't like the automatic assumption that she is mentally ill and bears no responsibility for her actions. Perhaps she is, but she appears to lead a normal life, so any claim that she is unbalanced is a hypothesis that needs to be tested.

"Attributing her delusions to a counsellor is pure speculation, yet you seemed convinced of this from the outset." When we're lost in a dark forest, can we be blamed for making out what shapes we think we see? I am still convinced that a quack counsellor is the most likely explanation. I know from Benito and from John that she did see a counsellor (or counsellors) for a long time. Yet I also acknowledge that the assumption may be wrong. I could point out that Fred is also making a supposition – that Verity is mentally ill – but I have to remember this guy is on my side. More correctly, he is on the side of truth, but that amounts to the same thing. This story doesn't have two sides.

"Benito was sure that she had been abused by someone, and he knows her better than you do." Yes he does, but his certainty that she was abused is not based on his knowledge of her, because it allegedly happened long before he met her. Benito is no better equipped than a stranger would be to decide what has made Verity what she is. He just generally buys into the "smoke and fire" connection, in this case and presumably in others.

"Some of your antics in your sleuthing period were rather troubling; it really could be called stalking." I expected this one. I did some things which I'm not proud of, which were out of character and which I can't imagine I would ever do again. Let that testify to the effect an accusation like this can have on an otherwise stable and rational person. People deal with such crises in different ways. For example, Angela wanted to soldier on and try to forget it, but one of my ways of coping was to submit to my urge to find things out. I have no regrets about this. Here's another way to look at it: if I had hired a private detective, wouldn't he or she also have tailed the target's car and eavesdropped on Heinrich's café conversation, and wouldn't that be considered legitimate?

"If you were writing this as a news story, what angle would you choose? What would be your opening sentence?" This is a real curve ball, and I protest I have no idea. All I can say is that the facts of time and place need to be positioned to leap out at the reader early in the piece.

"How can you be sure you haven't met her? Draketown is a small town." Yes, I have almost certainly run into her somewhere. I may even have met her, but that isn't the point. What matters is that I haven't met her knowing who she was. At no stage has anyone introduced me to her by name, because then I would have said, "Oh, you must be John's daughter." No encounter between her and me has given any reason for further contact.

Finally he asks what he seems to think are the two trickiest questions. First, "Are you still sure you want to go public?" Yes, I am. Secondly, he hits me with the sort of question a party secretary may ask a potential candidate for political office: "For your sake and mine, I have to ask you if there are any skeletons in your cupboard." Have I perhaps left any school after a scandal? So this is the reason he didn't want Angela to be there today: I would have the opportunity to come clean man-to-man about anything even Angela didn't know about. I reply that there is nothing. I am squeakily and boringly clean.

So the conversation ends. He has taken an intense interest and is now very well briefed. Of course, he can't just accept what I've said, so the next stage is for him to contact the police, tell them of the planned article and ask for their response. He regrets the fact that these days the police have a designated media spokeswoman who fields all questions. As a very experienced journalist, he fondly remembers the time when he was free to talk to anyone in the police, the city council, anywhere, including the top brass. Now he is bound to "the proper channels".

December 18

Another meeting with Lionel. The Men's Room is closing for the Christmas break, and this is his very last consultation for the year. I interrupt his writing of Christmas cards and cleaning the place up, but he doesn't seem to mind, and we chat for an hour or so. The main topic, of course, is my meeting with Fred Hurst and its likely outcome. When I happen to mention that the police have a documented procedure for dealing with rape and sexual abuse accusers (which I outlined in my July 15 entry), but the accused gets nothing except delays and brush-offs, he makes a very useful suggestion. At some point – perhaps in the news story itself if I can work it in – I should take a constructive line rather than a vengeful one. He means that I should offer to help the police develop a policy for sensitive treatment of anyone accused of sexual crimes. Circumstances have turned me into a reluctant expert, and even Arthur, the sergeant, conceded that I was treated poorly. In this way, something useful could come out of this fiasco, and the police and I would become unlikely allies. I have not the slightest doubt that the police need to halt the swing of the evidential pendulum against innocent men. My concern is that there may be little appetite for such a change. When it comes to sexual allegations, hunting down perverts is the only game in town.

December 23

The New Zealand Law Commission has just released a paper called *The justice response to victims of sexual violence: Criminal trials and alternative processes*. It looks at ways sexual crimes can be streamlined and victims better served. It suggests, among other things, specialised courts for handling sexual cases, because existing all-purpose courts are too unwelcoming for victims. It's all about the complainant, and at one point recommends that the commission "should give consideration to the most effective model for allocating and distributing funding to ensure wraparound care." The report is the length of an average novel, and I struggle through it to see what reference it makes to the rights and the peace of mind of alleged perpetrators. It has nothing except at one point a brief mention that shortening the harrowing delay before a case comes to trial may be of benefit to the accused man as well. No mention whatsoever is made of false accusations. What this all means is that if the present courts make complainants feel uncomfortable, we should make new courts to help them relax. If innocent victims of false accusers are terrified that their lives will be ruined, we should not give a damn.

This section interests me:

> ...complainants will be required to interact with a number of different people fulfilling various roles, which may be confusing to someone unfamiliar with the court process. The diffusion between various different people of responsibility for keeping the complainant informed makes it difficult to ensure complainants are receiving adequate information and support.

So the current problem appears to be too much wraparound – an embarrassment of support for accusers. Victims of false complainants should be grateful that we don't have all those official supporters tripping over each other in their determination to keep us strong.

Granted, we falsely accused are not a part of the commission's brief in this document. I support any reasonable measures to make the trial process more bearable for genuine victims – of sexual and any other crimes – but to be balanced this has to include victims of false accusations as well. Perhaps the paper's most useful section is when it suggests that new sexual charges may need to be brought in. I have implied this before in the section where I outlined the changing definitions of rape. From the complainant's point of view, one problem with the existing system is that if a charge brings a long prison sentence, defendants are almost certain to "defend aggressively", which increases the length and stress of the trial and increases the chance of an acquittal. A lesser charge than rape may increase guilty pleas and conviction rates in genuine cases.

Rape is a charged word. Applying it to sexual offences from which resilient women can easily recover may trivialise "true" rapes which really may destroy their quality of life. Even Australian matriarch Germaine Greer questions the value of the "all or nothing" crime of rape. In a column in The Independent in 2006, she wrote

> No one could take the uncorroborated statement of a complainant as sufficient basis for depriving a man of his liberty for years. But if what is alleged is common assault with a sexual component, and carries a lighter penalty, women's testimony could safely be given more weight. And we would not all be subjected to the silliness of protracted and hugely expensive trials involving inebriated undergraduates who collapsed in bed together and woke up unable to remember exactly what transpired.

The report has two recommendations that should ring alarm bells for the falsely accused. The paper advises that every judge who sits on a sexual violence case should be required to "have a designation to do so." I worry about where such a designation comes from. If it means that the presiding judge has had "training", who administers it, and what does that administrator believe about "rape myths", the number of false accusations and the role of corroboration?

It also says that defence and prosecution should agree on "a written statement for the jury dealing with myths and misconceptions around sexual violence." This looks terrifying for the innocent accused – as if those commonly held myths about rape myths are going to shape policy in order to – heaven forbid – make it even easier to get prosecutions. I doubt that rival figures about false rape statistics or rival theories about "recovered" memories ever find their way into a courtroom, but if they do, this provision does not convince me that the truth will get a fair hearing. For one thing, even defence lawyers will likely know nothing of the theories of psychology that may benefit their clients.

December 29

Fred Hurst emails me an update of sorts, indicating that the police tactic appears to be to hurry up and wait. They have told him that Sergeant Arthur G is "reviewing the file" and they are reluctant to reveal anything before until he gets back from holiday early in January. They also say that they don't want to comment while this case is still open as an active IPCA file. That seems odd, because the IPCA doesn't seem to be doing anything. Are the police stalling deliberately? Fred says he'll keep both the police and the IPCA honest by pressing them for any progress.

January 11

I get a letter from Arthur. It's quite long – 700 words or so – but it doesn't say much. It does confirm something all of us have suspected: that the investigation took "hundreds of hours". Many of the general points he makes are very reasonable: that these historic sexual cases are difficult because of the lack of witnesses and the clouding of memories. He insists that false sexual complainants are sometimes prosecuted, but he gives no numbers and, more important, says nothing of what charges are laid.

His comments about historic sexual cases in general misses the point about my specific one, so it's hard to see his letter as anything but a cop-out. He just doesn't see how different this is from a normal sexual allegation. Most outrageous of all is that it makes no mention of a formal letter of exoneration, even though he told me when we spoke in November that he would ensure that I got one...unless he thinks I think this is it.

Of course, he defends the actions taken by Eva. In fact, I was a very lucky boy to have her carrying my file. He says that "the New Zealand Police does not take any allegation of sexual assault lightly." Yes, I wouldn't challenge that; in my case, that was precisely the problem. He adds that sexual investigations are conducted by "trained investigators in accordance with a prescribed set of investigation guidelines and Detective Braun is such an investigator." Does he really think this should be some comfort to the accused?

"Rape myths" are clearly part of those guidelines. In fact, the letter even mentions one specifically, when Arthur writes that "genuine complaints can have elements of inconsistency, inaccuracy or even concealments of some facts, and this can be due to trauma." As countless tweets have told us, there's no perfect victim. In her specialist training, I wonder what would have happened if Eva had said to the instructor, "Wait a minute here. Maybe some complainants who take years to report are genuine, but wouldn't some just be after revenge, or attention, or maybe compensation?" or "Where do those stats on rape come from? They look doubtful to me," or "Reasons to lie can linger just as long as reasons to tell the truth." Would she still have been handed her certificate? Only if she did a retest in her summer holidays.

Arthur points out that Eva correctly offered me the opportunity to make a statement denying the accusation, an opportunity that may have played a role in having me cleared. But of course. Does he mean to imply that some investigators would not? Am I supposed to be grateful to have been granted my rights?

If what he says is true, this may mean that Charles' immediate advice back in February to get a good lawyer and front up to Eva was even more useful than I realised at the time. Some people told me not to utter so much as a single word to the police, with or without a lawyer. Maybe if I had taken their advice and refused to make a statement, I could have ended up trembling in front of an unpredictable jury, as so many falsely accused have to do.

January 14

I have my third meeting with Fred Hurst. He has seen my letter from the police, and it seems to disturb him a little. His first comment is that he suspects that it was not written by Arthur at all, but by the police legal team. This suggests the police are starting to get their wagons in a circle, and the job of making contact has been taken out of Arthur's hands. Fred asks if I still want to go public. The apparent determination by the police to leave me dangling for the rest of my natural life for a crime with no statute of limitations does not mean they actually intend to charge me. Fred agrees with me that if they couldn't build a case by September 18 they will not be able to build one in the future. Rather, he suggests that withholding the official clearance letter is a ploy to be used if and when the case goes public. If they formally exonerate me it will not allow them to say to the media and by extension the public, "Don't listen to this guy. We kept his file open because we still believe he may be the pervert Verity says he is." So maybe the police are finally concerned enough to get tactical.

This means that when Fred asks me whether I still want to go public, the new danger is not about prosecution but about an increased risk of mud sticking. He calls my determination to go public "reckless". But never mind, I tell him: it's a risk, but a calculated one. I also mention that when I recall the dark thoughts that haunted us for most of last year, during which I faced the possibility of a totally destroyed life, the prospect of a little mud seems tolerable.

He says this is a very interesting story, and he clearly wants to run it, but not at the expense of my safety or my peace of mind. I know that if I were to change my mind and call off the news story, he would have no regrets about all the time he's already spent.

He mentions one interpretation of decisions made behind the closed doors of the police station. It is a possibility I've also thought of, and my ex-policeman friend Cedric suggested it back on October 20. Maybe after the interview with John, Eva saw the truth, came back to Draketown and said, in effect, "It's all hot air. The woman is lying." The police then turned on Verity and told her she'd better retract her accusations voluntarily or they would charge her. This would be a praiseworthy action – a compromise of sorts – but I think it's unlikely, especially considering that Arthur told me he found it odd that such a thing can happen in investigations overseas.

January 15

Not a happy day. I can't focus on my lesson. Fortunately I have to teach for only half a morning, because we have a whole-school outdoor activity. Fred's comments from yesterday have reminded me that the police have terrifying power, and a semi-retired teacher has no weapons against it beyond the light of publicity and – at least on its best days – the IPCA. I admit that it's tempting to give it all up. Fred's concern for me starts to play on my mind. I respect his judgment, and the judgment of two friends who have both told me I am being foolish. So I have to weigh up one reckless and two foolishes on the one hand against…what? Against an action that is right and necessary.

One tells me I should forget about Verity and just get on with my life. By pursuing the story I am becoming obsessed, and this raises my hackles a little. I'd rather call it a commitment, and don't we all need to commit to something in our lives? In fact, since the verbal clearance in September I've been sleeping fairly well, and I teach and examine and play tennis and walk and cook and go to quizzes. Verity-related tasks don't take much of my time or thoughts. So how am I not getting on with my life? A job remains to be done, and I want to finish it. Unlike an obsession, it will have a finite end.

It would be easy for me to dismiss their advice with a huffy accusation that it's all right for them, because they aren't in this position, and if some unknown woman had threatened to destroy them in this way, they wouldn't be so quick to settle for a telephoned vindication from the police. But this would be smug and unfair. In this diary so far I've mentioned three people who have simply forgiven: Lance Boyle, Benito and that poor Australian man I mentioned way back on February 22. Perhaps my friends urging caution would act the same way.

Those three concerned supporters – the reckless and the foolishes – make a case that's so compelling that I can come up with just five counter-arguments which reinforce my commitment to carrying on. The police letter suggests their likely tactic will be to throw mud at me – or to discreetly encourage the public to. The two friends who called me foolish have warned that John or Jane Doe will do no more than read the headlines and connect my name, my face and the word "rape". Maybe I'm naively optimistic here, but I'm not so sure. Their pessimism may overlook what will be unique about this story: this is the first case that Fred or I know of when a man accused of a sexual crime will have sought publicity himself. That is a fact that even a distracted reader can pick up. Why would Mr or Mrs Doe think a guilty man would do that?

Another thought was prompted by a comment Fred made yesterday in a different context. He said that in more than twenty years in three local high schools, I must have taught thousands of local people – and he's right. The story will likely go national on the Stuff website, but my name and face will mean nothing beyond Draketown. As for local people, many will say, "Hey, I know that guy. He taught me. The bastard gave me a detention once, but I can't imagine him doing anything like this." Many people in Draketown know me or know of me. They will find it hard to believe what the police will want them to. Deciding I am not a paedophile because I come from a respectable background may not be very rational, but it has the great virtue of being an irrationality that works in my favour.

I also think about the reaction of people who are already in the V-loop. If the police "investigation" hadn't taken thirty weeks, not many friends and acquaintances would have known about it. But the way it's turned out, they do. Right from the outset I haven't been timid about telling the story, which means that most people who know me know about this accusation. No mud at all appears to have stuck. When they express such total support for me, and such outrage at the accusation, am I to assume they are just being polite and are whispering behind their hands about my outrageous perversions? Not a chance.

Here is another angle. Many people know someone, or know someone who knows someone, who has had an experience something like mine. When they read about my case, surely they are likely to say, "Thank god that someone is finally speaking out against cases like this." This is especially true of men, who realise that it could happen to any of them.

My final justification (or rationalisation) is hard to explain, but I'll do my best. I'm not sure that those who think I should fear publicity are really worried about mud sticking to me or my family. I think they're worried that some readers will think the same as they do: that I am naïve to think that mud won't stick. So what I have fear is not mud itself but others' expectation of mud. Put another way, the danger is not that some readers might think, "That guy's a paedophile" but "How naïve that guy is to think readers won't think he's a paedophile." But surely we can't navigate our already tricky course through life worrying about what our friends may worry other people may be worried we're not worried about. That should be clear enough.

One of the cautious friends has said that if I go public, all kinds of weirdos "will emerge from the woodwork." The relevant questions are these: who are these weirdos, how many of them are there, what will they actually do, will what they do have any effect on us, and why should we be concerned about them?

Just when I really need it, I get emails from two other friends in the V-loop and advocates of the Herb hypothesis: my Swiss friend Fridolin and Tony, both of whom urge me not to let things rest after a throwaway vindication by telephone. Like Herb himself, Tony even says he is prepared to contribute financially if I want to take out a private prosecution against Verity. This kind of support buoys me, though I wouldn't want to use anyone else's money.

Onward we go, then.

January 16

I have almost finished drafting quite a detailed response to the police letter when Alison makes a useful suggestion: I should send Arthur a very short "warm-up" email containing a handful of important questions about my current situation and about the police investigation. I should give him a week or so to respond, then send the long one. I come up with these, but don't send them just yet:

> Regarding my current status:
> You say my file has been "refiled". What does this mean?
> Will I still get a formal letter of exoneration? If so, when?
> Without such a formal vindication, will any "red flags" be raised if a prospective employer or anyone else requests a police clearance?
>
> Regarding the investigation:
> Did Eva check Verity's attendance records at Westchester High School and our local high school?
> Did she check my pay records (in effect, also my attendance) at Redwater College?
> If she did either or both of these checks, did she do so before or after my interview?
> How did Verity physically identify me?

I suspect that I stand little chance of getting a reply to the first group of questions, and almost no chance of getting a reply to the second, but at least I can say I gave the police the opportunity. Alison is right that these questions about school attendance are crucial, because that is where any proper investigation should have begun. Eva almost certainly made no such checks, and it must be embarrassing for the police if newspaper readers learn of that omission. Whatever the outcome of these questions, they will have served a useful purpose: either someone at Draketown police presses Eva about this aspect of her "investigation" or, at the very least, they are something for the police to stew on.

John and Gloria phone tonight, and we have a long talk, most of it on a common theme: what cynics might call confrontations, but we would prefer "approaches". Big news is that John and Gloria have booked to come here and stay with us in March, and it is almost certain that one or both of them will approach Verity and/or Charlotte, and perhaps also Benito. This has to be done effectively and safely, and we float all kinds of approaches to the approaches. I favour a more direct style, i.e. just turning up at their doors one after another. They are more circumspect, especially when it comes to Charlotte: they would prefer to make phone contact in advance and suggest a meeting in a public place. It's difficult even to decide who takes part. Do I go with them, for example? Probably not, though I'd love to. It's important that it doesn't look like a vigilante group, because we don't want either of them to call the police. In the case of Verity, a female has to be there, because a twenty-ninth sexual assault allegation against John plays no part in our plan – not that the police would pay much attention to it now. We make no decisions, and will talk about the options in more detail when they come down. This and the media exposure are the two big events on the horizon. I've made another decision: the diary will end when both of these have played out.

I'm mainly talking to John, but Gloria demands the receiver at one point because she has a pressing question to ask: "When we come down, can we use your binoculars?" I tell her that I've forgotten all about them, but yes, I'll dust them off.

We also discuss the puzzle of Jennifer, Verity's younger sister in Sydney. The letter John sent months ago to the business she has sometimes worked for on contract was returned unopened. That seemed odd to me, because don't all of us always open letters? Gloria suggests that Jennifer saw the New Zealand stamp and perhaps the Houwhanga postcode and figured out who it was from. But how strange that a formerly balanced and stable young woman would not at least want to know what her father had to say, even if she screwed up the pages in rage after she read the contents. The other possibility is that it just didn't reach her, because she doesn't work there any more and the firm can't contact her.

Jennifer matters. A long time ago she didn't believe Verity, and John thinks she can be won back. If she can, this may even sway Charlotte if her love for her daughter isn't totally blind. Verity's poisonous fantasies need to be isolated, and the chance to get John's more stable daughter to know about Verity's untruths is another reason to continue the campaign. I'd love to make the noble claim that getting Jennifer reconciled with John is my only motivation, but it isn't of course. Having Verity's sister and perhaps her mother know the truth about her is a satisfying outcome. Jennifer and Charlotte may not even know that Verity has accused anyone apart from her father.

January 18

I can add cousin Jackie to the supporters who are advising caution. She doesn't seem to be totally opposed to going public, but she suggests I shouldn't do so yet – not until after John and Gloria visit and make their approach. Once again she warns me about genies not going back in bottles, but I'm not sure about this analogy. All our lives are full of genies that can't go back into bottles and open doors that can never be closed again…not to mention locked doors that can never be opened...and open doors that we don't even notice.

She also suggests that she takes on the task of tracing Jennifer, hopefully to a physical address. The Gold Coast is a long way from Sydney, but at least being in the same country is an advantage. This would allow someone in the V-loop and in Sydney to go and talk to her. As an amateur sleuth with at least a little experience now, I operate under the assumption that it's only in movies that doors get slammed in faces. Recently some Jehovah's Witnesses confirmed that for me. Seriously – I asked them.

January 20

Information from Fred convinces me that, having no other strategy, the police are determined to stall. He tells me that the IPCA has "no open file" on me, even though the police offered this as a reason not to comment earlier. He says that he has finally got a response from the police communications manager, after several attempts. She simply said that Sergeant Arthur has no more comment to make about my case. Fred told her that he "will have to go higher," and that he will therefore communicate with the Draketown district superintendent tomorrow.

Fred tells me that if the police continue to say nothing the story can still go ahead, just with a comment that the police were asked to make a statement but declined to do so, but he reminds me that nothing happens without his editor's authorisation.

He also tells me he has an appointment with Lionel this week.

January 21

I email to Sergeant Arthur the brief questions I compiled five days ago. To my surprise,

I get a response just a few hours later, but all it tells me is that I've probably become a nuisance...though I can't be sure even of that. Not one question is answered clearly, and most are just ignored. He makes no response at all to any of the specific questions about Eva's "investigation". He repeats that accepting Eva's offer to make a formal statement back in February was a very astute move. He usefully defines "refiled" as "placed into filing" and adds that no further work is being carried out on it, presumably because that would require removing it from its cabinet once again. He says, "I do not believe you have anything to be concerned about as far as any future vetting process would be concerned." I'm cheered by the knowledge that he tentatively holds this vaguely optimistic opinion about my chances of being jailed for...oh, a decade or so.

His most puzzling sentence is "I have provided you with a dispositive style letter explaining the result of the investigation." This appears to be referring to the long letter I received from him on January 11, but I have no idea what *dispositive* means. Bill Gates doesn't know it, because the word is underlined in red on my computer. Is this Bluespeak? I check my fat 1980s Collins dictionary and it isn't there; there is an adjective form of *disposition*, but it's *dispositional*, and the meaning doesn't fit here anyway. My more recent Concise Oxford does have it, and defines it as "relating to or bringing about the settlement of an issue or the disposition of property," so it seems to be a legal term. But he says his letter was not dispositive but dispositive style. So the sentence now means that Arthur believes that his original letter was written the same way that letters attempting to settle property disputes are written, but that it wasn't in fact such a letter. Either he doesn't want to communicate with me any more or he's under the mistaken impression that he's bought our house.

January 22

I have another meeting with Cedric, my ex-policeman friend. He's read the January 11 letter and my detailed response, which remains unsent. I will still send it, but it appears that Arthur has finally unfriended me, so I am not sure who in the blue sanctum should be the lucky recipient. It has to be someone superior to him: either the Draketown commander or the area commander for the whole region. I want to check that Cedric agrees with my comments in that response. Have I been right about police procedures? Was I too disparaging about their omissions in my case?

He is as puzzled as I am about...almost everything. He also doesn't know what "refiled" means, and suggests that the word was chosen in order to obfuscate. It certainly can't be interpreted as a clearance. He adds that giving me a formal letter of clearance should be a straightforward matter, and the fact that Lance Boyle received one confirms this. He has no idea how Verity would have physically identified me, and he agrees that identification is an important issue in law. He agrees that the delay in clearing me was outrageous, and just shows that Eva had not done the required investigation to realise how different this was from the usual sexual accusation.

I am most interested in what Cedric has to say about one point. In my draft response I wrote, "I suspect that police districts may be assessed in crime categories that include clearance rates for sexual violence but not for false accusations." Was I being too cynical? He responds that, on the contrary, I "pretty well nailed it." If anything, I underestimated how thoroughly police districts are obsessed with statistics and crime clearance rates in definable categories. Officers in one police district in Auckland congratulated themselves on lowering their burglary rates by having almost all such crimes relabelled as thefts. When a whistle-blower revealed this, police at a very high level tried their hardest to suppress the facts, and a full investigation was never held.

Cedric says that getting me convicted would be filed as positive, not getting me to trial would be neutral, and prosecuting Verity or a false accuser would at best be anomalous, awkward, hard to file. More likely it would be scored as a negative. The police gain no credit for exonerating innocent people. That no doubt explains why Richard, the other sergeant I spoke to over the phone on September 22, said that Eva would be disappointed with the result. Hundreds of hours of "investigation", only to find that the complainant has not suffered so much as an accidental and fleeting nudge in a crowded bus. What diligent detective would not be shattered by such a grim discovery?

Justice classified can be justice denied. Arthur's long letter said that "no two cases are ever the same and each complaint comes with its own circumstances." Quite right: justice is an individual matter. But he seems to miss the significance of the very point he makes. This police fixation on clearance rates for categories of crime shows that when the circumstances of a particular investigation make it unique, they just carry on trying to pigeonhole it.

Cedric ends by encouraging me to go public. He says the tale needs to be told, and not just because it will expose police inefficiency, a complainant's delusions and widespread misconceptions about memory and false allegations, but for a more fundamental and universal reason: it's a good story.

January 25

A breakthrough in the subplot. A source I can't reveal (from the dark gumshoes) has found out that Jennifer still lives in Sydney somewhere. She married an ex-Draketowner, Michael, and they have two children. We know her husband's surname, and that Charlotte went to stay with the family over Christmas. She can happily visit any of her three grandchildren. John can visit none, and has to rely on determined people he's never met just to find out how many he has.

January 28

An interesting piece of information has been under my nose for over two weeks, and I've been too blind to see it. The top of Arthur's letter has my file number, and it just dawned on me that the first part of it looks like a date. I ring the police to ask if I can know the date when an accusation made against me was first lodged. The police receptionist asks me the number, and immediately confirms that the first part is in fact the date. So there it is: Verity first made this formal accusation with the police on February 27 2013.

This means that the police didn't make contact with me – or presumably any of the accused – until almost two years after she made the accusation. No wonder Benito said back on April 10 that Verity hadn't mentioned it for a long time. Dwight assumed the file would have been gathering dust, but this seems like an amazingly long time. Maybe the police gave it such low priority because they could see from the outset that Verity was just spinning yarns, or maybe this is just normal.

The police delay does nothing to diminish my anger at her. It means she had almost two years to doubt, to reconsider, to sidle sheepishly into the police station and say, "Look, I was going through a bad time, and I guess I was just looking for people to blame. I'm not so sure now that any of those men did anything to me." The police know that women with "issues" are always under pressure. They would have understood.

January 29

I've been sitting on my detailed reply to Arthur's "file review" for over two weeks now. It's clear he's said all he thinks he should, so my reply needs a new recipient – but who? I decide to go right to the top, and I address it to the Draketown-Schouten area superintendent, Hannah. She almost certainly knows about the case already, because Fred told me police silence at the medium level compelled him to go higher. It's early morning. The police station is open, but no one is on the counter. I drop the envelope a little behind the glass slide, with just that second of lingering apprehension I always get before I send something that may be life-changing: that little pause before clicking the mouse or dropping the letter in the slot. I can't get out of my head John's recent warning not to "tease rottweilers." Finally I summon the nerve to let go of it, and even give it a nudge so that it's safely inside the blue sanctum.

January 31

We – that is, a group of investigators including John and Gloria, Jackie, new recruit Anne C from Christchurch and I – seem to have found Jennifer's husband. The search I did with the name I was given for her husband yielded no results, but I changed the spelling of the surname, and of the Christian name to the less common Micheal, and something came up: a New Zealand news item about a bad sporting accident in 2012. The competitors were brothers, and the older one suffered a terrible injury to his leg. The name of the younger one, who emerged largely unscathed, matches the adjusted spelling of both names. His age is given as 34, so he would be 37 now, or three years or so older than Jennifer. It seems about right. The report says the brothers are Sydney-based, and a search in the Sydney telephone directory throws up the address and phone number of someone matching initial and surname. A photo search produces snaps of him relaxing at home, including two with young children. It all fits.

So we have the likely means to contact Jennifer now. But what do we do? Of course, it's mainly John's decision, and there are times when he says that if she wants to hide away, that's her own business. Jackie also tells me that thirty thousand people disappear in Australia every year, and some of those do so because they just don't want to be found. It's a fair point, but this is a special case. Most of those people who choose to break contact with their families probably do so because they are victims of complex family dynamics. It appears that Jennifer once had a happy relationship with her father (and Gloria even got along well with her), but it was suddenly poisoned when her sister finally convinced her that the outlandish allegations were true. Jennifer's standoff stems from a single series of related lies. John has always said that Jennifer was the rational one, and his unhesitating reply when I asked if Jennifer could be won back was "Yes." Recently he has been suggesting that the time may not be right yet, and that she may not be ready.

But if not now, then when? Or, put another way, if not next week, why in ten years? Reconciliation is possible, even likely, which will mean father and daughter can be friendly again early enough for John to witness his grandchildren's early years of development, at least from a distance. Jennifer has already believed dangerous untruths for at least three or four years, so perhaps it's time someone shook her and forced her to listen. Without some assertive and intrusive action to show her the truth, what would ever change her opinion?

Angela and I talk about the best approach. Uncharacteristically, she wants to be more direct. My idea is to contact Micheal. As he is outside the immediate family, he would be more likely to listen…or to read. Angela thinks that Jennifer may see such an approach as underhand – an attempt to present a case against her sister on the sly.

We don't even know whether any approach will be by letter, telephone or personal meeting. We have to see what John favours. Of course, he may veto all our ideas, but I hope not. What can be worse than the status quo?

February 1

The first anniversary of the start of this awful saga. Angela and I are feeling upbeat these days, but not so upbeat that we'll be getting Verity and Eva round for celebratory tea and cakes. What a year! Nothing like that will ever happen to us again, and how gratifying it is that the terror is behind us and we can determine for ourselves how and when the story will end. It's a trite comment, but this personal 9/11 has made us stronger.

February 6

I have a long talk with John and Gloria about approaches – mainly to Jennifer. We'll scrap the letter to her which I've been sitting on for months. We decide that I will write a short letter to Micheal at his place of work in Sydney. We think we know where they live, but we aren't sure they haven't moved somewhere else. If we send the letter to the home address and get no reply, we'll never know whether it was because they read it and decided to stay incommunicado or simply didn't receive it. For this reason it needs to be his work address, which we know almost for certain. I'll include a printout of the first ten days of this diary.

February 7

A link catches my eye on the Dear Prudence agony column of the Slate website: "Help! I'm scared of telling my husband I was molested as a child." The correspondent says that she was sexually abused by a school janitor when she was six. She says, "I repressed the memories for a very long time and only shared them with my therapist." Oh really? Any mention of repressed memories close to the word "therapist" has to look suspicious. Yet the advice offered by Mallory Ortberg ("Prudence") suggests that if she harbours any doubts that the correspondent's abuse happened, she is being very discreet about them. All "Prudence" says is that it isn't necessary to tell the husband, and she suggests that there is no fault in letting this event remain a secret "between yourself and your therapist for the rest of your life." Maybe it happened, but we would be naïve not to doubt it. This is surely evidence that not all the dodgy therapists have been flushed out of the woods yet, and not all journalists are suitably sceptical about them. As David Aaronovitch and his producer discovered when researching the podcast I mentioned back on August 4, false memory syndrome cannot yet be consigned to the annals of historic bad science.

February 8

The chance of being whacked for a sex crime when you are just going about your business seems to be even higher in the UK than it is here. Back on October 20 I wrote that rugby player Mils Muliaina was mercifully acquitted of sexual assault for some non-incident in a nightclub in Wales, but it went as far as a jury. Now Anne C sends me a link to a story in the Daily Mail UK about a man who was flung into what he called a "Kafkaesque nightmare" after momentarily brushing against "an award-winning star of film, TV, theatre and radio" in a packed Waterloo Station – Britain's busiest – at rush hour. She claimed that he sexually assaulted her "penetratively" for two or three seconds, and police traced him through data on his travel smart card. It sounds like a lot of work. Who says women's complaints aren't investigated?

The "case" would be laughable if it weren't so desperately sad. The complainant failed to identify him in an identity parade. CCTV cameras showed that he didn't even break stride, and the two made only momentary contact. She added that she also suffered a violent blow to her shoulder. One camera showed that in his left hand – the "penetrative" one – he held a newspaper, and in his right he held a bag. Regrettably, the famous woman cannot be named, but the man has been identified as Mark Pearson, 51. The reason he was named is that the Crown Prosecution Service actually took the case to court, where a forensic scientist engaged by the defence testified that Mr Pearson passed the actress for "half a second."

His lawyer said that the prosecution had slowed down the CCTV footage to make it appear that Mr Pearson had enough time to commit the crime. I wonder if a single rogue CPS official would be responsible for such evidence manipulation, or whether several of them sit in committee and decide if there is a case. Slowing the recording down must have been a conscious decision by someone unscrupulous enough to see that playing it at normal speed was no way to get a conviction. As in my case, a result mattered, not the truth. I've already mentioned the rape liars and their counsellors, but why are these crooks from the "Clown Prosecution Service" not put in front of a jury as well?

Mr Pearson commented, "One of the many frightening aspects is that this could have happened to anyone." Not strictly correct, because the victim would have to be a man. The article adds that the UK CPS has come under fire recently for its uncompromising pursuit of "perpetrators" accused by liars and fantasists who would have appeared credible to no one with a scrap of common sense.

This case had nothing to do with pursuing justice. It appears to have been taken to court because of a CPS witch hunt against innocent men, in line with a policy to get as many prosecutions as possible against sexual predators. Guilty men, innocent men – that's of little account. Mr Pearson received public support from Erin Pizzey, author and founder of the first shelter for victims of domestic violence. She said, "The CPS have recently been targeting men and it has got to stop…At the moment women seem above the law. They can do it in domestic violence cases – simply pick up the phone, no evidence required, and have a man removed from his family and his children – and they can do it with rape, too."

Yes they can, and in saying that I'm not referring only to cases like Verity's accusation against me. I've mentioned before the new, wider definitions of rape: it is about power rather than actual sex, and some would say that it isn't any less devastating if it's metaphorical. If this is true, then women can also be guilty, and that means the crime this unidentified actress has committed is attempted rape. She has sought to use her power to destroy an innocent stranger. Yet the consequences for her are…nothing. Not so much as a slap on the wrist with a wet train ticket for Waterloo. Despite Mark Pearson's acquittal, the perpetrator may even be eligible for a cash settlement.

Some of the headlines proclaimed that Mr Pearson's life was "ruined" by this charge. Given that he was acquitted, this goes too far. I've written many times that I am not particularly concerned about mud sticking to me if details of Verity's accusation go public, because only fools would think I'm guilty. The same applies to Mark Pearson, only more so. Everyone except his accuser and that select handful of women who hate all men would surely see him as a victim, even an accidental hero. Absurdly, his case went to trial, and no doubt this was an awful strain. I have no reason to doubt his claim that he had to have therapy, that he still has anxiety attacks, and that what he endured was "a form of mental torture sanctioned by the state." Of course it was, and this is unforgiveable. I don't wish to make light of what he has gone through, but what surprises me is that no one has mentioned the money. He got the result he hoped for, the one he had every reason to expect, but I presume no one reimburses him for his legal costs. With a preposterous case of this kind, the bill for innocence is enough of an outrage.

When I do a search for information and opinions about the Waterloo incident, I can find plenty of links, but not a single one to a women's group such as Women Against Rape or Rape Crisis. On the former's website I do find a video clip with their spokeswoman snickering at any suggestion that far-fetched sexual cases have been prosecuted. She says it's time the notion that the pendulum has swung too far was "put to bed." I also visit the news page of the CPS website, which has all kinds of snippets about the successful prosecutions they've brought, but not so much as a syllable about this very newsworthy case. How very odd.

February 10

I mail the letter to Micheal, Jennifer's husband. As I mentioned four days ago, it has a brief outline of what Verity has done. This part makes no reference to the accusation against John. I enclose a printout of the first ten days of this diary, and I also include my backup email address (not my main one) and an invitation to contact me for more detail. Why wouldn't he? Jennifer has surely told him what she believes is true about her father. Until now he would have no reason to doubt it, but surely this counter-claim would set him thinking, and he'd be burning to know more. I know I would.

It's strange to think that Jennifer, who is apparently very different from her sister in so many ways, appears similar in one important respect. She was supposedly rational, open-minded and balanced, but she has embraced Verity's story as unquestionably true. This is despite Benito's claim that for a long time, and much to Verity's anger, she was sceptical. Her refusal to have any contact with her father shows that this change is like a literal conversion to a new faith or cult. If she is to be de-programmed, I hope the approach through her husband will get the process started.

My sister Carol, who lives in New South Wales, tells me that under Australian law grandparents cannot under normal circumstances be denied access to their grandchildren. Grandparents are quite rightly assumed to be an important part of any child's upbringing. It throws up the question of how long Jennifer is (or, hopefully, was) intending to keep John out of her children's lives. As they get older, how is she intending to respond to the questions, "Will you tell us about your father, Mummy? Is he still alive? Where does he live? Can we see him?" I assume her response will be to say that he is dead.

February 12

Nancy, the daughter of my Christchurch friend Barry, works as an investigator in Australia. For some time she was trying to track Verity's sister down for us, but it was clear that Jennifer was trying to stay under the radar. Now that Nancy knows the married name, there is no stopping her, and within minutes she has found a statement of purchase for a North Sydney suburban property. The names are definitely right, so we know that Jennifer and Micheal bought this three-bedroom home recently for $1.3m. If his work contact fails, we can try this. Nancy even asks, "Do you want me to do a door knock? I'll be there at the end of February." Quite an offer, but I suggest we wait and see if we get a response from Micheal.

February 16

I read an online column in the UK newspaper The Telegraph, in which Martin Daubney offers some reflections on the "case" from Waterloo Station, when Mark Pearson didn't slow down sufficiently to sexually assault an unnamed aging actress. With its formidable Crown Prosecution Service out of control in its persecution of innocent men, matters in the UK appear to be even worse than they are here. Intolerable though it has been that the Draketown police took seven and a half months to clear me and apparently gave not a moment's thought to prosecuting Verity, if my "case" had happened in the UK it would probably have gone to court.

Daubney says that "the demonization of men is now an entire industry where lucrative academic, journalistic, charity and even governmental careers are forged." He adds

> At ground level, men are being made to feel increasingly hated by a society and legal system that seems to say "all men are capable of evil – if only you look hard enough"... Who can blame an increasing number of Men Going Their Own Way– the MGTOWs – who feel sex is so risky they are giving up on sex and dating altogether?

This has always been normal for men getting on in years. Even the great womaniser Jack Nicholson famously said in an interview for Newsweek after he turned 65, "It used to be that I didn't think I could go to sleep if I wasn't involved in some kind of amorous contact or another. Well, I spend a lot of times sleeping alone these days. That's different. And very liberating." But when young, red-blooded heterosexual men start thinking this way, it's a little scary.

I've only now learnt that this phenomenon has become well enough established that the acronym is now pronounced as a noun ("migtow"). There are now enough migtows that some heterosexual women are starting to worry that men are no longer showing any interest in having a relationship with them. At least, that's what some male bloggers are claiming.

February 18

I get a brief message from Fred, saying only that he hasn't heard back from Draketown-

Schouten district police boss Hannah. I also hear from John and Gloria. They've found out from Draketown police that Verity laid the accusation against John on the same day that she accused me.

February 21

It's obvious by now that I'm going to get no reply from Verity's brother-in-law in Sydney, but no matter: real sleuth Nancy D confirms that when she's passing through Sydney next week she'll knock on Jennifer and Micheal's door at number 9 just to confirm that it's the right place. With a bit of luck she'll even get to speak to her. Nancy asks what she should say and not say, but I tell her I trust her judgment.

February 24

In a brief message that only confirms police silence, Fred writes, "So far the police have not cleared you (i.e. they haven't said they believe the accusation was false) and that makes my position very difficult. I'm sure you can see that." He says he's going away for two weeks. It's unreasonable to expect him to be answering questions when he's on the beach in Hawaii or wherever, so I don't reply. But to be honest, I don't see it.

At least, not until I give it some more thought. For the police there are two connected issues: Fred's planned news story and my clearance letter. In our conversation back in November, Arthur assured me I'd get a letter, but this has apparently been overruled by someone higher up. At first I assumed this was a tactic that would allow the police to say for the news story, "Well, we haven't given a formal clearance because we still think this guy may be guilty." This would enable them to explain away all the delay and inefficiency of Eva's "investigation", in effect by claiming that the case is so complex that it still hasn't finished. If they officially cleared me, they couldn't make any such claim and their inefficiency would be exposed.

This comment from Fred may suggest that the lack of clearance and the refusal to talk to him are even more sinister: that they are tactics to prevent the story from being written in the first place. They are thinking that Fred cannot write about a clearly innocent man who has been treated unfairly, because the case hasn't gone to court yet. That's how I now read it. With the "case" still ostensibly open, perhaps it is legally dicey for him even to write a story. Or, at the very least, he is concerned that if it still goes to court and I'm convicted, he appears naïve to have believed me. This is outrageous because it means that the only reason Lance Boyle has a written clearance and I haven't is that he is behaving himself by loving and forgiving everyone. It has nothing to do with likely guilt.

If I'm right about all this, when Fred says his position is difficult he presumably means that he can't proceed with the article, now or ever, as long as I haven't been formally cleared. In chess there is a situation called zugzwang, when your current position may be strong but any move you make with any piece weakens that position. The problem is that the rules compel you to move, so there is no escape from changing the status quo. The police are in a kind of zugzwang. Tactically the safest thing for them to do is nothing, i.e. neither to give a formal clearance nor speak to Fred Hurst or anyone. The problem for me is that this isn't a chess game, so they don't have to move.

How bitterly ironic this is. After all those months contemplating whether I should or shouldn't, it now turns out that I can't even if I want to. There is no way I can get my story out there. This also means that when I spoke to sergeant Arthur, I made a tactical mistake telling him that I was intending to go public. If I hadn't said that, I would have a formal clearance by now and that would allow Fred to go ahead with his story about an innocent man.

Police are silent in the UK as well. The Daily Mail reports that Sir Bernard Hogan-Howe, the head of Scotland Yard, has blatantly refused to apologise for the shameful treatment of war hero Lord Bramall over unfounded paedophile claims as part of the discredited "Operation Midland". Bramall's home was raided as he was eating breakfast with his terminally ill wife, and police took months to clear him of the manifestly ludicrous allegations. Hogan-Howe said that the police apologise "only when there's good cause." He added, "There are difficulties with apologies to suspects." Tory MP Tim Loughton pushed Hogan-Howe in this case, insisting that the lack of an apology "undermined the competence and credibility of the force and public confidence in the police."

February 28

I get the email I've been anticipating from Nancy D. She's done the door knock at number 9 but no one answered the door. She tried the neighbours on both sides, and got no reply there either. When she was walking up the drive of one of these neighbours, she could see a woman with curly hair seated in the kitchen area of number 9, and thought the woman saw her. Nancy knocked again, but still got no reply. She took the registration number of the car in the driveway, and will do what she can to find out the owner, but access laws to this sort of information have changed, and this may not be possible.

At first I thought how odd it is not to answer the door when a stranger knocks. Paradise pedlars always canvass in pairs, so Nancy couldn't be taken as one of them. It seems rather pessimistic about people and about life in general that you assume a stranger at the door means trouble unless you know otherwise. Then I had an idea. I think Jennifer had a baby not long, so maybe she was breastfeeding. Even so, it does seem odd. That stranger at the door could turn out to be the person who transforms your life by bringing news that your great aunt Gwendolyn has tragically died but left you her house in Mayfair and her shares in General Electric. When Jackie heard about this, she said that if someone knocked on her door she would always answer out of curiosity, despite curlers, breastfeeding or anything else. People are strange. Not just strange but exasperating. Now someone else is going to have to visit number 9.

March 5

I phone Houwhanga tonight, and we talk about their forthcoming visit. John and Gloria are disappointed that Nancy missed Jennifer, but John, in particular, seems unenthusiastic about someone trying again. He says, "I think Jennifer needs more time." I just don't get this. She's believed lies for years already. Without someone muscling in and forcing the issue, what's to stop her believing them for ever?

Maybe there is another side to John's apparent unassertiveness. I've been thinking all this time that, having lost one daughter, he would be desperate to reclaim his other one. What I may have overlooked is how hard it may be to forgive a child who once believed you were guilty of such depravity, even if she was not the one who made the accusations. He hasn't said that's the way he feels, but if he thought "to hell with both of them," I would understand.

John also mentions something I confess hadn't crossed my mind: the number of women who would have known about these unmentionable deeds if Verity's claims had been true…and yet said nothing to anyone. This would include the supervisor at the swimming pool, the helper at the playground and – most critically – Charlotte. How could Verity's own mother have had no inkling that any of this was happening or, even worse, have known about it and not reported it? I've seen Verity's car in her mother's drive, and I've even seen her mother holding fort at Eagle's Nest, so they seem on good terms. Yet if Verity genuinely believes she was repeatedly raped through her childhood by her father and his friends, why isn't she still so furious about her mother's inaction that she refuses to have anything to do with her?

March 18

On the recommendation of Lionel, I pay a visit to Hugh, the lawyer who supports the Men's Room. He happens to be Monty's partner. He says that cases broadly similar to mine are a large part of his "daily grind". I ask about ways of prosecuting Verity.

He agrees that a private prosecution may amount to throwing good money after bad. He says that perjury is a possible charge, but notoriously hard to prove. I get the impression that people lie under oath all the time, and nothing happens. I ask whether there is any point just heading into the police station and saying, "A crime has been committed against me. Please investigate." He looks doubtful, but when I give him the bare bones of the Verity narrative, he says that in my case it may be worth a try, and I would certainly have nothing to lose.

He warns me that the police are lazy. "Not overworked…or underfunded?" I ask. "Not really," he says. "Lazy." Interesting. In my reflections just after my hurry-up call to Eva back on April 7, I mentioned that of all the possible explanations for the delay, laziness was the scariest. This is because the police would look at the accusation but not the specific facts of time and place and just casually say, "Hmm, tough one. We'll just let a jury decide." Hugh agrees that this happens, and it is a tragedy for the accused man, no matter what the outcome in the courtroom.

Hugh says this institutional laziness means that for the police to take any serious interest in my accusation, I would need to have done all the work for them, and present my case on a platter: names of witnesses who can testify where I was and when, my pay records and so on. He says this can only work if I have plenty of time. "No problem," I say. I've already done most of that work anyway. He suggests that it may be a good idea to lodge my complaint in another town – maybe take a drive over to Finchkey, for example. This is the best news I've heard in a while, and I'm keen. Maybe I'll do it next week, and John can come with me. All four of us could go, and make a day of it. A scenic drive, picnic with friends, visit to the police to lay a charge against the daughter of one of your fellow picnickers – how I love the Kiwi lifestyle!

Hugh also asks whether I've got my file from the police. He says I'm entitled to this under the Freedom of Information Act. A little sheepishly, I admit I haven't. How did I miss this angle? He even says I'm entitled to get a copy of Verity's statement. That should be a gold mine. I immediately apply to the police for all the goodies I can get. They tell me it will take a month, because everything is stored in the North Island. Time is never a problem.

Part Five

March 22

We pick up John and Gloria from the airport. Their first day is a time for all four of us to get reacquainted and make small talk.

March 23

This is it: the day when something finally gets done. Maybe, after more than a year, we will get some responses, if not answers. The first plan is for Gloria to talk to Verity's mother, so John and I drop her off at Charlotte's house and wait down the road a little in the car. No one home. Then we go into the city and Gloria strides into Eagle's Nest, courageously willing to improvise depending on who's there to confront. But the place is as dead as a tomb, with no browsers and only the woman who occasionally helps out sitting in the office.

We drive to the McDonald's car park to regroup. John decides to contact Verity, so we leave him alone in the car as he calls her mobile phone (a supporter found out the number months ago). This is the most important move of all, so why didn't we talk it through? After a couple of minutes he emerges and says he got through to her. He told her he's in town for a few days, and would she like to meet him for lunch one day? He says he kept a civil and measured tone. She was initially taken aback to hear from him, but recovered and said she would think about it. All very civilised, but that's not what I wanted. It just invites her to do nothing and have us wait for the remaining time of John and Gloria's visit, each day asking ourselves, "Will she make contact today?" But she won't, of course. John seems happy with his hands-off policy, as he has been with Jennifer. He's put the ball in Verity's court, and it's her turn now.

I can't see it this way. John needs to be more insistent. Someone has to make Verity see that she cannot fabricate such a monstrous story without suffering any consequences, and someone needs to force-feed Jennifer the truth. Verity has managed to avoid the wrath of the law, and to me this invitation to phone is just a way for her to avoid the justified wrath of her family as well. John can see I'm not happy with this, but what can I do? I may have been catapulted into his family, but when all's said and done, she's his daughter, not mine. I also accept that I'd be naïve to think he and I would agree on every way of handling every issue this awful saga throws up.

I don't stay despondent for long. We take Gloria back to Charlotte's house, and she hits the jackpot this time. John and I wait in the car just around the corner, and she's in there for about twenty minutes. An actual conversation then! This must be good news.

As soon as Gloria re-emerges we whisk her home fast for a debrief, before she's forgotten any of the details. Still outwardly cool but relieved it's over, she gives us her report. The only feeling Charlotte has for John is contempt. She refuses to see him or to have any contact with him, and clearly has encouraged both girls to do the same. She rejects any suggestions that Verity or Jennifer has treated him unfairly.

Charlotte still gets counselling help herself, because she says when John wrote to her last year about Verity's lies, she took the letter to her counsellor, who handily labelled the tricks John has been using to manipulate her as "minimisation". Charlotte concedes that she knows Verity has accused John of abuse, but she says she knows none of the details. She regards that as a matter between father and daughter. Nonsense. It's a matter involving father, daughter, two other innocent men and their families, so she may as well join the crowd…though I'd be astounded if she hadn't already played a crucial role.

Charlotte admits that Verity has been "ill". She concedes she has had counselling, but tests confirm she is not crazy. Charlotte avoids the direct question about whether she believes John abused her, saying only that his attitude to her was "not healthy". She objects to being put in the position of having to answer such a question. When Gloria mentions me, Charlotte implies she knows nothing about the allegation against me, and shows little interest. She knows my name, but only as someone John used to stay with when he came to Draketown. Gloria mentions the prosecution I'm threatening, but Charlotte quickly says that a private suit is ridiculous and wouldn't work. How does she know this? Has she been worried enough to find out, maybe after I spoke to Benito? In answer to the question about how I could have raped her daughter in

Houwhanga when we haven't even met, she says she is "not even going there." That makes two of us – I wasn't there either.

Gloria stresses the seriousness and extent of the allegations; she doesn't hesitate to say "rape", while Charlotte uses "abuse". Can it be that she really thinks it was just groping, or is she secretly ashamed of the horror of what her daughter has alleged? She says, "I am a mother with a sick daughter who is now much healthier." So that is her duty, and any innocent bystanders who get caught in the family crossfire are just collateral damage.

Charlotte's naivety confirms how much this whole outrage has to do with open skepticism on the one hand and, on the other, a combination of family loyalty and gullibility. She implies that she and Jennifer have heard from Verity at least a bowdlerised account of her sexual abuse (what Eva related to John was so depraved it was sickening), and decided that was all the explanation they needed for Verity's "issues". End of story. This means that, just like Benito, Charlotte and Jennifer assume not only that what smells like smoke must be smoke, but also that they know for sure where the fire is. An idiom that really does fit here concerns chicken and egg. To the family, Verity's mental instability is an effect of her real abuse, where we see the fake abuse as an effect of her instability – whose cause we cannot pretend to explain. Charlotte and Jennifer and Benito see Verity as a delicate and immaculate little bird savaged all her life by her father. It never crosses their minds that her "issues" may have a more complex cause and that he, Lance Boyle and I are the real victims.

For Charlotte, the sexual abuse neatly explains everything, not just Verity's "issues" but also what she calls John's bad behaviour. She's still furious that John criticised her and Verity for reading positive thinking books and using homeopathic treatments. She claims that he regularly shouted at them (which seems incredible to me), and that the girls were always miserable at the thought of visiting him and Gloria in Houwhanga. Gloria says she should look at the happy photos of their times there, but Charlotte says she knows how photos can be manipulated. Outdoorsman John is no techie. Is she suggesting he had them professionally photoshopped?

Gloria asks whether she or John can contact Jennifer, but the answer is a flat "no". She then asks Charlotte to ask Jennifer to contact her – not John. She says she will ask, but not to hold her breath, because contacting Gloria would in effect be contacting John. I doubt that she would even pass this request on. Charlotte bears no ill-will towards Gloria, and even gives her a hug. However, John is Lucifer incarnate, and she ends by saying that Gloria "has no idea how much he has hurt people."

So it's a mini-religion. Find a simple and reassuring dogma that conveniently answers the questions which are important to you, and stick to it. Pay homage to the professional priests. Convert the people around you who need to be converted, and spurn all attempts by outsiders to question the True Path. Never doubt; doubt is hard work and it offers no comfort that can rival simple belief.

In the early evening, John gets a call on his mobile phone from Verity's phone. But it isn't her. It's Heinrich, who raves at him while John listens passively. John had better leave "his family" alone. He screams that he knows a lot of people in Draketown, and John had better watch out. He expresses a desire for John to "rot in hell". That's always struck me as an odd curse. If everything they say about hell is true, wouldn't mere rotting be a luxury? Anyway, there was no mistaking his overall tone.

Interesting. When Verity heard from John a few hours earlier, she wasn't hostile at all. It seems that when Heinrich heard about John's call, he snatched her phone and vented his fury. This makes him seem to be the manipulator in the relationship. Perhaps this means he was behind the rape claims. God only knows. The good news is that his anger seems to confirm that their ship is starting to take on water.

March 24

We drive to Finchkey, which is the second-biggest town in Draketown province and half an hour's drive west, and I leave the others out in the car while I report the crime. This is the fifth conversation I've had with a police officer since the outrage began, and this guy would get the prize for the least approachable if it were not for Eva's matchless performance. In what follows I've used quotation marks at times. That doesn't mean I can recall every word, but my reconstruction recalls the spirit of the exchange as accurately as I can remember it.

He starts to write the details in his notebook. I'm carrying a folder with a copy of my pay records and the text of my interview with Eva, and I tell him that it contains the evidence showing not just that Verity's accusation isn't true, but that it cannot be true. He doesn't even glance at it. He says, "Can you wait a few minutes?" He leaves the room and while I wait for him to return I have nothing to do but look at the only two posters on the wall of the interview room: one that boasts of the twenty-five languages for which the police can supply interpreters, and another that has a list of types of interview questions with examples: "open", "closed", "probing" and so on. This seems odd. Do the police sometimes pause an interview to look at this chart?

This guy certainly needs no such help. When he saunters back in after five minutes or so, he has me figured and knows exactly what to do. He's reading from a printout and says, "I see you've reported this alleged crime before." I protest that I haven't – not as such. I have told other police in Draketown that the complainant's allegation is false, and that I think she should be prosecuted. He shrugs, so to his mind it amounts to the same thing. I can already see this will go nowhere. He says I still have an IPCA file open. This is the second time the police have used this excuse. "No," I say. "That's not true." He asks what evidence there is that she was not telling the truth. I reply, "The evidence is in this folder, if you would just –"

He has not the slightest interest. I may as well have been asking him to read a research report on elk migration. He says with a smirk, "You keep trying to distract me with that folder. I just want you to tell me why I should believe she hasn't been telling the truth…Look, hundreds of the cases we have to look at are about the way people perceive things. Like traffic accidents. The two sides involved in an accident look at the event in totally different ways." I want to explain that the facts in my folder are the real issue and the only distraction is the ridiculous comparison he's making between Verity's crime and a road accident, but I know a lost cause when I see one. He says, "The police in Draketown have looked at the victim's accusation and chosen not to prosecute you…or her. That's the decision." To him it seems like a fair compromise, and he looks at me as if to ask what I'm complaining about. My natural courtesy trips me up and I thank him for his time. Damn! I thanked him for refusing to investigate a crime. Why am I so polite with these awful people?

I go back to the car and join the others. I don't tell them very much about what happened, only the bare bones. But on the drive home I can't help dwelling on this exchange and on the way it relates to all the exchanges I've had with the police. I try to get to grips with that peculiar mindset that the pertinent facts of Verity's accusation – the time and the place – are of absolutely no importance. None of the five I've spoken to at length have appeared to understand that this is not a normal case of he said/she said. They seem to be such slaves to procedure that they can never escape from the general to consider the particular. It could be that they are just covering each other's backs, but I have another idea which is less sinister but more stupid.

If the police buy into the whole catalogue of rape myths, which they seem to, then no evidence that discredits a complainant's story would ever be enough to prove the event didn't happen. If the attacker was tall, blond and spoke with a Swedish accent, and the suspect is a short and balding Bangladeshi, this is discrepancy caused by trauma. They may have to let this suspect go, but someone must have raped her, because why would she not be telling the truth? Looking at my pay records, or any other facts, therefore serves no purpose. The police now see that John, Lance and I committed no crime, but they will *never* see Verity as anyone but a victim.

So here's how it all works. I can't be sure of this, but I'm almost sure. The police say they sometimes prosecute false accusers, but the truth is that this almost never happens, and when it does it is for one of those minor cases in which no perpetrator is named. No woman who tries to destroy a man's life ever faces consequences. I strongly suspect, then, that no final clearance letter is ever written. The fact that false accusers don't get charged justifies not giving unequivocal clearances, and the lack of such clearances justifies not charging false accusers. Neat.

March 29

We farewell John and Gloria. It's been an enjoyable week, because the two of us have got to know the two of them a lot better. We couldn't always escape the allegator in the room, but it's surprising how often she played no role in what we did, where we went and what we talked about. The visit didn't deliver many of the answers I'd hoped for, but it wasn't useless either.

March 30

The BBC has another story on Operation Midland, the trawling project conducted by the Metropolitan Police in the UK which took 80,000 police hours and resulted in no charges being brought (an investigation which I have referred to several times, beginning on September 7). The single accuser, whose outlandish allegations ended up costing the British taxpayer £1.8 million, will of course suffer no consequences whatsoever: he continues to be called just "Nick", he avoids prosecution and it doesn't cost him a penny. Harvey Proctor, a former Tory MP who had been accused and investigated, claimed that he had been "pilloried" and that the investigation had "irreparably ruined my life". In a sometimes tearful statement to the media, Mr Proctor called on the four Met chiefs to resign. This is a perfectly reasonable request, but Peter Saunders, spokesman for the National Association for People Abused in Childhood (NAPAC), commented:

> I don't think what's happened with Harvey Proctor has been entirely helpful to the whole process, but I hope it doesn't in any way deter victims and survivors - or complainants as Mr Proctor would call them - from coming forward where there are serious allegations.

"*…as Mr Proctor would call them…*"! Until a court finds their claims have merit, it's what they are, Mr Saunders. The point at which Mr Proctor started to break down in his press statement was when he was struggling to say that the manner of the investigation made him feel "disposable". Yes, that's it – that's the adjective that's eluded me. That is exactly how I have felt, and the way the police, media and spokespeople like Peter Saunders talk so glibly about "victims" and "perpetrators" just helps confirm the assumption of guilt that underpins these investigations. The accuser gets everything, including a positive label. The British police manipulate the language in other ways too. In their defence of Midland, they use the peculiar Bluespeak term "non-recent abuse", presumably because "historic" may suggest that it is over and done with now or – heaven forbid – just a story. I presume their investigations are handled by all sorts of officers, including both non-male non-uniformed and non-female non-plain-clothed.

Two investigations into Operation Midland will be held, but Harvey Proctor is surely right when he predicts both will be toothless. He says

> The outcome of these two fake inquiries will be a whitewash and a cover-up and a deliberate exercise in kicking the issue into the long grass until the architects of the scandal have moved on to collect their pensions.

April 11

National sexual abuse awareness week is due to roll around again, starting on May 2. Last year I did what I could to tell the other side of the story, by fronting up at the street stall and by writing that letter to the newspaper, in which I questioned the statistics. Of course, my challenge went unanswered. This year I'll try a different approach. Today I write an email to the "Nine to Noon" show on Radio New Zealand. I very briefly outline what has happened to me and suggest that as part of their coverage of sexual abuse during that week they may want to interview me. I point out that I can discuss matters that go beyond my actual case to broader issues such as the role of counsellors and the statistics war. This sounds fair to me. Why not hear another side?

April 15

I find out that the UK Crown Prosecution Service actually has guidelines for handling false sexual claims, and I manage to track them down. The fact that they exist at all is good news, because it means that the CPS at least concedes that false allegations happen. The bad news from the point of view of the falsely accused is that everything is stacked against prosecution. These guidelines confirm that the default attitude to an allegator is that she is by definition a victim, either of the assault which she alleges or…just of life. Pity can be a virtue, but not when it becomes policy.

The guidelines confirm that two charges are possible: perverting the course of justice (the more serious one) and wasting police time. It says that prosecutions for both offences "will be extremely rare." That seems odd. Why make such a prediction in a policy guideline? Why not just wait and see? Or is it not a prediction at all, but a piece of advice to prosecutors to make sure they drop charges except when the lies are too blatant and cynical to ignore?

Reading this document, I see that there are at least three obstacles to prosecuting anyone who lies about rape. The initial assumption, even if the complainant's claims appear untrue, is that she isn't lying. Apparently false accusations will require "sensitive handling", because true allegations may be retracted for many reasons. Investigators are encouraged to treat discrepancies in her story as a normal symptom of trauma. It stresses that all suspected cases of false accusation must be handled by specialist Rape and Serious Sexual Offences (RASSO) units. I have little doubt that what it takes to be a member of such a unit is to believe in "rape myths" with evangelical zeal. In fact, the document goes on to stipulate that "prosecutors must not resort to using myths and stereotypes", which it usefully lists as a series of bullet points. One myth is that victims always recall events consistently.

Let's assume the first hurdle is cleared, and the liar is exposed as such. Even then she remains a victim. The guidelines say that false allegations are made by fragile people, suffering from "mental health issues, learning difficulties, age, maturity and substance abuse issues". An allegator may be "a person who is vulnerable in the context of a relationship." All these issues mean that even when it can be confirmed that she has fabricated the whole story, prosecutors must have sympathy. Granted, her accusations could have destroyed a man, but was she old enough, smart enough, sober enough or sane enough to have formed such an intention? Did she even realise that her allegation was untrue?

For the tiny number of false allegations that come this far, there is a final and related hurdle to prosecution: public interest. This means that even if the accusation is manifestly untrue and the complainant is considered to be sufficiently in control of her own actions to be held responsible, investigators may consider that prosecuting her seems inappropriate or would do more harm than good. For example, perhaps she simply misunderstood the repercussions, or perhaps the case was abandoned before the victim of her accusation suffered any dire consequences.

These guidelines are not without merit in some cases, but they appear to be applied by default, which means that very few false complainants are ever prosecuted. This leads to the vicious circle I've referred to before: the low prosecution rate yields statistics that give the impression false accusations are rare, which reinforces the CPS policy of avoiding prosecution. Another report, to the UK director of public prosecutions by Alison Levitt, labels as a myth the belief that false sexual accusations are rife. This seems odd, because I'm not aware that many people ever make that claim. It acknowledges that false allegations do happen and that they can be devastating, but gives an assurance that they will be prosecuted "robustly", as long the evidence is clear and prosecution is deemed in the public interest – which sounds less robust than the manner in which suspects are pursued. It goes on to report that in the period covered, there were 5,651 prosecutions for rape, but only 35 for making a false rape accusation.

What should this tell us? The report implies that this proves false accusations are rare, but of course it does nothing of the kind. It is better seen as evidence that any investigators determined to prosecute false accusers – if any would be so bold – have too many hoops to jump through to bring a case to court. What the report goes on to say appears to confirm this. It consistently downplays the significance of false accusations. It mentions "alleged false accusations" and describes the complexities of the cases, such as the accuser's youth or mental state. It leans over backwards in its attempts to soften the crime of lying about rape. In one case study it suggests the complainant, who fabricated evidence, may have done so to increase the chances of her true rape account being believed. It also claims that frequent previous rape claims should not be used to diminish a complainant's credibility; it may just mean that she is vulnerable to being raped. All this confirms the general rule that male criminals go to jail, but female criminals need help.

The forgiving attitude shown by CPS towards false complainants is far from unique. Other organisations in other countries are determined to have them seen as anything rather than a crime. A report from the Australian Institute of Family Studies by Liz Wall and Cindy Tarczon suggests in its conclusion that false reports are not really false, only labelled as false, and the real harm is that such labelling deters victims from reporting:

> The stereotype of the "common" false allegation and the rape myths that contribute to incorrect beliefs about sexual assault, have negative consequences for victims and society in general, in that a willingness to report sexual assault is hampered for fear of being disbelieved or of being blamed for the sexual assault. What may be more useful is to understand more deeply, the contextual factors that play into a *label* (my italics) of false allegation.

This is yet another report that stresses the myth of the assumption that false rape complaints are common. I'm not sure where this comes from, because my perception is that most people believe false complaints are not as common as they really are. A cynic might even claim there is a conspiracy to keep a lid on the truth about the numbers of false complaints, especially in the UK. In 2010 two British lawyers, David Wolchover and Anthony Heaton-Armstrong, tried to get a breakdown of the numbers of false complaints by offence type, quoting "a huge number of established cases of concoction" in rape accusations, but they were turned down because separating out the data would be too costly. So where does the CPS get the evidence that makes it so certain false rape complaints are rare?

What I find most disturbing about the CPS report is that it seems to make no distinction between two very different groups: complainants who may have been lying but the police weren't sure enough to prosecute, and complainants who could be shown to have lied but were considered too vulnerable to prosecute. If almost none of either group are ever prosecuted, that cannot be used as evidence that false complaints are rare, so it is blindingly obvious that false reports must be more common than prosecutions suggest. We just don't know how much more common. What we can confirm is a new rape myth: that in the UK in the twenty-first century a woman who makes a rape complaint will not be believed. In fact, CPS policy has shifted so far towards believing complainants that the chance of a conscious liar being exposed as such is close to nil. Getting justice in false complaints would require a rogue prosecutor who throws away the current rule book.

Here in New Zealand the number of sexual assaults reported nationally rose from 2334 in 2001 to 5232 in 2015. A TV report calls this "not necessarily a bad thing" because it allegedly shows that victims – especially survivors of historic cases – are becoming more determined to report sexual abuse. The police have changed their policies and are now "more empathetic". Detective Inspector David Kirby, manager of the Adult and Child Protection section of New Zealand Police, says "There is an increased confidence that if [victims] come to us, we will believe them…and investigate their complaints." Yes, I know about that. In fact, the sea change in police practice guarantees that complainants will be believed long past the time when common sense should have shredded their stories. They will suffer no repercussions, no matter how outrageous their claims, how much stress they place on suspects or how much taxpayer money they waste.

May 2

Nothing from Radio New Zealand, from Fred Hurst or from the blue citadel. But just as I am about to bike into town to ask what has happened to my request to get my file under the Freedom of Information Act, I check the mailbox and there's an envelope edged with the blue chevrons of the New Zealand police. It's from someone in what is called the File Management Centre of the Draketown-Schouten Police District. FIA Requests are supposed to be handled within twenty working days, but it's now taken almost double that. Apparently my open-ended request for "a copy of everything I am entitled to relating to the historic rape accusation made against me by

Verity Rigby" has sent the File Management Centre into the sort of panic you might expect if I'd asked its Palermo division for everything it had on the Cosa Nostra. The letter politely informs me that "the request is for a large quantity of information or necessitates a search through a large quantity of information, and meeting the original time limit would unreasonably interfere with the operations of this agency." It asks for an extension until June 2.

Good grief! What has this woman put the police through? I have visions of Rigby House, a huge separate building to house Verity's statements, with rows of filing shelves reaching to the ceiling and nervous officials dreading that a request like mine will send them scooting around on forklifts for weeks. With uncommon politeness, the letter adds that I have the right to complain to the office of the Privacy Commissioner about this delay. No chance: I'm grateful for the apology and the assurance that the stuff will come. But where will we put it all?

May 3

It's sexual abuse awareness week, and right in the middle of the city, in the same spot as last year, there's the stall with balloons and banners. I lock my bike to the nearby post and approach the two women on duty. I say, "Do you want to hear about false rape complaints?" Before they have a chance to respond I add, "Well, I'll tell you." As I'm an exceedingly polite and mild-mannered person, at first I tell them that of course there are real victims of sexual abuse, and nothing I'm about to say should suggest I don't support the work they're doing. Then I outline the usual things about false rape figures, dodgy counsellors, the loss of presumption of innocence and all the rest of it. I'm surprised at how little they seem to know. For example, they had no idea about changes to the Evidence Act. However, they do nod in agreement when I mention the police obsession with statistics. I give them a one-minute outline of my case, and I feel some of the old rage welling up through my pores again. To their credit, they're paying attention and don't seem to take my anger personally, but when one says that the problem with actual abuse is that it has wide repercussions, I do become just a little…assertive. I point out that in my case the woman has formally accused her father of recruiting his friends to have sex with her when she was young – they both grimace at the depravity of this – and if she thinks that such an allegation doesn't have repercussions on the lives of large numbers of people she is sadly deluded.

They say that their director would be keen to hear my story, and I oblige with my contact details. But she isn't keen at all, and she won't get in touch, of course. I point to the banner at the front of their stall, about raising awareness of sexual abuse. I say that when every second person tells us that what we know about is just the tip of the iceberg, awareness doesn't seem to be a problem. When I tell them that stories like mine remain untold – that they are the ones crying out for more awareness – one says I should form my own support group. Sure, a group of men who are happy for people to know they were accused of raping children. I'm restrained enough to say nothing about the false information on their display headed "statistics". I must be mellowing.

May 4

I get two more reminders today about what does – and does not – need more awareness. The Draketown Post has an article about a sexual abuse survivor who was a victim of a recently convicted former priest. The offences occurred decades ago, when she was a teenager. I have no criticism of his trial or conviction, because he appears to be guilty (he may even have confessed), and the woman has shown a kind of courage by fronting up, using her real name and even agreeing to a photo. It is an increasing trend in such cases that actual victims are assertive enough to say, "I've done nothing wrong!" and to emerge from the shadows. The intro praises her for waiving name suppression "to make sure her story is heard."

The article says that her case gained some prominence in 2014, when she appeared in front of parliamentary select committee convened to look into funding for sexual violence. So the politicians, not just the media, are delighted to be seen to be doing something for sexual victims. Will there ever be such a committee to look into false claims? Possibly – just after the conversion of the Archbishop of Canterbury to Hinduism. Politicians are not keen for voters to see them chatting with paedophiles.

I have nothing against this woman telling her story. Good for her and for people like her. But that is the point: hers is far from the first such story we've read about. Survivor stories are almost turning into a genre. She has apparently had no trouble getting into the newspaper, and this is a full feature running to perhaps 1200 words. Compare that with my own persistent – some have said obsessive – attempts to get my own story heard or seen. Now, which issue needs more awareness? To anyone who has read this diary up to this point and still denies that false reports are common and serious enough for us to worry about, I would like to ask this: if you were wrong, how would you know? You certainly wouldn't learn anything from the media.

The great advantage of having a personal victim story told is that it allows readers or viewers to get beyond the abstract and identify with a real person who has been wronged. On March 27 last year, Angela commented after my visit to Rape Crisis and my attempt to tell the other side of the story that the two-percenters might change their tune if a brother or father became a victim of a false accusation. It's time we, the falsely accused, were given the chance to tell our stories and seize a share of all this understanding.

Society is so aware of sexual abuse of children that paedophiles are seen everywhere. I get a phone call from my brother Keith in Christchurch. After I give him a Verity update, he tells me that he was visited by the police because someone reported that he had been acting suspiciously in area where children were playing. What had he done? Parked his motor scooter near the seaside and sat on a park bench near the beach to take in the air. Fortunately they were just going through the motions and soon left when they saw they were barking up the wrong tree.

May 5

A thick white A4 envelope is bulging out of the mailbox, and it's got those blue police chevrons on the edge. My god, it's my file under the Freedom of Information Act. How strange, after the letter delivered just three days ago. Maybe this is just a taster, and a front-end loader will bring the rest next month.

But there's still plenty. I rip the envelope open and pages spill everywhere. There are even maps of ski patrol areas. I get everything back into some sort of order and start to sift through the files. I'll spend the next few days extracting the most relevant parts. Lots of pages are fully or partially blacked out with the comment "Section 29 (1) (a) Privacy Act 1993", so maybe what was threatening to bring down the Rigby House was the cost of toner ink.

When the accusation first hit us fifteen months ago, I mentioned that I had a feeling of having been stalked, knowing that all that time Angela and I had been going about our everyday lives, a menacing plot was being hatched behind the scenes. These files bring all that creepiness back. When I look at a standard form dated some time in 2013 with the heading at the top Offence: *male rapes female under 12* and the tag *Suspect 3: Peter Joyce,* it makes my flesh crawl. There's a new side to it now too. More police had a connection with this case than I'd ever imagined. In fact, nine are mentioned or suggested in these files, including the typist. They have all dealt with me by name behind the scenes, and may still think I'm a paedophile who just got away with it. They may only be police, but I'd still rather they knew for certain that I'm innocent. Who knows, maybe I even taught the typist years ago – or her mother.

Even a quick glance through tells me that I had one thing wrong. My cynical comments about the file yellowing in an in-tray were partly misguided. This woman's misremembrances certainly put the police through the mill, at least in the first months. There's page after page of references to documents and interviews and all sorts of research – of a sort, anyway – but the police were too incompetent to see the wood for the trees. I'll explain why a little later.

Interviews with Verity started way back in early 2013, almost immediately after she first reported to the police. They ran to a total of eight, with an accumulated time of seventeen hours and fifteen minutes. Cameras were used throughout, but unfortunately I don't get to see any footage; all these files show is the fact that each interview happened, its duration, and who was present. The first was the longest, at nearly four hours, and was conducted on February 26. She had interviews also on the following two days, each at around two hours. The remainder were spaced out every two weeks or so, finishing on May 15. Benito had told me the highlight of Verity's week was always her counselling appointment. And it makes sense: to be a victim of all these men is so rewarding, how could she ever let it go? No doubt these police interviews were the time of her life: hour after hour of sympathetic strangers hanging on her every fantasy, with the certainty that her accusations would even send unknown detectives scurrying around the North Island. It says, "It was apparent … that it would take some time to cover everything…due to…the lengthy time frame, the amount of offending and the strain it was putting on the complainant." Their concern is touching. Jon Chadwick of the Manchester sexual offences unit may want to headhunt these investigators, because they are clearly people people, not cold hard facts people.

Another female detective, not Eva, was named as the interviewer, though Eva was referred to as "monitor" each time. Maybe she was still learning the ropes. Even though she wasn't asking the questions from the outset, the fact that she (eventually) interviewed me and John shows that this was really "her" case: she was the only detective who stuck with it the whole time. It makes me wonder about the relationship she must have built with Verity. After learning about the importance of empathy with the victims and the prevalence of "rape myths", Eva would have earned her specialist sexual investigator's badge. I can't be sure, but I suspect that Eva soon became a Verity believer. Smoke means fire, after all. She invested a lot of time and emotional commitment into the case, and wanted to do right by this poor woman.

The police did spend some time on this case for a part of 2013, none more than their typist, who apparently had to make transcripts of hundreds of pages. What a waste that none of it gets used in court! On August 22 of that year someone spoke to Verity "about a number of matters arising from her interviews." Did the police start to see discrepancies? What still puzzles me is that the whole team seemed to take a sabbatical for all of 2014, because in that year absolutely nothing happened.

Back on November 12 I wrote that Linda Fairstein, the experienced American lawyer, said that false complainants "pile on features as they make them up." We all know that it's difficult to sustain any lie over multiple incidents and retellings. I am amazed that after more than seventeen hours of interviews, the highest level of skepticism the police managed to attain was – if my interpretation is correct – to ask Verity about "a number of matters" in her account. Clearly the result was not to see the light and call off the investigation. Aren't competent investigators supposed to develop a feel for these things? Aren't they supposed to notice the inconsistencies? My conclusion is that investigators who have certificates in handling cases of sexual abuse are the very ones whom we innocent suspects should fear most, because their training has taught them the need to understand rape myths, to put aside any discrepancies and to *believe.*

May 6

A few blacked-out pages appear to have contained photos, with just captions remaining. Some of these have been given by Charlotte, because the index contains a line that says "Exhibit list for photo album obtained from C Rigby". One caption says "Joyce's house in Westchester". Pity I can't see the sort of house I'd buy there. Another file refers to my house in Houwhanga. Oddly, another part of Verity's account says that when her father came down to Draketown he sometimes stayed with "his friend Peter Joyce," so she seemed to think I owned houses in three places – and actually lived in all of them. Didn't the police see that as suspicious? Or did they think she was a solo travelling act and I was such a fan that I bought a house wherever she performed?

Charlotte doesn't feature very much, but she was interviewed at least once. She was even asked about me in connection with John's visits to Draketown, when he stayed with us. She said they were both members of New Zealand Skeptics, a group "who get together and pick holes in things." Guilty as charged – things like believing without the slightest doubt any lies we or our children find comforting. When Gloria spoke to her, she played down her knowledge of the allegations, saying that it's Verity's business. But I suspect she had much more to do with it than she's admitted. I think I get her role now. To Charlotte, everyone's truth is her own. Her loyalty as a mother is everything, and whatever her daughter thinks happened, happened. Who could possibly be more deserving targets than these nasty skeptics?

Back at this early stage a sergeant whose name was new to me took over control of the case and drew up a timeline (details blacked out) and identified three named suspects (John, Lance and me) and said there were "at least another 3-7 (sic) males involved that could not be identified." I guess these were masked members of the ski patrol. Reports were obtained from three specialists (names blacked out): Verity's doctor, counsellor and chiropractor. The first two are expected, but the last one is a surprise. When I met Benito last year, he told me that Verity must have been abused, because her descriptions were so real. She even described how her hip hurt after each ordeal. I haven't paid much attention to this before, but I ring John tonight, and he tells me that when Verity was about five she lost control when learning to ride her bike with a back-pedal brake when she didn't back-pedal and went base over apex. She injured her hip quite badly. If she has tried to claim this minor lasting disability has been caused by sexual abuse, it may herald the return yet again of the money motive.

It turns out that Benito did tell the police I paid him a visit, which Eva found very puzzling. That's good news; as I've mentioned before, Lionel and Cedric have told me that the police are slaves to procedure. This means that any weird action of mine might unsettle them. The best surprises are always your own surprises.

May 7

Much of Verity's account of my raping her has – perhaps fortunately – been blacked out, but enough remains to provide some useful information. She alleged it happened twice. This is interesting, because Arthur said in the letter I received from him on January 11 that Verity made "a single allegation" against me. This tells me how thoroughly he reviewed the file. The first rape, which contains a fair amount of incidental detail, is titled *Eighteenth Incident – Peter.* This must be the eighteenth of all the incidents. Here is what she said about it:

> It was when I was at Westchester High School, living with Dad. I usually got the bus to HOAC, towards Houwhanga, because Dad ran HOAC. I was only there a term. I was new at school. I did bone carving. I walked out of school. There was a car there. A creamy yellow flat car, not a station wagon. I saw the car, it was a yellow car, with low brown seats, leathery with stitching. It was a sedan, had a gear stick. Westchester High School, walking out of school to car, I was wearing uniform, Peter was in the car. Other people saw me. Twins. One had short dark hair, her name was Nadine, and one was blondie coloured hair. I was wearing a white blouse, a checked maroon skirt and a maroon sweater. I got in the car. Went to his place in town. His name was Peter. He's been Dad's friend for years. He's a teacher or something. He was easily 40 to 45 at that stage with white skin, sandy brown shortish hair, my height. He had a wife, possibly an Asian wife and a sister in Rotorua. He had a broad forehead. He wasn't rough. Into the garage which was separate from the house. I got out of the car. He closed the garage.

> Go into the house into waiting room, kitchen was an open plan. *Next lines blacked out.* He goes and cleans up, comes back, we go through into another room with table and chairs. I sit down. He is in the kitchen cooking and talking. He puts food in front of me. I don't eat.

Everything centres on school. Even those people who subscribe to the "rape myths" explanation that genuine victims can have some discrepancies in their stories must concede that if I wasn't there when she was at school, her story just evaporates. Her description also doesn't fit. She is the first person to say I have a "broad forehead". I admit that it starts on one side and continues all the way to the other. Is that broad? Even in my prime, my hair was never "sandy brown". John suggests that she may have confused me with Gloria's late brother-in-law, who did have sandy hair and lived in Rotorua. Such confusion is understandable, because there's an excellent chance he also never raped her. For a long time I've been wondering how she visually identified me, and what's here seems to be all there is. If she'd offered the old standard joke description of "a little tall fella with a bald moustache", the police would have been out there tracking him down…or at least sending memos to each other about it.

The nineteenth incident also starred me, but had little detail. It just reported that it occurred in my house in Westchester, and that she stayed the night – claims which on their own should have cleared me very early. She added

> In the morning he gave me my uniform. I got dressed, feeling of "it's over". Walking out on concrete into garage and car. His wife was away. He took me to school the next day. A girl said something to me about it. She had dark hair, fancy tights, black with bright paint *(paint?)*. I don't know her name. I had a feeling the principal knew what was going on, everyone knew.

My house in Westchester. Right! Just at the time when Angela and I, along with our infant son, were getting on with our uncomplicated lives in the only house we owned, down here in Draketown. It makes me wonder if the police bothered to check records of house ownership. So she stayed the night, and it must have been during school term time. For a moment, let's assume as true what is false: that I owned even one house in the Houwhanga/Westchester area. A thirteen-year-old girl who is living with her father and stepmother doesn't come home after school, and they don't see her until school finishes the next day. Let's also accept Verity's primary claim that her father was the sexual recruiter. Her disappearance is no problem to him; maybe's he's even drawn up a schedule, and I was rostered on that night. But what about Gloria?

Didn't she wonder where her stepdaughter had got to, or are we to assume that she was in on it as well?

May 8

Nothing explains why they took so long to interview John, who was of course the main suspect and chief recruiter, so I guess we'll never know whether that was some sort of half-baked tactic or just inefficiency. However, some new stuff is interesting and unexpected. One report form requests a full explanation for the reasons no charges were laid. It seeks an "in-depth report outlining the investigation [and] evidence obtained." This is dated September 30 2015, which is two weeks after our clearance. I wonder if this means that Verity, perhaps prompted by a fuming Heinrich, refused to accept the decision and wanted a fuller explanation of why the police didn't manage to put these perverts away. To be fair, this is about a week after my phone conversation with Richard, Eva's sergeant, so it may have been a response to this. The wording suggests this is unlikely, however.

This brings me to the aspect of the "investigation" that is most outrageous: I see no sign that the police ever tried to find out where I was teaching from September to December 1991 – the only time Verity attended Westchester. This is despite the fact that the files confirm they knew this was when she stayed there. Eva has a summary of the findings of the interview with me. She says the events could not have happened the way Verity told the story because I was not living there at the time (quite right – I lived there only before Verity was born). Curiously, to Eva this doesn't mean it couldn't have happened.

Any complex system needs carefully allocated roles. The New Zealand Government appears to have assigned to the police and the Ministry of Education specific types of incompetence. The police have the role of asking inappropriate questions, but the task of providing inaccurate answers to those inappropriate questions falls to the Ministry. A detective called Sally, apparently based in Finchkey, was involved in an email exchange with someone called Joanna at the Ministry about my teaching records. One page in the files has a summary of my teaching jobs, as eventually supplied by this Joanna. It is incomplete and incorrect. It says that from mid-1974 until the end of 1975 I taught at an unnamed school. It had the initials CSC, but Joanna couldn't find what this stands for. Yes, I did teach at Central Southland College, but wouldn't we expect Ministry officials to know their own abbreviations? Also, I taught there for only a third of that eighteen month stretch; for a whole year I was driving a truck and working as a gardener. However, what is most disturbing is that it says I twice taught at Napier Girls' High School. I have never been near the place.

It is clear from this that the Ministry (or at least this official at the Ministry) is not competent to give correct information about where teachers have taught. On the surface, this may seem to reflect badly on the Ministry but not the police. Yet I'm not so sure. The public may not expect that professional investigators know all the answers, but should expect that they know where to look to get them. It's obviously important for the police to know this, for the sake of future investigations of teachers. A small number really are paedophiles. I email Arthur to suggest that the police attend to this. Of course, I have been unfriended, so I get no response.

Detective Sally should have done what I did: contact Novopay (the organisation which handles teacher salaries). What did it take for me to get my work details covering the time Verity was at Westchester? Not much. A two-minute phone call to the pay people, perhaps ten minutes to write the letter to them, eighty cents for a stamp and about five days waiting for their reply…and I'm just an amateur.

The incorrect work information the police obtained dates from before the alleged rapes. Why did they have so little interest in where I taught at the time of the alleged rapes? Police requests for my work records specifically ask for data from 1973 to 1990, and even suggest I may have taught at Westchester in 1990 – apparently convinced I had a house there. Granted, they may have needed to confirm my story about where I taught earlier in my career, in case I was trying to cover something else up, but these details would surely just be footnotes. The pressing question for anyone wanting to find out if the complainant's story has any truth must be to ask *Where was he when the rapes allegedly happened?* Nothing in the files suggests that they ever tried to find this out. All the requests to the Ministry end at 1990.

I thought for a moment that these requests may have been withheld from me, but what would be so secret about them? After all, they let me have the other requests to the Ministry about where I taught. Unless this was a deliberate attempt to avoid unearthing information that might vindicate me, the police performance here goes beyond everyday inefficiency; it is a masterpiece of rare ineptitude. It took them almost two and a half years to start asking questions, and then they asked the wrong ones.

In Eva's summary, which ends with her saying no charges will be laid, she says about me, "…he did do a house swap with Rigby at the time Verity talks about so could potentially have offended." Both Richard and Arthur have said the same. Yet this is nonsense on stilts; it is possible to believe this only if the notions *time* and *place* are foreign to you.

The police are all wrong; not just murky "he said/she said" possibly mistaken, but completely and demonstrably wrong. I was never in or near Houwhanga at the same time as Verity. She attended Westchester High School from September to December 1991, and her story falls apart if I can show I didn't pick her up from school. As I noted before, her whole narrative centres on school: she talks about her uniform, about the principal, the school gate, other pupils. She attended Westchester only during the third and final term of 1991 – from September to December. The records show I had not one day off from Redwater College down here in Draketown during that term. Why is this so difficult to grasp, after hundreds of hours of so-called investigation?

John and Gloria did indeed do a house and car exchange with us, but the police know that John and I were both teachers so we could have done this only in the school holidays when – wait for it – I couldn't have picked her up from school. Why would the four of us even arrange for such a house swap when either or both of John's girls were staying there? The girls would be staying with a family they had never met, and their father – Verity's recruiter – would have been in our house in Draketown. For the hard of thinking, that is what *exchange* means.

All this reveals that my eventual clearance had almost nothing to do with place and time. In what should be just a brief factual summary of the "investigation" and its outcome, Eva can't resist making what seem to me unnecessary comments about my uncooperative behaviour and attitude. She rejoices that neither of the IPCA complaints I made was upheld. Maybe so, but it would have been different if the IPCA had done its job properly and not totally ignored my specific complaint about the way she had acted. Finally she writes, "I advised the three suspects either by phone or letter that there were to be no charges laid…and the matter would be filed." The summary adds that none of the suspects have any police or criminal history. "Joyce and Rigby have both had jobs that have involved dealing with young females throughout their lives. There have never been any other complaints about them. Given the above I believe it would be unsafe to pursue any charges and as advised the matter will be filed."

Unsafe. I guess that means the police prosecutors think they would be unlikely to win over a jury. How they must hate juries ruining everything. It's ironic that our clean job history seems to have caused the accusations to be dropped eventually. I always insisted that this was – and should be – a minor aspect. The indisputable testimony of time and place was much more persuasive. So we got the right result, but far too late, and for the wrong reason. I find it exasperating that the police tossed the case out without ever having seen the significance of those simple facts.

May 10

Included in the files is an email from Eva to Detective Sally after my interview. This may have accidentally slipped past the censor. Too bad! It begins

> I have attached a copy of the statement I took from Joyce. He is an

> odd man, very suspicious. After I spoke to him he rang me a couple of weeks later demanding to know what was happening and believes that it is all a police conspiracy and that we charge innocent people all the time.

If Eva or anyone else finds me "odd", that is of course their prerogative. Yet such a value judgment does seem odd in itself. How can I reconcile her comments with Arthur's assurance to me that the police are concerned only with facts? What is more sinister is that her subjective comment seems to imply my likely guilt, and that she wanted to convey this feeling to a colleague who was also involved in the investigation. This seems to go some way to explaining why it took so long to have me cleared.

I did go through a stage when I did things some people might label odd, precisely between February 1 and September 18 last year. I wonder why. No doubt Eva has been taught that trauma can make genuine rape victims behave in unusual ways. Perhaps her next course can include the wide range of reactions that stressed suspects can display. We innocent accused need a Twitter campaign with the tag #TheresNoPerfectSuspect. And now that I and the other real victims have been cleared and Verity, the real perpetrator, has been shown to have put the police through hundreds of hours of ultimately fruitless work, I wonder if Eva thinks Verity herself is in any way odd. Or did her training as a sexual abuse specialist require her simply to believe that all complainants are by definition victims?

Eva's email put a spin on my statements to make me look unreasonable and impatient. She said I "demanded to know what was happening." Pure nonsense; I was particularly polite. She claimed I phoned her "a couple of weeks later." Not so. After the interview on February 10, my lawyer Monty quite reasonably and politely asked her when a decision was likely to be made. She said it might take two months. After enduring intolerable uncertainty, I rang her on April 9 – one day short of two months, so quite in line with the duration she herself suggested.

I write a letter outlining everything in my file which is unacceptable, incompetent or outrageous, including the contents of that email. I send it to Eva's sergeant, Richard. I say that, in the circumstances, it should be clear now that I am entitled to a letter unequivocally and permanently clearing me. Richard told me over the phone in September that the police can do this when they know someone is innocent, but they have too many doubts in my case. I don't anticipate getting a reply, let alone a letter of clearance. Some supporters have suggested I should make another IPCA complaint, but I'm not convinced that will achieve anything, especially since the IPCA have already told me they have no power to make the police issue such a letter.

In fact, I've come to think that the IPCA does little to bring the police to heel. After reading my entries from the past few days, one of my supporters said that the police should be embarrassed about the mistakes they made. Yes, they should. But we only get embarrassed when people can observe our mistakes. The police are used to having the power that prevents the public from seeing their incompetence. The IPCA probably helped to speed up the glacial pace of the "investigation", but has done nothing to hold the police accountable or to make their procedures any more transparent. Other innocent victims are suffering under the same callous incompetence right now.

One of my reactions back on February 8 to the preposterous trial of Mark Pearson for brushing past a woman at Waterloo Station in London was to ask rhetorically "Who says women's complaints aren't investigated?" His case shows that the UK Crown Prosecution Service is determined to impress the public with its pursuit of sexual allegations, even the most outlandish. My case shows the New Zealand situation is no different. A whole team of police spent so many hundreds of hours on Verity's transparently ridiculous allegations that I'm outraged not just as a victim but also as a taxpayer. The files tell any reader that the time spent on this case was no aberration: the procedural forms show that the police will follow these standard exhaustive stages every time, and the victim will be believed. By contrast, the suspect is afforded the sort of disdain usually reserved for pond scum. A form in my file has a list of final tasks to be done to wrap up the case, with checkboxes down the margin. One line has "Victim advised by…" followed by the options "phone/letter/personally". "Personally" has been circled. This means that when the police finally decided not to lay charges, someone knocked on Verity's door to give her, face to face, the unwelcome news that we may be perverts, but regrettably they had to let us go. That's a nice personal touch, but only in line with the police manual on how to treat "victims" with dignity. No complainant will ever get less. Innocent suspects who are cleared will most likely get the sort of sneered monosyllables that I received through the phone line.

Nothing in the files said anything about Verity's doubtful credibility after having falsely accused Benito a decade or so ago. Of course, it may have been redacted, but I suspect either that the police never did learn about it or chose to ignore it. It may even be policy to disregard a rape complainant's previous unsupported accusations. After all, just because her estranged partner wasn't prosecuted last time doesn't mean their daughter wasn't raped then, which means that Verity should still be believed this time. Properly developed policies for rape investigation must permit no scope for victim blaming.

All of this surely shows that anyone who says that sexual allegations are no longer taken seriously, or that complainants are not handled sensitively, is rowing with one oar in the water.

May 12

Last weekend's edition of the Draketown Post had an article about a trial of a local man on sexual charges, including historic rape. It said the trial was abandoned after the complainant became upset when the defence lawyer (Monty's partner Hugh, as it happens) "questioned her memory of when and where the assaults occurred." After a recess, the complainant refused to be questioned any more, so a mistrial was declared. Most interesting. I'm dying to find out more about this case, but I probably can't. Was she a genuine victim overcome with trauma, an innocuous but mentally unstable woman or another fabulist indulged by her family or the police but eventually terrified that she'd be caught out under oath?

I have another meeting with Lionel at The Men's Room. I bring in the envelope with my files, and show him the highlights. First I show him the email from Eva to fellow detective Joanna. I want him to share my outrage, but he just says, "Well, you *are* odd." Charming. But his jaw drops at the extent of police incompetence. He says that if any reporter can make it clear that the police got the facts so horribly wrong, my story is more likely to be told, but it's always an uphill struggle giving the men's side in any sexual matters. Two friends have told me some favoured advertisers might even threaten to pull their contracts with newspapers that run stories which rock the boat of comfortable assumptions about sexual abuse. I ask him if he thinks this is too cynical. No, he says it's very believable.

He also tells me that a young male student at a well-known university journalism school approached him recently. All students have to do a major investigative assignment, and he chose a new angle on sexual abuse: female abuse of males. This is a whole area my diary hasn't touched on. It's less common than the other way round, of course, but more common than most people think. Maybe any guy is just supposed to consider himself blessed to be the target of any female's sexual attention. The student admitted to Lionel that he had been a victim himself, hence his interest. An older woman sexually abused him a few years earlier. The school vetoed the topic, only relenting when he agreed not to have its name attached to any final report.

One comment Lionel makes gives me quiet satisfaction. He asks me to remind him what business Verity and Heinrich are involved in. "An auction room?" he says. "Seriously? In this era of online auction websites? I wouldn't give that long. It's about as sensible as buying into a DVD hire business." So Eagle's Nest may just die a natural death, and I won't have to send its coordinates to the Pentagon and call in a drone strike. Heinrich's looming third bankruptcy gives me a warm feeling as I cycle home in the cool autumn sunshine.

May 17

Following a suggestion from Alison, I email lawyer Hugh to try to get more information about the mistrial I mentioned in my last entry. I say that I don't expect him to tell me anything, but I suggest that he sends my contact details on to his client, so that he can contact me if he wants to.

May 19

I email Fred Hurst, asking if our story is dead and pointing out that I have my police file. I say that if he would care to look at it, he'd see that Verity's accusation, which he feared may have just been unfounded, has been confirmed as false and the police performance confirmed as hopeless. He replies, saying that his career at the Draketown Post is to end in less than two weeks. Presumably he's been made redundant. He's been working flat out on other last-minute projects and confesses he hasn't given my story much more thought. However, he's just sent a hurry-up email to the policeman whom area boss Hannah had put on the case. If he doesn't get anything, he'll try him again next week. He adds, "My difficulty remains that I've still only got your side of the story. Failing an admission by the police that they've erred, I'm stuck." Actually, no. Having my file from the police changes that, but I can't expect him to read it now. I reply, and ask if it's likely that another reporter may pick up the story, but I get no further response. So the answer to my opening question was *Yes:* the story is dead.

May 21

In crime movies the investigators investigate. It's their bread and butter. The detective inspector assembles her team in the main office, with grisly photos of the victim pinned up on the back wall. She snaps out tasks to the detectives. "Davidson! Paul Smith, the ex-boyfriend, says he was on the Staten Island ferry at the time of the murder. Get onto it." Davidson walks out and chases down the facts. The next day he brings details of witness statements and sailing times.

Can't real life ever be just a little like Hollywood? I've just noticed that the email Eva sent to her colleague Sally, asking her to track down my work records, was dated May 6. How did I miss this? So it took her almost three months from the time of my interview *even to begin* to find anything out. Actually, it's worse than that: it took her three months to ask someone else to begin to find anything out. Those pointless questions about where I was teaching before Verity was born and before she stayed at Houwhanga were asked a month after I phoned to ask Eva about progress. If Davidson had been so hopeless he would have been demoted to traffic duties in the next scene.

Of course, the research into my work record should really have been asked in late February 2013, immediately after the interviews with Verity. After all, that was when they learned from her that she was raped after school in Westchester. It would have been a simple matter to find out when she attended the school, and they could then have found out where I was teaching at the time. That way her story would have been discredited when it should have been, and no interview would have been necessary. After sixteen months living with this nonsense, it doesn't become any less maddening.

When I met lawyer Hugh back on March 18, he told me that the police are lazy. This surely confirms Hugh's claim, certainly in the case of Eva. It makes sense, too. The police have the sort of power that can prevent the public from peering through their windows to see what they aren't doing…unless odd and obsessed citizens take them to task.

May 26

I hear nothing from Hugh about the abandoned case, or from Fred Hurst about any contact from the police. I'd like to call this a conspiracy of silence – from the media, from police, from lawyers, from women's groups when I've challenged their statistics. It isn't, of course, because there's no collaboration among the groups, and each group has its own reason to clam up. However, this doesn't make their silence any easier to live with.

June 11

It's now over four months since the Mark Pearson Waterloo fiasco briefly made the news. I haven't read anything about scandalised demonstrators marching in the streets with placards, so it's time to see whether the outrage has at least stayed in people's imagination. I google "Mark Pearson Waterloo" and under "advanced search options" restrict results to the past month. The search throws up only three relevant web pages – all from concerned men broadly like myself. So the story was quickly bumped off the news sites, yet the charge against him was so absurd that it should have caused public anger and some serious and lasting challenges to prosecution policies and the whole notion of false accusations. It revealed that a delusional complainant can offer a description that doesn't fit of a person who committed a crime that couldn't have happened. With the cooperation of a prosecution service that will break any rules to make any fantasy appear credible to a jury, an innocent person's life can easily be destroyed. It should have been embarrassing for groups who campaign for more rape prosecutions, but they have the power to ignore it, so it has just faded into oblivion...

June 13

…but at least the story did make the news briefly, which is more than I can claim for my mine. Back on January 15 I said I was not obsessed, because this diary would have a finite end. My sense of outrage has barely diminished, but the time has come to quarantine it in my anger vault and climb the stairs the way other people do. I suppose I should be happy that I've fought Verity to a draw, which is the best result a falsely accused man can hope for under the unfair rules. John says that at least we don't have to live with a lie, as those in the enemy camp must. And he's right – the truth does matter as an end in itself. Yet we got no satisfaction in three specific goals. The most tangible would be official letters permanently exonerating John and me. I also tried to get the story out there into the wider world. Since a private prosecution against Verity was never a serious option, I wanted to pursue the Jennifer subplot, so that Verity would at least face some consequences within her own family, and maybe John would claim one of his daughters back.

On each of these I've come up against a mile-high brick wall, and it would be madness to keep beating my head against it for ever. Looking back, maybe I was naïve to expect that our saga meant anything – to the police, to news editors, even to Jennifer. For a while I thought the Draketown police might actually be worried about bad publicity, but at best I was an irritant, as a flea might be to a rottweiler.

When anyone is reduced to shaking his fist and shouting "This isn't over!" it's usually over. Metaphorically, this is where I've got to. My diary can't carry on with a never-fulfilled promise of a satisfying outcome, so here it ends. This is disappointing, but there is the diary itself. It is at least as complete as the unfinished story has allowed it to be. I hope it is read by those people who most need to read it – police, politicians, sexual abuse counsellors and women's groups – but I suspect it won't be. First, they probably won't even know about it, but even if they did, few people are receptive to ideas which challenge those dogmas which they find satisfying, which give purpose to their lives or which provide them a comfortable living.

I'll keep chasing the clearance letters and trying in any way I can to draw attention to the wider issues under the Herb hypothesis, but continuing the diary leads any reader to expect these will occur within it, and I have no reason to be so optimistic. The diary itself is unlikely to interest a traditional publisher. A friend of a friend, with some connections in publishing, was honest enough to say that mine isn't a compelling enough story because I didn't suffer enough. When I first hit upon the idea of the diary back on March 13 last year, I noted that the most interesting story would be the one that has me convicted, failing repeated appeals and getting maimed in a prison fight. In the finish I was questioned and eventually wasn't even charged, and where's the story in that? Innocent people are questioned as suspects and then not charged every day of the week. Likely readers are therefore friends and family.

I need to remind any of them who have come this far that September 18 last year confirmed me as one of the lucky ones. Yes, there is still a chance the police will bring charges but this is unlikely enough that we can sleep easily. Like a mild form of cancer, we'll probably die with this condition rather than of it. Everything I've written since our clearance has been because I've chosen to, so any sympathy should be reserved for those innocent victims who should never have been prosecuted and whose lives have been destroyed by a credulous jury.

June 16

Catherine Comins, whom I quoted on February 25 last year, would have no sympathy even for them. She was the one who brushed off the trauma and said that a victim of a false charge should treat the accusation as an opportunity to reflect. I've had sixteen months to reflect, but I'm not sure that the conclusions I've drawn would please her. Sexual accusations can be hard to prove, but I conclude that in these investigations police all over the developed world do not let the difficulty of unearthing evidence stop them from pursuing charges. However, the normal assumption that in our adversarial justice system police should seek to prosecute does not apply to false rape complaints, because they fall into no category on which police performance is evaluated. I conclude that some sane women have countless motives to lie about rape and sexual molestation, and that plenty of unscrupulous counsellors are happy to indulge their fantasies.

In fact, here are the motives my limited research has unearthed: to get revenge on a partner or a parent; to offer an excuse for looking at porn; to provide a motif for a gender-affirming conceptual artwork; to express dislike of a partner; to ride the victim express; to avoid a taxi fare; to hide sexual activity; to tip the scales in a custody dispute over children; to get attention; to have tuition fees paid; to provide a pretext for resitting a failed exam; to show how common rape is. The examples and data have come from New Zealand, Australia, the USA, Canada, the UK, Switzerland, Germany and Scandinavia.

A small number of men rape (or all men, depending on who defines rape), and a small number of women lie about rape. We can't pretend to know the numbers of either, but both are more than the numbers prosecuted. Some people say the public is cruelly skeptical about women's claims they have been raped, but I uncovered no evidence of this. In fact, many people suggest false reports are more common than the public assumes – people who are in positions to have informed opinions. In my account these are Draketown lawyers Dwight, Monty, David and Hugh, UK lawyer Chris Saltrese,

American lawyer and writer Linda Fairstein, writer and researcher Lynley Hood, advisor Josephine at the Draketown free law centre, my doctor, campaigner Felicity Goodyear-Smith, women's refuge pioneer Erin Pizzey, memory researcher Elizabeth Loftus, writer and reformed True Believer Meredith Maran, American journalist Ben Radford, Christchurch judge Brian Callaghan, German criminologists Erich Elsner and Wiebke Steffen, American social researcher Eugene Kanin, ex-policeman Cedric and Men's Room manager Lionel.

Their opinions should not be dismissed lightly. Yet in effect they are. My attempts to back up their accounts by telling my story or to question misguided common assumptions have come up against silence wherever I've turned, specifically newspaper, television, radio, the police, Draketown Rape Crisis, Auckland Rape Education and the Greater Manchester Police. The first two gave me some tantalising encouragement that I might be able to have my say, but nothing came of it in the finish.

Rape is often a terrible crime. Its new, broader definition guarantees that it isn't always, but the emotional association the word carries has not kept pace with the complexity of its changed meaning. The crime that some men commit is always seen as simple and wilful, and rigorous punishment serves public interest. All men know this, and expect the full weight of the law if they transgress – though new definitions of rape mean that a man often has no idea he has even broken the law. The crime that some women commit is always so inextricably complex that it will not be seen as a crime at all, because they have, in the words of the head of the Manchester sexual offences unit, "some sort of vulnerability". Anyone who doesn't see this or – heaven forbid – gets it the wrong way round is either a victim blamer or rape enabler, which amounts to the same thing. Having "discrepancies" in a rape account is a delicate matter, and we must strive to understand rather than condemn; our thinking about apparently false accusations must be refined enough to consider relationships and perceptions and myths and psychology and cultural nuances. Prosecuting false accusers almost never serves public interest, so it is fitting for society to pass "robust" legislation and then persistently ignore it.

Far from accusers not being believed, police have been trained to go out of their way to treat even the most preposterous claims as credible. Manuals have been written which prescribe how this is to be done delicately, but as far as I am aware no manual exists that prescribes how to respect the dignity of an innocent suspect. Those whom police may once have called liars are now treated as victims by definition. Any woman who lies about rape knows all this, and expects no prosecution if she transgresses, even if the accused man has never met her. I conclude that there is no chance of convincing the public that these conclusions are true.

We are expected just to live with this. Victims of rape are entitled to say that men can be bastards, but victims of false accusations are entitled only to shrug and say that life can be a bitch.

We praise a man who is angry on the right grounds, against the right persons, in the right manner, at the right moment, and for the right length of time.

Aristotle

www.ingramcontent.com/pod-product-compliance
Ingram Content Group UK Ltd.
Pitfield, Milton Keynes, MK11 3LW, UK
UKHW050919270726
13967UKWH00014B/2898